Barnes & Noble Critical Studies

General Editor: Anne Smith

Carlyle Past and Present

CARLYLE
PAST AND PRESENT

A Collection of New Essays

edited by
K. J. Fielding and Rodger L. Tarr

BARNES & NOBLE
BOOKS
10 East 53d St., New York 10022
(a division of Harper & Row Publishers, Inc.)

Barnes & Noble Books
Harper & Row, Publishers, Inc.
10 East 53rd Street
New York

ISBN 0-06-492078-X

LC 75-35036

For Beth and Jean

First published in the U.S.A. 1976

© 1976 Vision Press, London

Printed and bound in Great Britain
MCMLXXVI

Contents

Editorial Note

To study Carlyle is to anatomize the nineteenth century, for all the issues that stirred the age are present in his work, and his is now what he himself once called 'the articulate audible voice of the past'. But more than that, his influence on his contemporaries—poets, novelists, and historians alike—is evident everywhere in the literature of his time, and continued, long after his death, to have its effect on writers with a social conscience on both sides of the Atlantic. An appreciation of Carlyle, therefore, sends us back to Victorian literature with a new and critical awareness.

A.S.

Abbreviations

CL:	*Collected Letters of Thomas and Jane Welsh Carlyle*, Duke-Edinburgh edition, vols 1–4, 1812–28, edited C. R. Sanders, with K. J. Fielding, I. Campbell, J. Clubbe and Janetta Taylor (Durham, N.C. 1970).
Dyer:	I. W. Dyer, *A Bibliography of Thomas Carlyle's Writings and Ana* (Portland, Maine, 1928).
Froude, *Life*:	J. A. Froude, *Thomas Carlyle, A History of the First Forty Years of His Life, 1795–1835*, and *Thomas Carlyle, A History of His Life in London, 1834–1881* (London, 1882 and 1884), 4 vols.
Harrold, *Sartor*:	ed. C. F. Harrold, *Sartor Resartus* (New York, 1937).
LDP:	*Latter-Day Pamphlets*
NLS:	National Library of Scotland.
Reminiscences (Froude):	ed. J. A. Froude, *Reminiscences of Thomas Carlyle*, 2 vols (London, 1881).
Reminiscences (Norton):	ed. C. E. Norton, *Reminiscences of Thomas Carlyle*, 2 vols (London, 1887).
TC:	Thomas Carlyle: for personal references and for titles given in the notes.
Wilson, *Carlyle*:	The biography of Carlyle by D. A. Wilson, in six variously entitled volumes (London, 1923–34).
Works:	Carlyle, *Works*, Centenary edition, 30 vols (London, 1896–9).

Some accepted abbreviations for periodicals have also been used.

Chronology

1795	Born, 4 December, Ecclefechan
1806(–09)	Attends Annan Academy
1809(–14)	Attends Edinburgh University
1814(–16)	Mathematics master at Annan Academy
1816(–18)	Schoolmaster at Kirkcaldy
1817	Gives up intention to enter ministry
1818(–19)	Returns to Edinburgh, begins study of German, contributes to *Edinburgh Philosophical Journal*
1820(–23)	Contributes to *Edinburgh Encyclopaedia*
1821	Meets Jane Baillie Welsh
1822	Tutorship with the Bullers (until 1824); reviews *Faust* for *New Edinburgh Review*, and translates Legendre's *Elements of Geometry* (published 1824)
1824	Visits London; *Wilhelm Meister's Apprenticeship*
1825	*Life of Friedrich Schiller*
1826	Marries
1827	*German Romance*
1828	Moves to Craigenputtoch, "Burns" and "Goethe"
1829	"Voltaire" and "Signs of the Times"
1830	Writes "On Clothes" the germ of Sartor
1831	"The Nibelungen Lied" and "Characteristics"
1832	Visits London. His father dies
1833	*Sartor Resartus* in *Fraser's* (November 1833–August 1834)
1834	Moves to Cheyne Row, Chelsea, London
1836	First American edition of *Sartor*
1837	*The French Revolution*
1838	First English edition of *Sartor*; first American edition of *Critical and Miscellaneous Essays*; "Scott"

11

1839	First English edition of *Essays, Chartism*
1841	*Heroes and Hero-Worship*
1843	*Past and Present*
1845	*Oliver Cromwell's Letters and Speeches*
1848	Articles for *Examiner* on Ireland
1849	First meets Froude; tour in Ireland; "Occasional Discourse on the Negro Question"
1850	*Latter-Day Pamphlets*
1851	*Life of John Sterling*
1858–65	*History of Frederick the Great*, vols 1 and 2 (1858), vol. 3 (1863), vol. 4 (1864), vols 5 and 6 (1865)
1866	Inaugural Address as Rector of University of Edinburgh; death of Jane Carlyle
1867	"Shooting Niagara: and After?"
1869	Audience with Queen Victoria
1875	*Early Kings of Norway* and *The Portraits of John Knox*
1881	Dies 5 February. *Reminiscences* published

A Preface by Carlyle

AND BY THE EDITORS

Carlyle remains one of the most enigmatic Victorians. Looming over his contemporaries, he has been worshipped, distrusted and decried, but is still imperfectly understood. The magnetism of Carlyle seems even stranger because of his relationships with his fellow artists, whose various and often contradictory impressions have led to our own uncertainty. How is it, for example, that Ruskin can refer to him as "Master", Meredith as a "heaver of rocks, not a shaper", and Arnold finally as "dangerous", when each at some time came directly under his sway? Yet the proof of his importance still lies in his relation with his contemporaries, and modern students of Carlyle still have to come at the essence of the man.

No doubt the nemesis of Carlyle is the result of his writings. The transcendental *Sartor Resartus*, the apocalyptic *The French Revolution*, the elitist *Heroes and Hero-Worship*, the polemic *Past and Present*, and the historical and prophetic *Oliver Cromwell*, together with his earlier critical and historical essays, have brought him even more than the usual favour and disfavour that surround a controversial writer. But with "The Nigger Question" and *Latter-Day Pamphlets* he invited the stoning of a prophet. A result has been that it is still extremely difficult to approach Carlyle dispassionately, especially with the added offences of *Frederick* and "Shooting Niagara: and After?"

The present volume, therefore, is a survey; it is a series of fresh attempts to examine his work; they are *new essays* in that none has been published before, yet they chiefly return us to his own period; and we hope that they are part of a now widely renewed reconsideration of Carlyle. It may be too soon to assess how far this has gone. Some of it has taken the form of re-editing, as in the on-going *Collected Letters of Thomas and Jane Welsh Carlyle* which will give us at least a view of almost the whole Victorian age by two of its keenest observers. Yet many of the problems of revaluation remain to be resolved: stones are being moved, but many are not yet overturned. These studies are contributions to a work which must essentially be a co-operative one.

Future study of Carlyle lies in seeing his relation to the past. As Swinburne wrote of him and Newman in "Two Leaders" (1876):

> Honour not hate we give you, love not fear,
> Last prophets of past kind, who fill the dome
> Of great dead Gods with wrath and wail, nor hear
> Time's word and man's: "Go honoured hence, go home,
> Night's childless children; here your hour is done;
> Pass with the stars, and leave us with the sun."[1]

It is because of this that his relations with men and movements of his time are important for understanding the period. Whatever he wrote, he was concerned with its effect on his own age; and he was caught then, as now, between past and present. If we are to show this dispassionately, therefore, we should like to argue that the best preface to any review of his work may lie in his own words, and that this is a good reason for taking advantage of a happy accident that there are newly-discovered and unpublished *disjecta membra* of Carlyle's which recall us to what he sought to express.

First, a brief word as to their nature. They come from some papers which have long been in the Forster Collection of the Victoria and Albert Museum Library, which are among the earliest drafts of his attempts to write the life of Cromwell during 1841–2.[2] There is a more detailed study to be made of them, which will bring out even more clearly than we have always known how impossibly difficult Carlyle found the work to write.[3] In fact it was never written as he intended: the form of *Oliver Cromwell's Letters and Speeches* was partly an evasion as well as a solution of the problems of a considered *Life*. Over the years

14

spent in arriving at his method (as we have always known) Carlyle even broke off in the midst of his struggle to give three or four months to writing *Past and Present*, a historical study in which he more squarely faced the challenge of addressing his own times.[4] But before and after this, day after day, he sat at his desk and drove his pen across paper trying to discover what he wanted to say by the familiar process of writing it down first and then seeing what it meant.

As art this is dubious; as a means of understanding how Carlyle worked it deserves more thought; as an entry into his mind, especially at a time when he was re-examining his opinions, it has considerable interest.

Sometimes he goes back over past routines, rehearses ideas for *Past and Present* and *Cromwell*, agonises over the condition of England, and returns to his belief in *Heroes* as he had lectured on them in May 1840.[5] His "radicalism" of the thirties may be thought to have begun to change and fade, and it seems that his determination in spite of all difficulties to write about Cromwell came from his faith that his ideal hero should be a Puritan, inspired by a deity recognizably like the God of his fathers. His whole effort to find a fit form for his shifting beliefs helps to reveal the preconceptions underlying Carlylism of the early eighteen-forties. It may leave us with Swinburne, praising the thunderous art of Carlyle though believing it to belong to the past: yet not so much because what he says is only indirectly applicable to the present, but because his whole message is that we must continually try to discover the truth for ourselves.

Yet for our prefatory purposes we may take up three of his themes. First Carlyle's concern for the condition of England. Secondly, his problem in reconciling this with the study of History. Thirdly, the way in which these are related to an urgent insistence on sincerity, or even inspiration. Familiar such ideas may be; but they return us, in his own voice, to the fundamentals of *Carlylism*.

That *Cromwell* was written out of a concern with his own age is not new, but the insistence with which it comes through and the trouble it caused is one of the more striking features of the Forster manuscript. So tightly is it interwoven with all he writes in draft, that it is often inseparable; yet, as Carlyle's patience

15

breaks at the inaccessibility of the past, he bizarrely invokes Cromwell himself:

> *Enter the Ghost of Oliver Cromwell* (by way of Prologue, *loquitur*) on another Stage than that of Dr Laud. Who art thou of friendly mortal voices that hast awoke me from the iron sleep? . . . Who art thou? What meanest thou?—Ye people and populace of this Amphitheatre, aye there you are, new English faces, male and female, beautiful, young and old, foolish and not so foolish, even as our own were! The same and yet so different. Not Christ's Gospel now, and a Godly Ministry; but the People's Charter and Free Trade in Corn. My Poor beloved countrymen,—alas, Priests have become chimerical, and your Lords (Law-wards) do stick the stubble ground with dry bushes in preservation of their partridges. . . . My Children, my kindred, it is a comfort to me that I am dead, that I have not again to fight, and in such a cause as yours has grown.—And say, good unchristian people, why have you summoned me into the daylight? . . .

Then follows Carlyle's own comment: "What an amazing piece of work is this. Where *will* all this end; anywhere?—Ach." (f. 54v.)

Carlyle is convinced that "the epic of the Present is the thing always to write; the epic of the Present not of the past and dead" (f. 95v.); yet he has "funded" such toil in his study of the seventeenth century (f. 105v.) that he cannot give up. He thinks (at one moment) that a straight history, like *The French Revolution,* is not wanted: "Probably no one will ever make much of endeavouring to resuscitate (as in F.R.) the whole business— rather try to bring up the *soul* of it" (f. 103v.),—which may be found in Cromwell:

> —*Oliver Cromwell* (27 Septr 1841; Monday 1½ p.m.)!—
>
> O Oliver my hero . . . what is the use of man's writing; of man's understanding, which should be the basis of writing? That man may *see* the great things which are, which have been, which probably will be, in God's world here below.—If an Oliver Cromwell stood close by us, in the vesture and dialect of this our own time, he were of all men the worthiest to be written about. Two centuries lying heaped over him obscure the man; have abolished much that was transitory in the man. . . . He existed, he exists; can we not discern him, decipher him, present his lineaments to men?— [not likely I think!] (f. 107.).

It is likely that Carlyle's asides show that he had begun to recognize that though a history may aim to bring out the *soul* of a past period, it is hard to reconcile this with the set purpose of reflecting on the present. The problems of ordering a faithful interpretation are difficult enough without confusing the two ages. In August 1842 he confesses to Emerson, "One of my grand difficulties I suspect to be that I cannot write two Books at once; cannot be in the seventeenth century and in the nineteenth at one and the same moment."[6] For Carlyle's draft comments on the Long Parliament, for example, drift into topicalities, which were eventually to be no part of his terse introductory remarks on the same subject in the final text of *Cromwell*:[7]

> The English Parlt still exists; the last of our traditions in which some men still hope. I have looked upon it myself, not without astonishment, not without some earnestness of curiosity. There it still sits and simmers, passing thousands of acts yearly, delivering acres of printed talk yearly, at present in what they call the Reformed State. . . . Young men and old in frock [coats] and trousers with their legs folded . . . or sitting in ranged benches with their hats on, free and easy, mutually conversing humming Manifold; unfortunate dull orator entirely inaudible amid the din. . . . It is one of those 1001 private-bills about canals, highways, harbour-duties, turnpike rates, which pass here yearly, which have all to come hither that they may pass. It is the best way, sayst thou? Well, who knows! . . . But bills that wanted persons to pass them, surely at first thought one would fancy they might as well look out for somebody who *would* listen to them first of all! These are mysteries of State (f. 55v.).

It is much the same with his comments on the Church of his own day, which are implicit in *Cromwell* but not as direct as even in the surviving fragments of manuscript.[8]

Much of the Forster Manuscript was to be condensed into the opening chapter of *Cromwell*, "Anti-Dryasdust", expressing Carlyle's hope that History has something to teach, his exasperation with records, his contempt for historians and his aim to resuscitate "a Heroism from Past Time". Clearly he sees the paradoxes in History. He sets the highest value on "truth", which means that he must depend on documents, facts and firsthand authorities; but his real concern is with what is true in principle, which

17

may be very loosely related to any one of these. Then, any historian must trace a path for us through a limitless past universe of action, for "Narrative is *linear*, Action is *solid*". Yet it is he who makes this path, "tracking it out with the eye not, as is more common, with the *nose*,"—that is, using "insight" not just laborious "research". Carlyle's half-simulated impatience is a way of dramatising his problems:

> For indeed the History of the Past is the real Bible. So did the god's which made this Universe manifest itself to us . . . even so if thou wilt think of it. That is the true series of incarnations and avatars. The splendour of God shone thro' the huge incondite chaos of *our* being, so and then so; and by heroism after heroism, we have come to what you see. The Bible of the Past, rich are they that have it written as some old Greeks, old Hebrews and others have it. But looking in Collins's Peerage and the illegible torpedo rubbish mounds I am struck dumb. English *Literature* (is a thing yet to be born) if Literature mean *speaking* in fit words what the gods were pleased to *act*. . . .
>
> "God is great," say the Moslems: yes, but Dryasdust and Human Stupidity are not small. It too is wide as Immensity, it too is deep as Hell; has a strength of slumberous torpor in it, the subduing of *which* will mean that the History of this Universe is complete. . . . [Yet] the gods will never conquer it, sings Schiller and say I (f. 4v.).

> Wilt thou look, O reader; shall we two endeavour to look earnestly together. Vain is Whitelocke, vain are Knebworth, Hardwick State Papers, Somers' Tracts Harl [eaian] Miscelly, and that fatal rubbish mound of "original documents", documentary of little, except of the stupidity of mankind. . . . Read no more there: believe me I have read till my soul is near extinction, and much I have read which no following son of Adam will ever more read; and in all this there is nothing visible but an undecipherable universe filled as with dirty undecipherable London fog (f. 111v.).

> He is a conservative (one of the truest) who brings back the Past vitally visible into the Present living Time. . . . Your dreary constitutional Hallams, your (who's?) are the true revolutionists, that would cut us off sheer asunder from whatsoever went before; representing all that went before as lifeless ashes, as a thing one blesses God one has no further trade with (f. 100).

18

The past belongs to Hela the Death Goddess . . . overspread with pale horror, with dim brown oblivion. And who are these, evidently kinsmen of the death goddess, that stand as Janitors admit[t]ing you, under heavy fees, to some view of the matter here and there? They are the Historians, bless their singular countenances,—on the whole as strange a people as I have ever seen. What an indistinct mouldy Whiteness overspreads their faces, so that no human feature can be clear, discovered; the features all gone, as in long-buried men, into a mealy damp-powdery, blank. . . . See with what amazing amorphous wrappages, like huge Irish watch-coats, quilted out of all the rags of Nature, they have indistinctly wrapt themselves; and stand, all winged, undecipherable, without form . . . By Heaven, the inner anatomy of one of these necromantic watchmen is a thing Science longs for; such a one I would go some miles to see dissected, and know what it was that he had within him, if aught (ff. 54–54v.).

It was not long after this that he came on the Camden Society's *Chronica Jocelini De Brakelonda*, and turned from Oliver to the Abbot Samson. At one moment he is writing about Cromwell's first letter, addressed to "Mr. Storie, at the sign of the Dog." Then, on the same page, he launches into a long continuous passage on "Jocelin of St. Edmundsbury. . . . One of those vanished Existences, utterly grown dark, whose works or footprints are still clear to our eyes" (f. 56v.).[9] What is common to both books and men is that, in Carlyle's sense, they are heroes, and such heroism means the ability to grasp what is true. As he says in *Past and Present*, it means " 'Hero-worship', if you will,—yes, friends; but, first of all, by being ourselves of heroic mind."[10]

This may not be a new light; but, again, what the draft shows is what came to Carlyle when he set himself to write *something* even though clear that it was not the subject of his new book. He is too bitter at his failure for it to be called almost automatic writing, but he is trying to draw on the well of his own belief. As he says: "We have written lately often of *Silence*: but how deeply at present do we feel that Speech too were glorious and blessed. Forms unutterable struggle like spirits in prison within us. . . . Thought, like the gods, is born of chaos; like lightning out of the black vague-rolling tempest: all chaos is the mother of thought, as Venus (Urania?) sprang from the foam of the sea" (f. 95). The basis of his thought is his belief in morality. As he was to re-

19

state it in *Past and Present*: "All religion" reminds us "of the quite *infinite* difference there is between a Good man and a Bad".[11]

But is there not, human at the heart of all, strangely hidden, sunk, overwhelmed yet not extinct, a light-element and fire-element, which if you but awaken it shall irradiate and illuminate the whole, and make life a glorious fixed landscape, rock-borne, sure, the home and conquest of the brave, no longer a shoreless, skyless wavering chaos wherein cowards weep and die. It is infinitely respectable this fact that poor man's convictions are primarily moral; that his life-theory, never so stupid logically, has ever a moral truth in it whereby it first became credible to him. Wild Odin with his red-bearded Thunder*god*, with his hoary *Jotun* Frost the glance of whose devil-eye splits rocks, found credence and apotheosis among the Northmen not for these things which are become foolish false, but for another thing which remains for ever wise and true. Ye Northmen, ye shall not fear death; a Supreme Power presides over that and all things, and has appointed *Valkyrs* Choosers. Death's appointers, unerring inexorable: them ye shall follow unreluctantly, nay joyfully; and know that He on high takes only the valiant to his bosom, tramples all cowards down to Hela and the realms of Night! Not a well-conditioned Norse heard that but answered, Yes. To the great-hearted melancholic Norsemen, sitting sulky, vacant there, . . . the whole universe a shimmering mask of vague unintelligibility to them, such news was as a spark of lightning, awakening their own inner light,—which then blazed and burnt! I myself to this hour have respect for it, and hope always to have. Neither do we find that Christianism, this faith of Oliver's, propagated itself much by publication of "Evidences," Bridgewater Treatises and such like in these early times. No: curiously enough it was by other ways. Infinite pity and admiration, infinite assent to a new form of nobleness again kindled all hearts nigh sunk unto death. . . . If you will have a man believe, convince his heart; let the poor man see face to face a truth, palpable veritable, of which there is no doubting: it is strange to what extent his logicalities on all sides will accommodate themselves to that (f. 106).

What seekest thou for new Gospels, religions of the Future? In the heroic hearts born into every generation, lo *there* is a new Gospel and religion, not of the Future only but of the Present, direct and indisputable revealed once more by the Almighty Highest! What wouldst thou, fool? Did not the Highest God make —thee. The small still voices that speak, if thou wilt listen, in thy own heart of hearts, are not these His voice withal,—monitions from the unfathomable ever-sacred heart of things? Thunders from Sinai &c; these may be needed for rude boyhood; a grown man can understand what is said to him without these! The heroes of any age are the true Gospel of that age. . . . ["intellect and virtue inseparable, nay identical": how very gently this began with me; and it goes swelling and deepening, so as to look really like a most important thing! The thought, all diluted into irrecognisability in the above, is nevertheless a true one: "Honour the able-man; and for this end (first of all) know him, know where to seek for him."] [Last night, 7 jany 1842, at H[enry] Taylor's talked of this].—(pen spoiled!) (f. 95v.).

Aber es kam Nichts auf das Blatt!—Worship of Heroes the only kind of Worship that remains to us? The only one, intrinsically, that man ever had? The "religion of the future" is even *this*;—and those wearisome confused adjustings of Church to State and controversies between High Church and the Voluntary Principle will, for one thing, abolish themselves and trouble us no more. Church and State being all one . . . and indeed all manner of true free universal principles, coalescing into Catholicism very difft from the poor old Pope's, as the seven coloured rays into floods of pure light. It will be a blessed time.—"O Jerusalem, Jerusalem, thou that killest the Prophets and stonest them that are sent unto thee!" O England, England, thou that doest even the like,—thou that misknowest the Heroes, hangest their dead bodies on gibbets, who rejoicest over the Quacks, saying, Be *ye* king over me;—and art now arrived at the gates of ruin and inanition by the leading of these same! Open thy heavy eyes, foolish country, look and see. Quacks lead thee, even hitherward; to no other goal, but to ruin and destruction only, could or can these leave thee: gravitation tends not more surely to the centre than Quackery does to the Devil. . . . (f. 154).

Even apart from the merely historical notes there is much more than this in the manuscript, which is not only of editorial interest. For part of its value lies in the sense it gives of bringing one closer to Carlyle in piecing the scraps together. It is even a reflection on his own technique in his published works: we ourselves play Editor to Teufelsdröckh and Sauerteig, seeking for inspiration in these fragments of Manuscript. Nor is this just a forced coincidence. Carlyle's mode of thought and expression

21

depend on his breaking down accepted forms and recreating them according to his inner convictions, and here they wait to be re-assembled. In a somewhat similar way this meant that as a historian he had to master his subject so that he could identify himself with figures of the past, and make a forced use of their concerns to focus and express his own convictions about the present.

Other contributors to this volume have noticed how this is an essential part of Carlyle's method, and so it needs less comment here. It is certainly part of his *process* and a means of allowing the mere narrator to participate in, or to re-create the past, by playing roles.[12] He is still fascinated by the fancy he had indulged in *Sartor* (p. 261) of the "Time-annihilating Hat" which will bring periods together telescoping Time, though even that would not be enough:

> Every Historian should be provided with a *Time-Hat*: what . . . an amazing implement/. Fancy him entering one of those supper-parties where Edward Hyde sits listening . . . where Shakespeare etc sits incountering of wits with Benj*n* Jonson! But he would be a melancholy *foreigner* withal; the people's thoughts as strange to him as their costumes: we belong to our own century as to our own parish, and have to gaze with blank sad wonderment. . . . The vocables men utter with their tongues are hardly more diverse, than the thoughts they cherish in their hearts: what we can say is that one alphabet spells them all (f. 53v.).

The historian must be able to become one with his subject, as Carlyle is drawn to be with Abbot Samson, Cromwell or Frederick.

This is curiously revealed in the Forster manuscript, which has two striking passages which Carlyle did not publish; for it is not only fancy which sees in them his self-identification with Cromwell. Their interest lies both in this and in their being another newly-caught echo of that voice of his, like so "few other voices". The first passage comes in an account of his action at Cambridge, on 15 August 1842, to prevent the University Plate's being des-patched to the royalists:

> Peace, ye Heads of Houses; go into your Lexicons again; suffi-cient for *this* day be the evil thereof. Mr. C in this work of his has authority which *he* is willing to venture on. The man wishes to be civil too; but urge him not. In those grey troublous eyes of his,

in that unbeautiful rough countenance of his, there is something
dangerous. Ye hear how his common bass voice rises easily into
harsh querulous tenor; and argumentative speech—like a prophetic chaunt becomes austere canto-fermo. His face will suddenly
flush red, and again it will suddenly flush blackish bluish, and become of slate colour: I judge that his temper is none of the
blessedest. He has an unpleasant breadth of jaw. Besides he
preaches, plays, and has warts on his face. A man probably not
without madness in him (f. 55).

Then, again, as he composes the letter "To Mr *Storie* at the Dog":

In some small chamber, warmed with wood faggots in a house
on the South outskirts of St Ives, sits a robust middle-aged man,
penning this epistle. . . . By intense inspection something of this
man can be discerned. A man of simple farmer aspect; very far
from beautiful, sorrowful rather, [*word uncertain*] cloudy-browed,
what the common run of men call ugly. In those deep anxious eyes,
plays for the present no smile;—yet have I seen them beam with
honest laughter, and their sternness melt in the softest tears, for
he is a living man this angry farmer. Between the brows what an
ugly wart. The jaw too has dangerous squareness, under each ear, a
dangerous angularity: dangerous if strong mean dangerous, as to
the common run of man it does, the man's voice too is none of the
musicalest: strong nor can you call it flatly dissonant, yet I think
there is something of the metallic gong in it, oppressively impressive; and then alas it so easily rises into alt! and belches you
forth a bellow withering men's very heart like few other voices of
which you never heard, or speaks in a kind of inspired recitation or
glowing canto-fermo, much too impressive on the auditor (f. 56).

History, said Carlyle, is "a looking both before and after",[13] and
may even mean trying to look at one's own image. And if History
is "the essence of innumerable Biographies"[14] it will remain un-
intelligible to the reader who cannot understand himself. Thus
to read Carlyle's works is also to try to understand Carlyle.

NOTES

1. *The Athenaeum* (8 Jan. 1876), p. 54, after the tributes to Carlyle on
   his eightieth birthday, 4 December 1875: "Night's childless children"
   is a phrase applied to the Furies by Aeschylus.

2. The Forster manuscript (F. 48.E36) was part of the original bequest of the Forster Collection, in 1876, to what is now the Victoria and Albert Museum, London; and soon after its receipt it was rather approximately put in order and bound. Since it was then even more approximately catalogued under John Forster's name, as " 'Statesmen of the Commonwealth' [1840] MS. and proofs, letters etc. . . . Also notes &c. by Mr. Carlyle", it has eluded notice, and I came to examine it only after it was kindly drawn to my attention by Mr Anthony Burton, Assistant Keeper. The present account is intended to be no more than a summary. The manuscript consists of 180 miscellaneous sheets, mostly on paper of the same size as used for *Past and Present* (8 by 13 inches), but with some odd letters and scraps. It is incomplete even as a draft: some of it having gone the way of all manuscript, and some apparently parcelled off separately and used as the basis of the *Historical Sketches* (London, 1902, uniform with the Centenary *Works*), edited by Alexander Carlyle. Much of it is made up of notes from Carlyle's reading. It is really *not* in chronological order, so that one of the first problems for future study will be to see what this was. Actual dated comments range, in the main sequence, from 20 December 1841 to 27 Nov. 1843, but it also includes some letters of 1844 and one of 1846 (KJF).

3. The difficulties were fairly well brought out by Froude through quotations from letters and the *Journal*, and he correctly inferred that "many pages were covered with writing of a sort". But he never saw this writing, and seems to have accepted that Carlyle burnt it. There has been a natural tendency to accept TC's self-reproaches, and some failure to see how thoroughly the ground was being laid for his book. (*Life*, III, 332–5.)

4. See especially Grace E. Calder, *The Writing of Past and Present, A Study of Carlyle's Manuscripts* (New Haven, 1949), Yale Studies in English 112. This is the authoritative work, based on the manuscript of the first draft (British Museum) and the printer's copy (Yale University Library). In spite of being written without reference to the miscatalogued Forster manuscript its authority remains, although a few conclusions might be questioned. We still do not know exactly when Carlyle started *Past and Present*, any more than we can give a precise date for the beginning of *Cromwell*.

5. "Heroes", of course, recur in *Past and Present* and *Cromwell*, but the drift of the manuscript sometimes appears to be back towards the lectures, and even the Clothes-Philosophy is revived (f. 111v.), and dropped only after an "Ach Himmel! O *where shall* I begin?"

6. *The Correspondence of Emerson and Carlyle*, ed. J. Slater (New York and London, 1964), p. 328.

7. *Works*, VI, 107.

8. The visit to the House of Commons was paid on 15 June 1842, and is described in similar terms in a letter from TC to his mother, 17 June,

NLS, MS, 521.5. He went to hear Charles Buller, since Mrs Buller wanted Carlyle to hear her son speak on the Church Patronage (Scotland) Bill. Evidently Carlyle barely exaggerates: on a "technical objection" the hearing was put off until 5 July, and it was then postponed for a further six months, to be followed by the Disruption of the Scottish Church. For "comments on the Church of his own day", see Forster manuscript, f. 52.

9. Cf. *Works*, X, 40.
10. *Works*, X, 35.
11. *Works*, X, 227.
12. See pp. 98 and 207 for method, and pp. 98, 178–80, and 208–9 for identification. Carlyle undeniably uses it from *Sartor* onwards, the parallels between *Frederick* and *Cromwell* being particularly clear. It is conceivable that the re-writing of part of the *French Revolution*, without "foul papers", made it less obvious there, though still a fundamental principle.
13. "On History," *Works*, XXVII, 83.
14. *Works*, XXVII, 86.

I expect to undertake a further study of the Forster manuscript in an attempt at least to solve unanswered questions about Carlyle's progress with Cromwell, just when he turned to *Past and Present*, and the relationship of the more important passages to the *Works*. (KJF).

1

Carlyle Today

by G. B. TENNYSON

In the National Portrait Gallery in London there is close to an entire floor devoted to portraits of figures from the nineteenth century. At the end of a long corridor, off which are situated various rooms for artists, literary figures, actors, and anti-slavery agitators, one enters at last a large octagonal room. In the centre of this room stands a pedestal topped by a rectangular glass case; inside the case stands a bust of Thomas Carlyle by Joseph Edgar Boehm. Behind the bust on the opposite wall hangs the very large, unfinished but superb portrait of Carlyle by John Everett Millais. On the left hand of the father, as the viewer sees it, hang portraits of John Stuart Mill, John Ruskin, and William Morris. All of these portraits are disposed around large relief letters which read—PROPHETS. As one enters the room Carlyle appears not only larger than life, but in a kind of double focus; his eminence in the portrait, higher and to the right of the bust, seems to be shimmering through the glass which enshrines his brooding countenance in three dimensions; and through the same glass gleams the legend of his role. Mill, Ruskin, and Morris recede as accent marks or satellites; the rest of the room scarcely has any existence: stray figures of explorers and scientists adorn the walls, but the room is unquestionably dominated by the image, one might almost say the presence, of Thomas Carlyle.

To a student of Carlyle the display is both awesome and gratifying. Awesome because Carlyle always appears to be sitting in judgment (a quality of the living Carlyle admirably captured by the more successful portraitists and sculptors), and, perhaps because he is shown twice, he seems to be following one with his

27

eyes through the room. Gratifying because the arrangement also seems to be a judgment of posterity itself on Carlyle's place in Victorian life; gratifying, moreover, in a way that the fine statue on the Embankment, or the splendid Herdman portrait in Edinburgh can never be. The Embankment statue, after all, cannot be moved, fixed as it was by public subscription shortly after Carlyle's death. The Scottish National Portrait Gallery, for its part, can well be expected to have a display of one of Scotland's most illustrious sons. But the selection in the National Portrait Gallery seems one determined less by accident and more by choice than these other two, to be in fact the judgment of Britain on Carlyle. Never mind the fact that the National Portrait Gallery happens to have a treasure trove of Carlyle portraits, more perhaps than that of any single figure outside of recent monarchs. It has much else besides[1] and it could have arranged its Victorian display in ways that would have placed quite a different emphasis, or none at all, on Carlyle. So one must acknowledge that this display represents something quite intentional and something quite contemporary in terms of the present view of Thomas Carlyle.

Now, in one sense the display could not be more obvious. To students of the nineteenth century the presentation of Carlyle as an eminent Victorian and one whom it pleases critics to call a "prophet" must seem almost a cliché. But this is academic habit, and the National Portrait Gallery in following that habit in a contemporary exhibition for the average museum-goer serves to raise questions about the habit itself, questions which it is the academic obligation to answer.

The first question, it seems to me, is: how has Carlyle come to the eminence ascribed to him by the display in the Portrait Gallery? Has he always enjoyed it? What was his position in, say, July 1914 when the Millais portrait was slashed through the forehead and left eye by a suffragette, presumably on the grounds that Carlyle's well-known opposition to democracy and the ballot box was a contributory factor in the denial of the vote to women.[2] What in general has been the course of thought on Carlyle that has brought him to the present position of such prominence in the eyes of the keepers of the National Portrait Gallery? In short, what has been the history of Carlyle's reputation?

Another question raised by the display in the National Portrait

Gallery is suggested more specifically by the *mode* in which Carlyle is presented. Unlike Newman, who is to be found in company not only with Dr Pusey and the saintly John Keble, as is fitting, but cheek by jowl with a bust of Thomas De Quincey, stared at ruminantly by George Eliot, and on the very same wall with James Anthony Froude (all an illustration no doubt of T. S. Eliot's contention that old combatants are in death folded in a single party); unlike Macaulay, who looks prosperous among a category called "Men of Learning"; unlike the rather haunting Darwin portrait properly displayed next to his "Ape", T. H. Huxley, on a wall labelled "Scientists"; unlike all these, Carlyle and his satellites are labelled "Prophets". As I have said, this is a critical commonplace. But if we stop to think on the matter a moment it is a rather astonishing commonplace. In what other country and in what other age could we expect to find a category of writers publicly labelled "Prophets"? Indeed, outside of the Bible can we think of any *assemblage* of prophets? In the National Portrait Gallery itself no other age has a group of portraits so designated. The Victorian presentation is unique. The question that is thus raised is, what in fact *is* a prophet? And further, why is Carlyle one?

The question of Carlyle's prophetism and the question of Carlyle's reputation raised by the display in the gallery are curiously intertwined. They may almost be said to be one question. It is to this double-pronged question that this paper is addressed.

The raw material that one uses as the basis for generalizations about a writer's reputation is exceedingly difficult to itemize. It is, of course, not only those written treatments of the author's reputation (in Carlyle's case these are relatively few[3]), it is also the mass of material written about an author in general (in Carlyle's case the mass is relatively large), and beyond that it is the body of references and reflections in other works, in biographies, in contemporary accounts, in critical studies primarily devoted to matters other than reputation, and so on. Above all, it is the "feel" one acquires in going through scholarly and critical and historical material; and this cannot be pinned down to single works. My own recent massive encounter with Carlyle-related critical material has exposed me both to the specific treatments of Carlyle and his reputation and to the general feel of intellectual and critical response to Carlyle for the past one hundred and fifty years.[4] It is largely on the basis of this encounter that I shall endeavour to outline the state of Carlyle's reputation.

For purposes of seeing Carlyle's reputation in perspective, it is easiest to view it in three main stages. They are in the first instance chronological:

> I. Carlyle's lifetime (to 1881)
> II. From Carlyle's Death to about 1930
> III. From 1930 to the Present

But each period has its own character too and can be designated by an appropriate adjective as follows: The Popular, the Reactionary, and the Scholarly-Critical. And each period has its own book, or books, that sum up the dominant tone of the period. These works in turn were undertaken by characteristic types of Carlyle scholars for the period in question. Finally, each period and its dominant attitude cast some light on the idea of the prophet as exemplified in Carlyle.

Before looking at each period in greater detail it may be useful to summarize the general trend of Carlyle's reputation throughout the three periods. If it is a commonplace that Carlyle was an eminent Victorian and another commonplace that he is often viewed as a prophet, it is the greatest commonplace of all in Carlyle scholarship that his reputation, along with that of most of his fellow prophets and even most of the men of learning and the writers of the Victorian age in general, suffered an almost total eclipse after his death. Perhaps no one other than Ruskin plummeted more precipitously in public esteem and in general reader devotion. Of course this observation indicates that Carlyle had reached a rather high eminence, else his fall would not have appeared so dramatic. If we were plotting the whole course of Carlyle's reputation through the three periods on a graph, we would note a generally rising curve in Period I up to a very high peak towards the end of his life, a drastic plunge in Period II to a valley almost as deep as the peak was high, and a cautious rise in Period III to a modest eminence but with perhaps a further rise in prospect.

Let us trace this curious pattern in somewhat greater detail

30

through the three main periods of Carlyle's reputation, with special stress on The Popular Period since it offers within itself a paradigm of what happened later.

The Popular Period. This runs from the late eighteen-twenties to Carlyle's death in 1881, for it is not until the late twenties that Carlyle can be said to have a reputation at all, following what has been described as the longest literary apprenticeship in English letters. While the graph described above pictures an upward swing throughout the Popular Period, a closer look reveals that only the main thrust is upward; there are some downturns as well. Or one could say that, while Carlyle's reputation increased consistently in his lifetime, the esteem in which he was held by knowledgeable people varied a good deal. From the point of view of simple notoriety, of course, Carlyle began in total obscurity and ended in total celebrity. But from the point of view of esteem the path was rockier and in some ways anticipated the period since his death.

Carlyle began by baffling readers, came to have an enormous hold on them and to be revered by them, and then he startled and disappointed his readers by his social intransigence, and finally more or less redeemed himself towards the end by another great work and died in honour. The illustrative documents in this phase are in fact Carlyle's own works, or at least the response to them. The early literary essays and *Sartor Resartus* (1833–34) represent the first stage, that of bafflement, though of course these works came to have an almost biblical force with later generations. Even from the start the bafflement was mixed with admiration and respect, but initially Carlyle seems to have enjoyed a reputation as a kind of brilliant eccentric. The second stage, that of adulation, is best represented by *The French Revolution* (1837) and *Past and Present* (1843). It was Carlyle's triumph with the twice-written *French Revolution* that rehabilitated his earlier writings and secured him a future reading public that would devour any word he chose to publish. Some of that public, though continuing to read him, felt considerable dismay with the publication of such works as *Latter-Day Pamphlets* (1850), and for some years while Carlyle traversed the vale of tears of research on *Frederick the Great* there were many who felt towards him primarily disenchantment. But at last, with *Frederick the Great* (1858–65),

31

Carlyle entered the fourth and last stage of his reputation in his lifetime, that of honour and reverence, and, though there were dissenters, it was essentially in a state of honour and reverence that Carlyle died.

This overview of the state of Carlyle's reputation in his lifetime lends itself fairly readily to documentation from his contemporaries. John Sterling, for example, on *Sartor Resartus* has rightly been much reprinted. His admiration for many of the sentiments mixed with his dismay at, and even distaste for, many of the modes of utterance in the work well captures what proved to be the contemporary reaction:

> The sense of strangeness is also awakened by the marvellous combinations, in which the work abounds to a degree that the common reader must find perfectly bewildering. This can hardly, however, be treated as a consequence of the *style*; for the style in this respect coheres with, and springs from, the whole turn and tendency of thought. The noblest images are objects of a humorous smile, in a mind which sees itself above all Nature and throned in the arms of an Almighty Necessity; while the meanest have a dignity, inasmuch as they are trivial symbols of the same one life to which the great whole belongs. And hence, as I divine, the startling whirl of incongruous juxtaposition, which of a truth must to many readers seem as amazing as if the Pythia on the tripod should have struck-up a drinking-song, or Thersites had caught the prophetic strain of Cassandra.[5]

Emerson's enthusiasm for the early Carlyle is also well-known, as is Mill's. Indeed, the three early enthusiasts, Sterling, Emerson, Mill, were heralds of the second phase of the Popular period, the phase of adulation, and they figured representatively in that phase. Mill, for example, was moved to a warm review of *The French Revolution* in his own Journal, *The London and Westminster Review*, which began:

> This is not so much a history, as an epic poem; and notwithstanding, or even in consequence of this, the truest of histories. It is the history of the French Revolution, and the poetry of it, both in one; and on the whole no work of greater genius, either historical or poetical, has been produced in this country for many years.[6]

John Sterling took extensive space in the same publication two years later to write an encomiastic account of Carlyle's works in

32

which, significantly, he devotes considerable attention to the question of prophetism and of Carlyle's "teaching".[7] Indeed, Sterling in his review very largely captures what would come to be the dominant tone of the Victorian response to Carlyle, the tone that characterizes all of the Popular period.

Other adulators could be cited, not least among them Dickens who paid Carlyle the compliment of using *The French Revolution* as part of the raw material for a novel. But the point should be sufficiently clear: as a result of his triumph with *The French Revolution* Carlyle established himself as one of the great writers of the age. Even the setbacks of the period of disenchantment during the eighteen-fifties and the semi-reclusiveness of Carlyle's life after the death of Jane Welsh Carlyle in 1866 and after the publication of *Frederick the Great* never entirely dimmed the lustre of the reputation that stormed all before it in the eighteen-forties. Matthew Arnold, writing in the eighties, recalls some of that glory as it appeared to the Oxford undergraduate Arnold had been when Carlyle came fully into his own:

> Forty years ago, when I was an undergraduate at Oxford, voices were in the air there which haunt my memory still. Happy the man who in that susceptible season of youth hears such voices!
> There was the puissant voice of Carlyle; so sorely strained, over-used, and mis-used since, but then fresh, comparatively sound, and reaching our hearts with true, pathetic eloquence.[8]

Arnold was obviously writing with full awareness of the years that had elapsed since Carlyle's puissant voice had stirred Oxford. He would have known that Carlyle's social views in "Occasional Discourse on the Negro Question" (1849), and especially the *Latter-Day Pamphlets* (1850), had quite turned much enlightened opinion against him. Mill and Carlyle ceased to be personal friends and Mill retorted to Carlyle's views with "The Negro Question" (1850). Emerson and the New England intellectuals were alarmed. Many agreed with Trollope, who said: "I look upon him as a man who was always in danger of going mad in literature and who has now done so."[9] Ruskin remained a notable exception to the prevailing view of the fifties, the period of disenchantment with Carlyle, and almost alone of prominent persons he congratulated Carlyle on the blistering *Latter-Day Pamphlets*. Arnold, however, sided with such as Mill and Emerson and Trollope and it was the Carlyle of this phase that Arnold dubbed a "moral desperado".

But the publication of *Frederick the Great* (1858–65) went far towards redeeming Carlyle in public esteem (though perhaps not in Arnold's esteem). The upturn in the sixties was also signalled by the election of Carlyle as Rector of Edinburgh University in 1866 in competition with none other than Benjamin Disraeli. By 1875 Carlyle was the reigning grand old man of English letters: a distinguished roster of literary figures presented him with a testimonial in that year affirming that Carlyle had in his own life comported himself as the Hero as Man of Letters. He had earlier declined a decoration and pension offered by Her Majesty's government through Disraeli, though he had been willing to accept in 1874 the Prussian Order of Merit proffered by Bismarck. When Carlyle died and by his own request was *not* buried in Westminster Abbey, the Dean of that foundation nevertheless preached a moving funeral sermon which contained the following observations characteristic of the Victorian estimate of Carlyle:

> It was customary for those who honoured him to speak of him as a 'prophet'. And if we take the word in its largest sense he truly deserved the name. He was a prophet, and felt himself to be a prophet, in the midst of an untoward generation; his prophet's mantle was his rough Scotch dialect, and his own peculiar diction, and his own secluded manner of life. He was a prophet most of all in the emphatic utterance of truths which no one else, or hardly any one else, ventured to deliver, and which he felt to be a message of good to a world sorely in need of them.[10]

Dean Stanley's remarks are a fitting terminus for considering the estimate of Carlyle in the Popular Period, for things would not be the same afterwards. But before moving to the next phase it is appropriate to look back and in looking back on the pattern of more than fifty years of Carlyle's reputation we are struck first of all by the enormous success of it. Carlyle succeeded against every odd; he simply imposed himself on his contemporaries. He would be heard; and he was heard. It is improbable, but it is true.

Carlyle's contemporaries viewed him with admiration bordering on reverence; even his enemies treated him with respect. If one had to settle upon a single word to characterize the general Victorian view of Carlyle, that word should be—Teacher. Victorians did not think of Carlyle primarily in literary terms; that is, they were not overly concerned about the proper literary category to place him in—essayist, historian or social critic. Nor did they preoccupy themselves unduly with analysis of Carlyle's style. Not that they were indifferent to it, not that they did not occasionally satirize it, and even from time to time, as in a Sterling or an Emerson, make valuable contributions towards understanding it. But they kept their eyes on Carlyle the Teacher.

Nor do I think the Victorian reaction to Carlyle was misplaced. It was the response he sought from his readers and in the main they made that response intelligently and thoughtfully. We should not let ourselves be misled because Victorian zeal for Carlyle the Teacher occasionally led to Victorian excesses of discipleship. To be sure, many Victorian readers made an easy transition from Teacher to Philosopher to Theologian and endeavoured to extract from Carlyle's writing the "system" that they felt sure must lie buried there. Something of this impulse must lie behind the Victorian equivalents of "The Thoughts of Chairman Thomas" that one still meets with in second-hand book-shops. These, of course, have fallen into great disrepute today; but I would suggest that the disdain aroused today is provoked really more by the idea of such compilations than by Carlyle himself. I have recently, for example, been working in an area where it is natural to come across such volumes as *The Christian Year Birthday Book* and *Heavenly Promises*, these being extracts from John Keble's *The Christian Year* arranged in special sequence for Victorian instruction and delight. They must seem a little superfluous to the twentieth century, considering how many copies of *The Christian Year* itself were (and are) available. But no matter: the twentieth century has found all of Keble superfluous. The volumes in question, though, do testify to the Victorian propensity for such collections and for making any favoured author into a teacher. They can be duplicated for most serious Victorian writers. There may be, for all I know, such a volume culled from the less incendiary passages in Swinburne. Carlyle, of course, was better suited than Swinburne for such treatments; he seems at times to have written with an eye towards them.

At all events, the key Victorian word for Carlyle was Teacher. And by that they meant not only the obvious, the didactic, the

35

hortatory, the reproving, but even something of what we would understand by prophet. In fact, there is almost a formula in typical Victorian commentary on Carlyle, and it runs something like this: "Carlyle says so-and-so, or Carlyle does so-and-so, it is true, but the fact is that Carlyle is not a —— [here fill in "novelist", or "historian", or even "philosopher"], but a Prophet, and it is as a prophet that he is to be understood." Usually this sense of prophet equates with teacher and sage. Sometimes the analysis of prophetism is deeper, of course, but I think the Victorian emphasis always falls on the prophet as teacher. It is, in my judgment, far from the worst emphasis.

In great part the monument of the whole Victorian estimate of Carlyle is James Anthony Froude's four-volume *Thomas Carlyle* (1882, 1884), which appeared with almost indecent speed upon the death of Carlyle and which has been held ever since to be the "standard" biography. It is in a curious way both the shining example of the Victorian view of Carlyle as Teacher and the herald of a new and not very auspicious period in Carlyle's reputation— the Reactionary Period. As the capstone of the Victorian view of Carlyle as Teacher, Froude's *Life* really has no equal in breadth and in detail. Froude's view of Carlyle is in many ways entirely consistent with the widespread nineteenth-century view of him— Carlyle the rugged peasant's son emerging from the wilderness with his "Message" and his Teaching—indeed, these are among Froude's favourite words in connection with Carlyle. Froude sums up much of the Victorian attitude of sometimes uncomfortable reverence toward an acknowledged moral leader. Froude even seeks to justify the more debatable aspects of what he likes to call Carlyle's "creed", thus showing himself loyal to the end.

But Froude's *Life* is something other than a pious biography. Almost upon its appearance, coupled with that of the hastily-edited (by Froude) *Reminiscences* (1881), there was an outcry. The Oscar Wilde quip that every great man has his disciples and it is always Judas who writes the biography seemed to many the proper description of Froude's attitude toward Carlyle. Certainly today, it seems to me, the more interesting aspects of Froude's biography are not those having to do with Carlyle's emotional state but those having to do with Froude's. There is some reason to suspect that, when he came to write Carlyle's biography, Froude

felt toward Carlyle not unlike the way he felt toward the Tractarians when he came to write *The Nemesis of Faith*. Is it any
wonder that Froude's enemies sensed the same and titled one of
their anti-Froude works, *The Nemesis of Froude?*[11]

Thus at the very moment that Froude's *Life* stands as a sum-
mation of Victorian reverence towards a great teacher, it also
ushers in a new and rather untidy phase of Carlyle's reputation
that was to last for many years. It is the era I have dubbed the
Reactionary.

If the key word for the Popular period of Carlyle criticism is
Teacher, the key word for the Reactionary period is—Denouncer.
Now this phase, lasting for about fifty years following Carlyle's
death, is in many ways confused and at first seems not to lend
itself to easy categorization. It saw the appearance, for example,
of some notable works of scholarship—editions of letters and
occasional unpublished Carlyle works, for much of which we stand
indebted to the industry of Carlyle's nephew, Alexander Carlyle.
It was also the age of Traill's "Centenary Edition" of Carlyle's
works (1896–99) which for lack of a better still qualifies as the
standard edition. It saw, however, also a great quantity of biographical and quasi-biographical writing, especially that which
swirled around the Froude-Carlyle controversy, as it came to be
called, though I prefer to call it simply the Froude Controversy.
It saw too some specialist works of scholarship, editions of such
works as *The French Revolution* (by C. R. L. Fletcher, 1902, and
J. H. Rose, 1902), *Heroes* (by A. MacMechan, 1902), *Past and
Present* (by A. M. D. Hughes, 1918), and *Sartor Resartus* (by
MacMechan, 1896, and 1905) that continue to be of scholarly and
critical importance. It saw also many of those droning German
dissertations lauding the Sage. But still it had a dominant tone,
and that tone was set by what seemed to be Froude's undermining
of Carlyle's reputation as man and thinker. It was the negative in
Carlyle that came to dominate all consideration of him. Even
documents not directly involved in the Froude Controversy were
still animated by their stance one way or another on the Froude
issue.

It has been the fashion for many years now for scholars to say
as little as possible about the Froude Controversy, to pass over it
with a few discreet words as one of the displays of especially bad

temper on the part of our ancestors. Space prevents me from departing radically from this procedure, but I will say that I do not
entirely endorse it. The effects of the Froude Controversy linger
on today among undergraduates who ask confidently: "It's true,
isn't it, that Carlyle was impotent?" or in glancing sneers at
Carlyle from rather less innocent intellectuals. There is supposed to
be a kind of gentleman's agreement among scholars that Waldo
Hilary Dunn, after a lifetime of exculpating Froude, has con-
clusively proved (in *Froude and Carlyle*, 1930) that Froude was
more sinned against than sinning. Personally, I find this absolution
rather too generously given and in need of re-examination, but
here I only want to cite the Froude Controversy to illustrate the
temper of Carlyle criticism over a long period and not to reopen
the controversy itself.

That temper, I have suggested, tended to turn Carlyle criticism
into a battlefield over the negative aspects of Carlyle's life and
thought. To write in denunciation of the great Denouncer was an
act of courage, so it was thought; to write in defence of the great
Denouncer was equally so, and an act of loyalty as well. Though
I personally delight in this phase of Carlyle criticism as offering
byways of such quaint interest as even the Victorian chresto-
mathies do not provide, I recognize that this is a personal and
quixotic taste. Most readers do not care to know that Carlyle wore
a truss, or that Jane Welsh was thought by Geraldine Jewsbury to
have died *virgo intacta*. It is not squeamishness, I don't think: it is
on the contrary a case of modern taste being too jaded for all this.
The Froude controversy is simply no longer salacious *enough*! But
what it did to Carlyle criticism cannot be so easily overlooked.

For fifty years Carlyle scholars and critics debated the nega-
tives of Thomas Carlyle. We can divide most writers on the
subject into two camps—the Loyalists and the Revisionists. The
Loyalists were composed at first largely of those who had known
and admired Carlyle, such men as his nephew Alexander, or
the medical man, James Crichton-Browne, who became embroiled
in the matter on Alexander's side. They were joined later by
those who came under Carlyle's spell in the usual way, through
his writings. Among these we may number most of the German
academics whose tribe extended up to the second World War.
For the most part they simply muddied already turbid waters by

38

dragging Carlyle in to stand Godfather to whatever policy they wanted to defend at the moment on other grounds, the two most notable ones being Prussianism and Naziism. In a sense these men actually belong among the revisionists since they revised Carlyle to suit their own needs, but they felt themselves rather to be Loyalists, preserving in Germany even when it had been cast aside in Britain the true faith and the memory of a true Hero. There were, of course, also second generation Loyalists in Britain as well, and I will speak of two of these shortly. But Loyalists of whatever generation or country had this in common —they were defending a beleaguered holy place against the infidels and they fought with all of the zeal of a persecuted minority.

The Revisionists, for their part, looked to the Froude portrait as their standard, and also the subsequent Froude publications, not only Carlyle's own *Reminiscences*, which splendid book one can consider a casualty of the Reactionary phase since it was so rarely seen in its own right—not only, then, the *Reminiscences* and Froude's *Life*, but the posthumously published *My Relations with Carlyle* (1903), wherein Froude sought to justify the imputations he had made about the domestic relations of the two Carlyles, but only succeeded in making more explicit what was seen as treason to Carlyle and in provoking even more frenzied denials from the Loyalists. Even the valuable *Love Letters* (1909), which only now are being superseded by the *Collected Letters* (of Duke University and Edinburgh University) were provoked by the Froude "revelations" rather than by their inherent interest. Thus the Revisionists succeeded one way or another in dominating Carlyle scholarship for many years and in seizing at least most of the headlines during the Reactionary Period.

Revisionist documents of enduring value, apart from Froude's *Life* seen in its revisionist aspect, are actually very few. Certainly revisionism coloured everything said about Carlyle during these years, and thus the biographies and hence the received view of Carlyle may be said to have been deeply affected by the reactionary-revisionist ethos. Moreover, it continues today, and in contemporary scholarship on Carlyle's social and political views, revisionism may still be said to be dominant. One is still obliged to denounce the Denouncer on such matters as democracy, the vote, heroism, and discipline. I read in a book published in 1969 that only an occasional campus Carlylean still seeks to exonerate Carlyle of the darker charges hinting at Naziism that are levelled against him, these being taken simply as proven facts.[12] So, like the 1914 suffragette, we are still slashing Carlyle from forehead to eye on certain topics. One ought to add that, though this is Froude's legacy, it is doubtful that it was ever Froude's intention; for on these social matters Froude always sought to support Carlyle's views. Still it is the fruit of the revisionist spirit that has made Carlyle's name a dirty word in certain sacred modern precincts and Froude is its godfather. Despite all this, there is no outstanding purely revisionist document, as distinguished from the reactionary-revisionist *spirit*, that has survived the passage of the years. W. H. Dunn's Froude studies come as close as any to qualifying. The genteel mockery of a Lytton Strachey, while still entertaining, is not substantial enough to qualify. If one wanted to find a pure example of anti-Carlyle revisionism, one could go to Norwood Young's *Carlyle: His Rise and Fall* (London, n.d. [1927]), a late reactionary-revisionist document of a thoroughly vilifying nature, but it survives rather as a curiosity than anything else.

On the Loyalist side, there are more enduring documents. I have referred to some editions and volumes of letters. These are still of great value. There are also two works which stand, like Norwood Young, at the end of the period and, like Froude, both close it and open a new era. The first is David Alec Wilson's six-volume biography of Carlyle; the second is Isaac Watson Dyer's *Bibliography of Thomas Carlyle's Writings and Ana*. Wilson published his volumes over a ten-year period from 1923–34 (the last volume being completed after Wilson's death by D. W. MacArthur). Dyer's *Bibliography* appeared in 1928. Now Wilson's is the more backward-looking of the two works. His *Life* is clearly oriented towards the Reactionary period. It is an effort at total and documented vindication of Carlyle. It is not a wholly successful effort, although its industry is enormous. Wilson was the last of a dying race, that race of those who had known or almost known Carlyle in person and who felt it a personal duty to clear his name of the evil associations that had grown up around it. One would with reluctance send any but the most specialist readers to Wilson today, but his volumes do mark a new era in their commitment to a thoroughly documentary approach to Carlyle and in their assumption that Carlyle is to be taken seriously again as a writer, though in Wilson's view the operative word would be "still".

Dyer's *Bibliography* reinforces the Wilson approach and subjects it to even greater rigour. It, too, enshrines the past in that it lists any and everything by and about Carlyle, which means a great deal of fugitive material from the Reactionary phase. But it also means much Victorian material and above all it means the fixing of the canon of Carlyle's writing and even such useful extras as a supplement on portraits of Carlyle. That Dyer too is a Carlyle disciple is evident time and again in his *Bibliography* in his frank pro-Wilson and anti-Froude sentiments. But what is uppermost is the accurate listing of works by Carlyle and works about him. There have been from time to time minor additions to Dyer, but no major overhaul. His book still stands as the definitive bibliography up to its time and as a continuing reproach to scholarship that there has been no successor to cover the forty-odd years of Carlyle scholarship that have succeeded upon Dyer.[13]

If the tone of open partisanship in Wilson and Dyer marks them as the last gasp of the Reactionary period with its personal animosities and its aura of denunciations and defences of Carlyle the man, the emphasis on scholarship, on accuracy, on amassing a wealth of detailed information that also characterizes these two works marks them as the beginning of a new era altogether. It is, of course, the Scholarly, or perhaps more precisely the Scholarly-Critical era in which we still find ourselves. The Popular period was dominated by the image of Carlyle as Teacher; the Reactionary period was dominated by the image of Carlyle as Denouncer, often as not turned back upon the Sage himself as Carlyle the Denounced. The Scholarly or Scholarly-Critical period is dominated by the image of Carlyle as Influence.

Perhaps the contentiousness of the Reactionary phase had been too bitter, perhaps it was just that the passage of years and the departure of persons who knew the period and the principals from first-hand experience had softened tempers, perhaps it was simply that Victorianism and those who made it were now phenomena of historical interest and could be placed along with mediaevalism, or Elizabethanism, or the attitudes of any era now definitely over and closed. However it was, in the thirties the scholars began to move in. Tentatively at first and not without setbacks over the next decades. The Second World War, for example, threatened to revive the hard feelings toward Carlyle generated by the First. And even more recently, the preoccupation, one might almost say the obsession, of modern times with race and racism has provoked ritual denunciations of Carlyle reminiscent of the Reactionary phase. But the main drift of the past forty years has been upward, and it has in Carlyle studies been directed toward seeing the man the Victorians venerated as a Professor-of-Things-in-General and the late Victorians and Edwardians alternately venerated and deplored as a Denouncer-of-Things-in-General, rather more as an Influence-on-Things-in-General.

The Influence approach is both safer and more in keeping with the supposed objectivity of scholarship than either of the previous approaches. One can, for instance, explore an influence without having to support it. One can for that matter lament it while still chronicling carefully how it was manifested. Thus it has been possible in the Scholarly period of Carlyle studies to write about Carlyle without necessarily appearing either as his sycophant or his grim-eyed detractor. Not that persons interested in Carlyle do not even today meet with charges of being at least crypto-Fascists merely because they are interested in Carlyle, but I am happy to say that that attitude is gradually being tempered and is restricted primarily to the academic groves in America and Britain that can always be relied upon to express in loftier language the sentiments of the popular press of thirty years ago. Still, to give credit where it is due, I should point out that the Scholarly revival itself stemmed from the Academy, once Wilson and Dyer and others had pointed the way.

It will not be surprising to learn that in the modern scholarly revival Americans have been in the forefront, although in its full extent the scholarly revival is very much an Anglo-American endeavour. But American graduate education was not modelled on German to no purpose, nor did American scholarship forget that Emerson set an example of American pioneering in Carlyle studies when he saw to it that *Sartor Resartus* appeared as a book in Boston before it did in Britain. In the early years of the modern scholarly revival we must look to such scholars as Emery Neff and Charles Frederick Harrold in the thirties and later to Hill Shine, Carlisle Moore, and Charles Richard Sanders for the most substantial work in Carlyle studies. I shall not itemize their achievements but simply say that they ranged from studies of influences on Carlyle to studies of his thought and to occasional editions of his work, though these have not in the main been the chief work of the scholarly period. Much else has been generated by the revival of interest in Carlyle. There is even a scholarly article on Carlyle's poetry, of all things. Of course it is American. British Carlyle scholarship was somewhat slower, although today there are notable Carlyle scholars in Britain too.

Doubtless the crowning achievement of the scholarly phase of the Scholarly-Critical Period will be the Duke-Edinburgh edition of the letters of the two Carlyles under the general editorship of C. R. Sanders. The project, which has already borne its first fruits in the first four volumes of Carlyle's letters (1971), is almost certain to stand as the greatest single monument to Carlyle produced by the Scholarly period, unless, wonder of wonders, a really scholarly edition of his works is undertaken in our time. The *Letters* edition is not only a work in the tradition of careful and accurate scholarship which has been the byword of the Scholarly period, it is also testimonial to Carlyle's pervasive Influence; for the publication of so many letters over such a long span of time is posited on the assumption that Carlyle's correspondence (and Jane's as well) not only tells us a great deal about a remarkable man, but that it casts light on the whole Victorian world, that it reveals the ideas and attitudes of an age, through one who both shared and shaped those ideas. I think that the scholarly labours of the past forty years, as well as what survives of the previous hundred years, amply confirm that the assumption on which the *Letters* edition has been undertaken is a very sound one, and the undertaking of the *Letters* edition is proof that the scholarship of the previous forty years has not been in vain.

There remains, then, in the survey of Carlyle's reputation only to say a word about the Critical phase of the Scholarly-Critical period. A critical dimension is, of course, evident in almost all that has been done on Carlyle and cannot be said to be a wholly new interest. But the way in which it has been pursued in recent years does represent a kind of new emphasis. For one thing the critical interest in Carlyle has become much more literary and technical than it used to be. There are in all periods valuable literary analyses, but the attention to nonfictional prose, Carlyle's chief medium after all, as a vehicle deserving the same kind of literary-critical analysis and consideration as, say, poetry or the novel is a growth of quite recent date. In Carlyle studies the chief spark for what is now a healthy and growing fire of critical studies was John Holloway's *Victorian Sage* of 1953. Here British criticism gave something to American and subsequent studies of Carlyle the literary artist are certainly indebted, for pioneering the topic if for nothing else, to Holloway's study. I have myself contributed in a modest way to the critical (and I hope also to the scholarly) phase of contemporary Carlyle studies, and I find in Holloway something fresh and exciting in approaches to Carlyle. Such scholar-critics as George Levine or Albert LaValley, show too that they too have been receptive to a more literary and aesthetic approach to Carlyle than has been common in Carlyle studies of earlier periods or even of the early part of the present Scholarly period. And to come very much up to date there are now booklength studies of Carlyle's impact on Dickens and countless other Carlyle studies underway. Most of the current work shares the twin interests of the Scholarly-Critical period—Carlyle as Influence and Carlyle as literary genius. Thus from the modern academy has come a kind of Scholarly-Critical palingenesis to Carlyle studies which can only serve to confirm, as perhaps it has helped to shape, the judgment of Carlyle as pre-eminent among Victorians.

Such a survey as the foregoing serves to confirm that the National Portrait Gallery display that began my reflections is right insofar as it is a judgment of Carlyle's *importance*. After all, any man who can generate more than 1,200 books and articles on his life and work cannot be entirely without interest. But there still remains the second question, the *mode* of Carlyle's appearance in the Gallery, that deserves a brief comment or two. It might seem that the three periods I have outlined do not tell us too much one way or the other about Carlyle as a Prophet, but

44

in fact I think they tell us a great deal, even, as we shall see, the Scholarly-Critical with its striving toward objectivity and merely establishing the facts.

The things that the three periods tells us are suggested by the secondary terms that I applied to each phase. These are: Teacher, Denouncer, Influence. I think it would be hard to find three terms more essential in delineating what a prophet is. I know that in vulgar use the word *prophet* is often synonymous with fortune-teller or predictor, and of course that *is* an aspect of prophetism. Recently I came across (in *The Times*!) the rather awkward word *futurologist*, which appears to be a man who specializes in extrapolating what life will be like 25 or 50 or 100 years hence based largely on statistical circumstances today. Well, perhaps a prophet is a kind of futurologist. But not, I think, quite the same kind as is domesticated in the Rand Corporation. A prophet may see into the future sometimes because he has seen so well into the past. A prophet is thus not merely someone who can predict the growth rate of the steel industry, but some-one who can predict the growth rate of human industry, if I may Carlylize for a moment. Nor may a prophet be content merely to pass on his statistics to the next office, for his statistics are always alarming and must be communicated to the world at large for its own benefit. The world must be instructed, it must be taught. The Victorians were very much on the right track in seeing Carlyle as a teacher, for that is what a prophet by the nature of the case must be.

But a prophet must be more than a teacher. It is not just a case of passing on the received word, which, I might add, comes to the prophet in a variety of ways, not the least important of which is the ancient wisdom which has fallen into desuetude. No, a prophet must do more than say what is right; or perhaps the way to put it is that a prophet often says what is right by pointing out what is wrong. Denunciation is as essential to prophetism as teaching. We might even venture a definition of prophetism as "teaching by denunciation". Now Carlyle was a great denouncer, one of the best we have ever had. It is not surprising that his denunciations got under the skin: they were so often right and so often tellingly put: they were *supposed* to get under the skin. But it is not surprising either that there was retaliation. The later years of Carlyle's life, as one reads the biographies, seem to be a series of encounters by Carlyle with impertinent visitors to the Chelsea House. And the encounters always seem to be occasions of irritation. The inevitable Americans, following Emerson, come and get their come-uppance. It must have been terribly exasperating. Something of the same feeling must have gnawed at many readers who never had the opportunity, or misfortune, to meet Carlyle in person. And when a man has spent fifty or sixty years infuriating people, it is no wonder they grow weary, however right many of his pronouncements may be. I am not suggesting, as has often been done, that Carlyle would be better off if he had died twenty or thirty years before. I am one of that small company that enjoy even the later Carlyle, even *Latter-Day Pamphlets* and even the insulting and testy old man who frightened off American pilgrims with roars of scorn. Not that I should have enjoyed receiving any of it personally and not that I personally agree with Carlyle's every utterance, but it is all a kind of sport that one can admire at spectator distance—bear or bull-baiting in which the bear or bull always wins.

Still, all this has its perils. And one of them is in sowing discontent and in provoking people to ideas of vengeance. I mean this now not only in a personal way but even from readers. And since Carlyle was, like all of us, only human, even if a prophet, he had the same clay feet that Froude had, or that Froude's elder brother had been shown to have as early as the eighteen-thirties. Besides, what better way to avoid the implications of a prophet's denunciations than to denounce the prophet himself? Hence the dominant tone of the second period of Carlyle studies. But it serves to remind us that Carlyle was not, could not be—no prophet can—a gentle teacher, sweetly leading his lamblike disciples down the flower-strewn path to the temple of Lady Wisdom. Carlyle was not cut out to be a John Keble or even a John Henry Newman, who could insinuate his criticisms with that subtlety that is at once his glory and the cause of most of his troubles. I hesitate to speculate on such matters, but perhaps if we were more aware of the genuine fire that was in Keble, we would have been less likely to relegate him to such quasi-oblivion as he now endures; and perhaps Newman survives so undefiled as he does because even his sweetest utterances have a sinewy toughness that doesn't let go. Carlyle in any case had plenty of fire and toughness. Maybe too much. But that too is essential to prophetism. If the prophet singes the consciences, he has done a good part of his work. So the Denunciatory phase of Carlyle criticism is a phase that had to come and that should continue to serve as a reminder of just how much of a prophet Carlyle was. Nobody ever called Jeremiah soft.

As for Influence, it too is essential, unless one is going to remain a closet-prophet. A prophet worthy of the name must somehow affect people; he must strike that chord. And Carlyle did. He changed England in ways more profound than the railway. That story has still not been fully told. Perhaps it will be by future Carlyle studies. Robert Sencourt in his memoir of T. S. Eliot offers the kind of suggestion that scholars in the modern period have been exploring and will surely explore more extensively in the future. He writes:

> While still an undergraduate at Harvard, Tom Eliot had read *The Symbolist Movement in Literature*, by Arthur Symons, and found a gate opening into a new world. Symons began by taking up the conclusion of *Sartor Resartus* that the path to the supernatural ran along the external world. "It is in and through *Symbols*", Carlyle had written, "that man, consciously or unconsciously, lives, works and has his being." A symbol is a representation, but does not aim to be a reproduction: it denotes an idea or form; the seen points to the unseen. "In a Symbol," said Carlyle (or rather, his spokesman Teufelsdröckh), "there is concealment and yet revelation: hence therefore, by Silence and by Speech acting together, comes a double significance . . . In the Symbol proper, what we can call a Symbol, there is ever, more or less distinctly and directly, some embodiment and revelation of the Infinite."
>
> In the mid-nineteenth century this metaphysical vision had swept consciously into French literature, at first through Baudelaire and later through the poets Verlaine and Mallarmé. Now, in the elegant precision of Arthur Symons' book, Eliot became familiar with Rimbaud, Verlaine, Mallarmé, Maeterlinck and Huysmans.[14]

T. S. Eliot as a Carlyle epigone? Carlyle as a precursor of the Symbolist Movement? These are not fantastic notions at that. For the time is ripe, or soon will be, for another period in Carlyle studies that will correspond to the last stages of his own career. It is certainly true that few who have taken up the cross of Carlyle scholarship in modern times have been hostile to the man who taught Britain how to see herself in the modern world. But few also have yet been ready to take on and defend Carlyle steadily and whole to a new age that has not known him. These will be those who usher in a fourth stage.

Yet Carlyle is sometimes painted as a lonely and disillusioned old man who never suceeded in saving England. Well, it is of the nature of a prophet not to succeed too much; otherwise we should all be saved and the Jews would never have known the destruction of the Temple or the Babylonian captivity. Total success would deliver us not merely from present danger but from future peril as well. Not even Carlyle can do that. For the Oxford English Dictionary tells us that prophet comes from the Greek for "speaking forth". It defines prophet as:

> One who speaks for God . . . as the inspired revealer of his will; one who is held or (more loosely) claims to have this function; an inspired or quasi-inspired teacher.

It does not say a prophet must be successful, only that he be inspired with the will of God and speak it forth. Of course Carlyle says it better when he defines for us the special role of a prophet and offers proleptically, or prophetically, the justification for the mode of his own presentation in the National Portrait Gallery and for the attitude that modern criticism is again coming to hold towards him:

> Poet and Prophet differ greatly in our loose modern notions of them. In some old languages, again, the titles are synonymous; *Vates* means both Prophet and Poet; and indeed at all times, Prophet and Poet, well understood, have much kindred of meaning. Fundamentally indeed they are still the same; . . . .
>
> . . . the *Vates*, whether Prophet or Poet, . . . is a man sent hither to make [the divine mystery] more impressively known to us. That always is his message; he is to reveal that to us,—that sacred mystery which he more than others lives ever present with. While others forget it, he knows it;—I might say, he has been driven to know it; without consent asked of *him*, he finds himself living in it, bound to live in it. Once more, here is no Hearsay, but a direct Insight and Belief; this man too could not help being a sincere

man. . . . He is a *Vates*, first of all, in virtue of being sincere. So far Poet and Prophet, participators in the 'open secret,' are one.

With respect to their distinction again. The *Vates* Prophet, we might say, has seized that sacred mystery rather on the moral side, as Good and Evil, Duty and Prohibition; the *Vates* Poet on what the Germans call the aesthetic side, as Beautiful, and the like. The one we may call a revealer of what we are to do, the other of what we are to love. But indeed these two provinces run into one another, and cannot be disjoined. The Prophet too has his eye on what we are to love: how else shall he know what it is we are to do? (*On Heroes and Hero-Worship*, Lect. 3)

And in this way Carlyle delineates for us his own role and anticipates the modes in which subsequent criticism will approach him. Vates-Prophet, certainly; but with much of the Vates-Poet about him as well, as has become increasingly clear in our own time. Thus the matter of Carlyle Today leads inevitably to the matter of Carlyle Tomorrow. That is when I hope we will move to a new stage in our understanding of Carlyle and see that the prophet and the poet are one.

NOTES

1. At any given time the National Portrait Gallery displays only a third of the more than 5,000 portraits in its collection.
2. The record of this event, including a photograph of the damaged portrait, is in the files of the National Portrait Gallery. The attack was presumably unaffected by the fact that TC himself had been a trustee of the Gallery, 1875–68; see also pp. 225–6.
3. The most notable reputation studies are: H. L. Stewart, "Carlyle and His Critics", *Nineteenth Century*, 86 (1919), 505–14, and his "Declining Fame of TC", *Transactions of the Royal Society of Canada*, Series 3, 14 (1920), 11–29; Frank Luther Mott, "Carlyle's American Public", *PQ*, 4 (1925), 245–64; Alan Carey Taylor, *Carlyle: sa première fortune littéraire en France (1825–1865)* (Paris, 1929), and his *Carlyle et la pensée latine* (Paris, 1937); Howard D. Widger, " TC in America: His Reputation and Influence", unpublished dissertation, Univ. of Illinois, 1945; and *TC, The Critical Heritage*, ed. Jules P. Seigel (London, 1971). See also "Carlyle's Reputation", in my chapter on Carlyle in *Victorian Prose, A Guide to Research*, ed. David J. DeLaura (New York, 1973).
4. The encounter in question was for the chapter in *Victorian Prose*. I

examined more than 1,200 separate items. This did not include all of the treatments of Carlyle in his own lifetime, though it included a good many of them, nor did it include all dissertations on Carlyle, though it included a large number of them also. As it happens, Carlyle is the single most frequent topic of doctoral dissertations in the field of Victorian literature, in part because of the considerable number of German dissertations on him. (See R. D. Altick and W. R. Matthews, *Guide to Doctoral Dissertations in Victorian Literature 1886–1958* [Urbana: Univ. of Illinois Press, 1960]).

The purpose of my examination was not to consider Carlyle's reputation *per se*, but to evaluate the existing body of scholarship and criticism on Carlyle. However, it is largely on the basis of the examination of this material that it has been possible to generalize in this paper about Carlyle's reputation.

5. John Sterling, letter to TC, 29 May 1835, quoted in Carlyle's *Life of John Sterling* (1851), and Harrold, *Sartor*, pp. 307–16.

6. *London and Westminster Review*, 27 (1838), 17.

7. *London and Westminster Review*, 33 (1839), 1–68.

8. "Emerson", *Discourses in America* in *The Works of Matthew Arnold*, 15 vols. (London, 1903), IV, 351.

9. *The Letters of Anthony Trollope*, ed. Bradford A. Booth (London, 1951), p. 15.

10. Arthur Penrhyn Stanley, funeral sermon on TC (1881) in *Sermons on Special Occasions*, reprinted in *TC, The Critical Heritage*, p. 516.

11. A. Carlyle and James Crichton-Browne, *The Nemesis of Froude* (London, 1903).

12. This unfortunate statement appears in that otherwise entertaining study by John Gross, *The Rise and Fall of the Man of Letters* (London, 1969), p. 30.

13. For a discussion of most of the post-Dyer works up to 1965, see Carlisle Moore, "TC" in *The English Romantic Poets and Essayists*, ed. C. W. and L. H. Houtchens (rev. ed.; New York, 1966), pp. 333–78, and up to 1971 the Carlyle chapter in *Victorian Prose*, ed. D. J. DeLaura, and the annual survey of scholarship in the autumn number of *Victorian Poetry*. See also R. L. Tarr (assisted R. E. Dana), *A Bibliography of English Language Articles on TC: 1900–1965*, Univ. of S. Carolina, Dept. of English, Bibliographical Series, 7 (1972).

14. Robert Sencourt, *T. S. Eliot, A Memoir* (New York, 1971), pp. 27–8.

2

Carlyle on *Sartor Resartus*

by JOHN CLUBBE

Several of Carlyle's major statements on his most enduring work, *Sartor Resartus*, have lately come to light. Until recently they have either remained unpublished or are known chiefly through the inaccurate transcriptions given in the first volume of Froude's biography. Froude refers to these and other statements by Carlyle on his life and works only as "a series of brief notes upon his early life".[1] At one point he cites "a German biography in which he was said to have learnt Hebrew" (I, 17), but otherwise he fails to indicate his source. The "German biography" is Friedrich Althaus's *Thomas Carlyle: Eine biographisch-literarische Charakteristik.* It appeared in the German periodical *Unsere Zeit* in July 1866,[2] and, in English translation, in 1974.[3] Althaus's work came upon the scene shortly after Carlyle had enjoyed one of his greatest triumphs delivering his inaugural address on 2 April as Rector of the University of Edinburgh. Three weeks after the address, Jane Welsh Carlyle, his wife for nearly forty years, died, and he plunged into a profound gloom and remorse that ended only with his life in 1881.

Sometime in July 1866 Carlyle received, probably from the author himself, Althaus's biography. Recognizing its importance, he thought "of having the poor Piece *interleaved* . . . and of perhaps correcting one or two blunders here & there" (*TR*, p. 23). Beginning on 29 August and continuing through the first ten days of September, he wrote his comments—some a few words, others the length of several paragraphs—on the inserted sheets or in the margins. Despite his referring to Althaus's work as a "poor Piece", he viewed it with unusual regard: "this," he said, "on the whole, is considerably the best Sketch I have yet seen on the subject" (*ibid.*). No greater praise could come from one who had long advocated firm and demanding standards for the art of literary biography and who had despaired that anyone would "ever know my poor 'Biography' " (*ibid.*). That he fully intended his notes to Althaus to be used by subsequent biographers his preface makes clear. "The *fewer* errors they set afloat . . . on this subject, the better it will be" (*ibid.*), he writes there, and concludes in the afterword: "Here and there a bit of certainty may have its advantages" (p. 122). Some of the notes served as trial runs for incidents more fully narrated in the other reminiscences, in particular "Edward Irving", which he began soon after he completed the Althaus. Stimulated by the biography to look inward, he wrote the notes as a first thinking-through of much that he found painful to recall.

Carlyle's notes to Althaus range from the extensive and highly significant comments on *Sartor Resartus* to various autobiographical reminiscences: of his schooling and university career, of his plans for the ministry, of Professor John Leslie and of his relationship with Edward Irving, of the gradual working out at Hoddam Hill in 1825–1826 of his 1822 conversion, of his possible emigration to America in the 1830's, and of his father and mother and brother Alexander. He leaves valuable statements on the extent of his acquaintance with classical literatures and on his first knowledge of German, on other works beside *Sartor* (especially the *Life of Schiller, German Romance,* and *Frederick the Great*), on his intellectual debts to Goethe and to Jean Paul, on the development of his singular literary style, and on the "might is right" maxim popularly attributed to him. His clarifying comments on a host of other points, biographical and critical, will require significant modifications in subsequent accounts of his achievement. Althaus's biography, which owes much to statements obtained from Carlyle himself by their mutual friend Joseph Neuberg, has in itself new and authentic information. Althaus gave Neuberg questions to pose to Carlyle; and Neuberg, in turn, transmitted the answers to Althaus, "the greater part in Carlyle's very words".[4]

In the 1870's, along with Carlyle's other personal papers, the interleaved copy of Althaus's biography came into the hands of

Froude, whom Carlyle had entrusted with the task of writing his life. Froude made selective use of Carlyle's notes, published a few of them inaccurately and incompletely, and based statements in his narrative on others. Upon completion in 1884 of his four-volume biography, he returned Carlyle's papers to Mary Aitken Carlyle, Carlyle's niece. A family friend, Charles Eliot Norton used the notes to Althaus sparingly in preparing his edition of the Goethe-Carlyle correspondence,[5] and twenty years later Mary's husband, Alexander Carlyle, used them to support his thesis that much in *Sartor* was autobiographical.[6] The interleaved Althaus remained in his possession until his death in 1931. On 14 June 1932 the manuscript was sold as part of lot 203 at the great Sotheby sale of Carlyle's books, letters and manuscripts. It brought £23, a fraction of what it would bring today. Lot 203 also included a typed translation of Althaus's biography, two typed copies of Carlyle's notes, two letters from Althaus to Carlyle, and other biographical material by Carlyle or relating to him. In April 1934 the National Library of Scotland purchased the interleaved Althaus from Messrs Maggs, along with a typed copy by Alexander Carlyle of most of Carlyle's notes. The Library did not purchase the other items in lot 203, and I am unaware of their present whereabouts. The interleaved Althaus and Alexander Carlyle's typed copy are now catalogued as MS 1799 and MS 1800.

No other biographer or critic of Carlyle besides Froude, Norton, and Alexander Carlyle has, to my knowledge, made use of Carlyle's comments in the interleaved Althaus. Even David Alec Wilson, a close friend of Alexander Carlyle, did not have access to the Althaus manuscript in preparing his monumental six-volume biography of Carlyle (1923–1934).[7] Yet Carlyle himself intended the notes to complement his more extended biographical recollections in the other reminiscences. Not only, then, do they constitute a document of major significance in understanding Carlyle's life, but they also provide one of the few instances in literary biography in which the subject of the biography had the opportunity to comment extensively on his biographer's account. And when that person is Carlyle, whose writings on the art of literary biography have been influential and controversial and who denied that a true biography of himself could be written, the comments should prove of interest to the historian of literary biography.

The Althaus biography remains the closest we have—with the conjectural exception of Froude—to an authorized or approved biography. That Carlyle included a preface and an afterword to it indicates that he judged it in some degree valid as an interpretation of his life. Although he felt that Althaus had done a creditable job, there remained a great deal he did not know and could hardly be expected to know. Perhaps it was while writing the commentary to Althaus that Carlyle realized it had to be supplemented still more. It is even possible, though unlikely, that he might not have written his other autobiographical writings if the Althaus biography had not crossed his path when it did. In any event, Carlyle came to realize the necessity of clarifying many points about his life and his works that would be obscure to the inevitable biographers of the future. No other explanation begins to account for his protracted labours in the years following his wife's death when he wrote the reminiscences and edited her correspondence. Only through this work could he put his own life into perspective and attempt to come to terms with it. The concern that his biography be accurate explains his careful correction of dates and statements in Althaus's account; the concern that it be true explains his clarifying and interpretative comments. His desire both for accuracy and for truth is nowhere more evident than in the pains he took in preparing his observations on *Sartor*.

Since Carlyle had little to say about *Sartor* in the other reminiscences, unquestionably he meant his comments in Althaus to constitute his major statement. Despite his later professed depreciation of *Sartor*, he may have unconsciously divined that it was to be his most enduring work. While he explains in several letters what he is attempting to do in *Sartor*, only in the interleaved Althaus does he discuss its autobiographical significance. In a long appendix to the *Love Letters*, Alexander Carlyle affirmed *Sartor*'s value "as an autobiography of Carlyle in his early years" (II, 361) and on several occasions quoted in support of his views Carlyle's notes to Althaus. Critics since then have often ignored or denied the autobiographical elements in *Sartor*. Yet it is not necessary that *Sartor* be interpreted as literal autobiography for us to realize that Alexander Carlyle hardly exaggerates when he contends that chapters 5 through 9 of Book II are "founded on incidents and experiences in Carlyle's own history" and are "in fact a sort of autobiography for the period mentioned, delineated poetically, spiritually and figuratively, yet true to life as regards the chief incidents and events, and not far from the truth even in the details" (II, 366). Indeed, his contention derives its chief support from Carlyle's own carefully considered observations. Their publication here, set within the context of the Althaus biography, should help to clarify the extent to which *Sartor* is autobiography.

Eight separate comments by Carlyle have to do with *Sartor*. They are printed below as Carlyle wrote them, except that his abbreviations (written in the crabbed shorthand of his later years) have been expanded. The method of presentation is ordinarily as follows: (*a*) a brief summary of the context in Althaus in which Carlyle's note appears; (*b*) the note itself; (*c*) indication of publication in Froude and, if published there, the importance of any major differences from his text; and (*d*) briefly, the note's significance for the interpretation of *Sartor*.[8]

1. Althaus quotes two paragraphs depicting the idyllic youth enjoyed by Diogenes Teufelsdröckh (*Sartor*, pp. 97–98). Carlyle comments: "*Sartor* is quite unsafe for details! Fiction *founded* perhaps on fact—a long way off" (*TR*, p. 28). Froude refers to, but does not quote, this comment (I, 15 and 26).

2. Althaus quotes or paraphrases several short passages describing Teufelsdröckh's early schooling (*Sartor*, pp. 104–105) and concludes: "Who does not already recognize in these traits the prototype of the sensitive soul, the stern, dissatisfied, idealistic, resigned 'weeping philosopher' of later years? Even if his discontented spirit sought refuge from the routine of school existence in tasks that he picked out for himself in the workshops of the real world, still the solid learning acquired in his school years did not serve him badly." Carlyle comments:

> *Sartor* here, in good part; not to be trusted in details! "Greek", for example, consisted of the *Alphabet* mainly; "Hebrew" is quite a *German* entity,—nobody in that region, except my reverend old Mr Johnstone, could have read one sentence of it to save his life. I did get to read Latin & French with fluency (Latin *quantity* was left a frightful chaos, and I had to learn it afterwards); some geometry, algebra (*arithmetic* thoroughly well), vague outlines of geography &c I did learn;—all the Books I could get were also

55

devoured; but my "Hang" [*the "bent toward abstract reflection"
mentioned below by Althaus*] there is a myth. Mythically *true* is
what Sartor says of his Schoolfellows, and not half of the truth.
Unspeakable is the damage & defilement I got out of those coarse un-
guided tyrannous cubs,— especially till I revolted against them, and
gave stroke for stroke; as my pious Mother, in her great love of
peace and of my best interests, spiritual chiefly, had imprudently
forbidden me to do. One way and another I had never been so
wretched as here in that School, and the first 2 years of my time in
it still count among the miserable of my life. "Academies", "High
Schools", "Instructors of Youth"—Oh ye unspeakable!—(*TR*, pp.
31–32).

Althaus goes on to write that Carlyle's "memory was as retentive
as his diligence and ability to learn were great" and that "he had
in equal measure the gift of being able to cope with a mass of
details and the bent toward abstract reflection". Froude publishes
the passage inaccurately and with omissions (I, 17–18) and
Alexander Carlyle a part of it accurately (*Love Letters*, II, 365).
Froude's chief omission—leaving out at the beginning after
"*Sartor*" the words "here, in good part"—alters the emphasis to
imply that *Sartor* is nowhere "to be trusted in details", when
clearly Carlyle intends to affirm that he based many details
not only in the account of Teufelsdröckh's education but elsewhere on actual experiences. The second omission—"but my
'Hang' [*the "bent toward abstract reflection"*] there is a myth"—
strongly suggests that the young Carlyle was more firmly rooted in
the everyday world than Althaus (and later biographers) realized.

3. Althaus describes the grimness of Carlyle's life between the
period of his abandoning schoolteaching in Kirkcaldy in November
1818, and of his agreeing to tutor Charles and Arthur Buller in
January 1822. Carlyle, in a long passage containing three references
to *Sartor*, indicates that in these years he "was entirely unknown
in 'Edinburgh circles'; solitary, 'eating my own heart', fast losing
my health, too; a prey, in fact, to nameless struggles and miseries,
which have yet a kind of horror in them to my thought. Three
weeks without *any* Sleep (from *im*possibility to be free of noise),
&c &c." Further, he continues:

I had spent the winters [*of 1818–1822*] in Edinburgh, 'looking
out for employment' on those dismal terms; the summers (had it

only been for cheapness' sake) at my Father's. Nothing in *"Sartor"* thereabouts is *fact* (symbolical *myth* all) except that of the *"incident* in the Rue St Thomas de l'Enfer",—which occurred quite literally to myself in Lieth [*Leith*] Walk, during those 3 weeks of total sleeplessness, in which almost my one solace was that of a daily bathe on the sands between Lieth and Portobello. Incident was as I went *down* (coming *up* I generally felt a little refreshed for the hour); I remember it well, & could go yet to about the place.— (*TR*, pp. 48–9).

This passage is published inaccurately by Froude (I, 101), with two words—"thereabouts" after " '*Sartor*' " and "those" before "3 weeks"—omitted, and accurately by Alexander Carlyle (*Love Letters*, II, 380). Carlyle's note refers to the climactic moment of Teufelsdröckh's despair in "The Everlasting No" (*Sartor*, pp. 166–168), and Froude's omission of "thereabouts" significantly alters the sense of the passage. "It does not follow", Alexander Carlyle observes perceptively, "that because the work is mythical 'here' or 'thereabouts' (i.e. in one or two specified passages) it is mythical throughout."[9] He convincingly places Carlyle's conversion, set by Froude in June 1821, in July or early August 1821 or, more likely, 1822. The latter date is generally accepted today. That the conversion was not as abrupt as implied in *Sartor* and that his recovery extended over many years is the contention of two important articles by Carlisle Moore.[10] Several of Carlyle's notes to Althaus not given here corroborate that the recovery was not sudden, but imply that the idyllic year at Hoddam Hill in 1825–1826 marked the termination of the recuperative process.

4. In the long passage covering the years 1818–1822 Carlyle writes:

Try Scots Law [*1819–1820*]; write (pitifully enough) 'Articles' (as said was) for Brewster's *Encyclopedia* [*Feb. 1820–Jan. 1823*]; fight with the dismallest Lernean Hydra of problems, spiritual, temporal, eternal;—"eat my own heart"; but authentically take the Devil by the nose withal (see 'incident in Rue St Thomas'), and fling *him* behind me, 1820, '21, '22; till *Legendre* [*Dec. 1821; April–July 1822*] &c with *rather* improving prospect of wages; and finally on Irving's call to London, Charles Buller arrives, summer of 1823 [*Jan. 1822*], and pressure ["tightness" *crossed out*] of finance as good as disappears for the time. (*TR*, pp. 50–51).

This note again refers to Teufelsdröckh's conversion (*Sartor*, pp. 166–168). Though Froude alludes to the passage (I, 64, 78), he does not publish it, nor, to my knowledge, is it published elsewhere.

5. The third excerpt from Carlyle's long comment follows:

> In Edinburgh from my fellow creatures little or nothing but *vinegar* was my reception—cup [*i.e., a slight bow*] when we happened to meet or pass near each other;—my own blame mainly, so proud, shy, poor, at once so insignificant-looking and so grim and sorrowful. That in *Sartor*, of the '*worm* trodden & proving a *torpedo,* and sending you ceiling-high to be borne home on shutters' is not wholly a fable; but did actually befal once or twice, as I still (with a kind of small not ungenial malice) can remember. (*TR*, pp. 51–52).

Froude publishes this passage inaccurately (I, 57), omitting "—cup" and the clause "and sending you . . . on shutters". Carlyle's language in 1866 echoes the passage referred to in *Sartor Resartus*: "An ironic man, with his sly stillness, and ambuscading ways, more especially an ironic young man, from whom it is least expected, may be viewed as a pest to society. Have we not seen persons of weight and name coming forward, with gentlest indifference, to tread such a one out of sight, as an insignificancy and worm, start ceiling-high (*balkenhoch*), and thence fall shattered and supine, to be borne home on shutters, not without indignation, when he proved electric and a torpedo!" (*Sartor*, p. 129).

6. Carlyle's final three (unpublished) comments on *Sartor* have to do with his efforts to find a publisher for his manuscript and its reception by the public. When Althaus incorrectly states that in 1832 he settled permanently in London, Carlyle comments:

> no; went up [*from Craigenputtoch*] August 1831, with *Sartor* in my pocket, intending to be back in a month; could not get *Sartor* published (Reform-Bill agitation &c &c); . . . returned [*to Craigenputtoch*] (still with *Sartor* in my pocket), March 1832. . . . [*There*] I wrote *Diamond Necklace, Cagliostro*, and various things (*translation* a good part of them, *Mährchen* &c); was publishing *Sartor*, slit in Pieces (but rigorously *un*altered otherwise) in *Fraser's Magazine* . . . (*TR*, p. 69).

7. Althaus later observes that "further attempts to publish *Sartor Resartus* as a book also proved unsuccessful", opposite which Carlyle notes: "there were none made" (*TR*, p. 74).

8. Althaus goes on to say that *Sartor* was "apparently much revised" in the interval between Carlyle's stay in London and its serial publication in *Fraser's* (Nov.–Dec. 1833; Feb.–April, June–Aug. 1834). Carlyle, denying this, writes:

> Not a letter of it altered; except in the *last* and the *first* page, a word or two! — — Nothing whatever of *"spätere Versuche"* [*further attempts*] either (as already marked): Fraser's Public liked the *Johnson* so much (which I had left with him, written there that winter) that he was willing to accept *Sartor* in the slit condition; had it so (probably on cheaper terms), went on with it obstinately till done,—tho', from his Public, he had a sore time with it: "What wretched unintelligible nonsense!" "Sir, if you publish any more of that d——d [*stuff?*], I shall be obliged to give up my Magazine!" and so forth,—in the whole world (so far as could be learned) only two persons dissentient, 1° a certain man called *Emerson,* in Concord Massachusetts, and 2° a certain Irish Catholic Priest, Father O'Shea of Cork (whom I have seen since, & who yet lives)[11] writing to him, each for himself, "So long as any thing by that man appears in your Magazine, punctually send it me."[12] So that Fraser conceived a certain terror, if also a certain respect, of my writings & me; and knew not what to do,—beyond standing by his bargain, with an effort. (*TR,* pp. 74–75).

Carlyle makes here the important disclosure that he did not alter significantly the manuscript of *Sartor* (completed late in July 1831) between its several rejections by London publishers in the autumn of 1831 and its serial publication in *Fraser's* in 1833–1834. Contrary to general opinion,[13] he did not submit it to Edinburgh publishers after the attempts in London had failed. Elsewhere in the notes to Althaus Carlyle stresses that, in changing nothing in *Sartor* except on the first and last pages, he bent neither to public opinion nor to pressure from the magazine's publisher, James Fraser. That he made no significant alterations in *Sartor* became a point of honour with him. G. B. Tennyson correctly notes, however, that in February 1833 Carlyle emended the name "Teufelsdreck" to the more subtle "Teufelsdröckh".[14]

Carlyle's comments on *Sartor Resartus* given here indicate that even in his old age he looked back with interest upon a literary work of whose ultimate value he was never altogether certain. Still, he wished to leave behind a record that would aid others in understanding this complex book and its relationship to his own life. Taken together, the comments to Althaus provide a valuable statement of his attitude toward the work by which he is most likely to be remembered.

NOTES

1. Froude, *Life*, I, 16. Carlyle's notes on *Sartor* should be read in conjunction with two other important statements on the work: (1) in a letter to his publisher William Fraser of 27 May 1833, in *Letters of TC 1826–36*, ed. C. E. Norton (London, 1889), pp. 364–7; and (2) in a letter to John Sterling of 4 June 1835 in *Letters of TC to John Stuart Mill, John Sterling and Robert Browning*, ed. A. Carlyle (London, 1923), pp. 191–4.

2. (Leipzig), II, 1–41. Reprinted with minor revisions in Althaus's *Englische Charakterbilder* (Berlin, Verlag der Königlichen Geheimen Ober-Hofbuchdruckerei [R. v Decker], 1869), I, 237–322.

3. As part of *Two Reminiscences of TC*, ed. John Clubbe (Durham, N.C., 1974). I have thought it useful to bring together in this essay Carlyle's various pronouncements on *Sartor* scattered through the Althaus biography, in that they constitute, in effect, his only sustained commentary on *Sartor*. Further references to my edition (abbreviated *TR*) will be inserted parenthetically within the body of the essay.

4. Althaus, "Erinnerungen an Thomas Carlyle", *Unsere Zeit*, I [n.s.] (June 1881), 826. My translation.

5. *Correspondence between Goethe and Carlyle*, ed. C. E. Norton (London, 1887), pp. ix–x, 156.

6. *The Love Letters of TC and Jane Welsh*, ed. A. Carlyle (London, 1909), II, Appendix B, 365–81 *passim*.

7. See his *Carlyle*, IV, 124, 194.

8. I have placed editorial comments and conjectures within brackets in the text.

9. NLS, MS, 1800. Cf. *Love Letters*, II, 365–6.

10. "*Sartor Resartus* and the Problem of Carlyle's 'Conversion' ", *PMLA*, 70 (1955), 662–81, and "The Persistence of Carlyle's 'Everlasting Yea' ", *MP*, 54 (1957), 187–96.

11. Carlyle eventually met Father O'Shea in Cork and described his encounter in *Reminiscences of My Irish Journey in 1849* (London, 1882).

12. Cf. *The Correspondence of Emerson and Carlyle*, ed. Joseph Slater (New York and London, 1964), pp. 16, 98, 103.

13. E.g., Harrold, *Sartor*, p. xxvi, based on Wilson, *Carlyle*, II, 322.

14. *Sartor Called Resartus* (Princeton, 1965), p. 152.

3

Carlyle, Mathematics and "Mathesis"

by CARLISLE MOORE

On Poetry and geometric Truth,
The knowledge that endures, upon these two,
And their high privilege of lasting life,
Exempt from all internal injury,
He mused. . . .

Wordsworth, *The Prelude*, V, 56–60

When *will* there arise a man who shall do for the science of mind
—what Newton did for that of matter—establish its fundamental
laws on the firm basis of induction . . . a foolish question—for
its answer is—never.

Carlyle, *Collected Letters*, I, 84

Biographers of Thomas Carlyle who have noted his early interest
in mathematics when he was a student and struggling writer in
Edinburgh have accepted his own statement that the subject ceased
to interest him about 1820 or 1821.[1] When at about the same time
he discovered Goethe and the German philosophers, and began to
make his way towards the Clothes Philosophy, it seemed clear
that mathematics faded quickly from his thoughts leaving hardly
a trace. It was indeed a transfer of allegiance, as if he had written
"Close thy Newton, open thy Goethe". By 1831, in *Sartor Resartus*,
he was soaring on such poetic and near-mystical heights that one
might well grow sceptical of his earlier "mathematical prowess"
and doubtful of its importance in his mature thought. More than
most men of letters Carlyle appeared to be unlogical and un-

scientific. His manner of reasoning and arguing alienated many scientists of his day and prompted Darwin to remark of him, "I never met a man with a mind so ill adapted for scientific research",[2] and Herbert Spencer to call him a sloppy thinker, of little or no consequence in the history of English thought.[3] Darwin's judgement, if not Spencer's, seems true enough. Carlyle on the *Beagle* or in a Cambridge laboratory is hard to imagine without amusement. But research is one thing and comprehension is another. A fair rejoinder to Darwin may be found in the testimony of John Tyndall: "I do not know what Carlyle's aptitudes in the natural history sciences might have been," he wrote, "but in . . . physical subjects I never encountered a mind of stronger grasp and deeper penetration than his. . . . During my expositions, when they were clear, he was always in advance of me, anticipating and enunciating what I was about to say."[4] Lyell too respected him, and even Herbert Spencer felt his influence.[5] The Cambridge mathematician Augustus De Morgan praised his early mathematical work, particularly an original essay Carlyle wrote on Proportion, which was "as good a substitute for the fifth book of Euclid as could be given in the space", and showed that Carlyle "would have been a distinguished teacher and thinker in first principles".[6]

Such views are speculative at best. Carlyle did not become a mathematician or scientist. His struggles to find a career and his impulse to preach led him into the "other culture". During his early Edinburgh days, however, this course was hardly visible to him, anyway not practicable, and he spent a considerable part of his time and energies from 1809 to 1822 in learning, teaching, or writing mathematics. It has been suggested that under only slightly different circumstances he might have made it his career.[7] That he did not is perhaps most simply explained by his admiration for Goethe and by Jane's urging him to write a novel; but there are deeper causes, and it is just as obvious that he had literary ambitions from a very early age. His surprising talent in mathematics, his prolonged serious interest in it, and his eventual shift to literature, invite closer examination. It is proposed here to trace the course of that serious interest, through his reaction against mathematics, to his postulation of an ideal science as he groped towards a formulation of the Clothes Philosophy.[8]

The talent cannot really be explained; it was no doubt part of the intelligence he was born with. As for the serious interest, Carlyle himself attributed it, but only partly, to the inspiration and encouragement of his distinguished mathematics teacher at Edinburgh, Professor John Leslie, whose genius "awoke a certain enthusiasm in me". Froude laid it to Carlyle's temperament being "impatient of uncertainties" so that he "threw himself with delight into a form of knowledge in which the conclusions were indisputable".[9] For another dozen years, however, he was not only able to tolerate but even espouse uncertainties, if these could be balanced against one another. Only in the middle 1830's did impatience begin to harden his opinions, and even then uncertainties remained to humble him.[10]

"For several years," wrote Carlyle, "geometry shone before me as the noblest of all sciences, and I prosecuted it in all my best hours and moods."[11] Two conditions account for this. One was his cultural inheritance. In early nineteenth century England Isaac Newton was revered as the founder of new Truth—a Truth which was needed to strengthen the weakening faiths of orthodox religion. He was the genius who had geometrized space, who had brought mathematics into the arena of intellectual discourse, and had "explained" the phenomena of the heavens and the earth by a single mathematical law. His discoveries were taken as having re-established the idea of design and were regarded as counters to eighteenth century scepticism, for they were implicitly neither anti-Christian nor anti-Trinitarian, but brought mathematics, physics and astronomy together in a triumphant demonstration of cosmic order which pointed to God as creator of all things: "God said, Let Newton be! and all was light". At Cambridge, Wordsworth saw from his window the Roubiliac statue of Newton "with his prism and silent Face" which he would later describe as "the marble index of a mind for ever / Voyaging through strange seas of Thought alone."[12] And Carlyle, reading the *Principia* in 1817, observed that with Newton science enabled man to see past, present and future in a single view, to predict the future, and to ascertain permanent truths: "Assuredly the human species never performed a more honourable achievement" (*CL*, I, 103). In this he was only reflecting the general opinion.

Back of Newton was Euclid with his *Geometry*, even more than Newton the symbol of imperishable truth. Although a non-

Euclidean Geometry was then evolving in the work of such continental mathematicians as Gauss, Bolyai, and Lobachevski, it was hardly known in England where geometry remained basically and ultimately Euclidean, resting firmly on demonstrable proof derived from self-evident assumptions.[13] Euclid was still alone in looking on beauty bare. The Book of his *Elements* stood like a rock against the flux of changing forms and ideas. To Wordsworth it was the "Stone of abstract Geometry" which, as Auden puts it, offered one of the two routes of salvation from the anxiety of the dreamer—the other being the "Shell" of imagination and instinct—and which represented "the transcendental stable reality desired as a haven for the storm-tossed mariner".[14] For Carlyle too the appeal of geometry lay in its clarity and precision, its sure road to truth: "Where shall we find her in her native purity," he wrote his friend Robert Mitchell, "if not in the science of quantity and number" (*CL*, I, 120, 16 Feb. 1818). There is a special significance in his having been educated at Edinburgh where mathematical thought was still dominated by synthetic geometry at the expense of the analytic algebra which flourished on the continent. While the Bernoullis, Euler, Laplace, and Lagrange were employing the more modern methods of algebraic analysis, Scottish mathematicians like John Playfair and John Leslie, though they were not unfamiliar with these methods and on occasion admitted their superiority over the ancient geometry, continued to teach geometry "to the almost total exclusion of modern analysis".[15] Despite Newton's pioneer contributions, British and Scottish mathematical thought and practice fell behind. Scotland had particularly strong reasons for maintaining this attitude. One of these was epistemological. Philosophers of the Common Sense School like Thomas Reid and Dugald Stewart, reacting against the earlier, Platonic conception of mathematics as not needing empirical verification (an attitude shared by James Beattie and John Playfair), insisted that mathematics must not lose sight of its basis in sensory data.[16] The danger of analytic algebra was that it threatened to lead mathematics away from the very basis upon which its claims to authoritative truth rested.

For this reason Leslie, who shared most of the views of the Common Sense School, objected to the use of "imaginary" or "impossible" numbers like the square root of minus one, since they could not be related to external objects. He also deplored the algebraists' concepts of "quantities less than nothing", or negative numbers, as well as complex numbers. The scope of mathematical inquiry had to be deliberately limited in order to protect its epistemological claim to truth.[17] This claim was important also to the Scottish moral philosophers; both James Beattie, and Dugald Stewart who gave the compulsory two- or three-year sequence of courses in Moral Philosophy at Edinburgh, brought mathematics to bear against Hume's attack on the bases of human morality. Nearly every University student learned in his moral philosophy class that the surest means of obtaining certain knowledge was to be found in the study of the foundations and principles of mathematics.[18] Both moral and intellectual training resulted from the process of mastering the axioms, theorems, and corollaries of Euclid and of solving original geometrical problems. Such training was seen as a prerequisite for all other studies, and for this purpose geometry was regarded as superior to analytic algebra. For John Robison, algebra with its symbolic methods was "little better than a *mechanical knack*, in which we proceed without ideas of any kind, and obtain a result without meaning and *without being conscious of any process of reasoning . . . .*"[19] Geometrical methods might be slower but they exercised and disciplined the mind as algebra did not. Dugald Stewart recommended "the study of Greek geometry to strengthen the power of steady and concatenated thinking", and Leslie, also recommending "the geometry of the ancients", wrote in his *Elements of Geometry* (1809) that "While it traces the beautiful relations of figure and quantity, it likewise accustoms the mind to the invaluable exercise of patient attention and accurate reasoning. Of these distinct objects, the last is perhaps the most important in a course of liberal education." For Leslie, therefore, geometry belonged to the general culture by virtue of its intellectual, moral and aesthetic nature.[20]

Professor Leslie's influence on Carlyle is undeniable. Carlyle attended his classes for three years and received his personal advice and assistance on many occasions. If he and the Common Sense philosophers were right in thinking that geometry trained the intellect we may well ask how it trained Carlyle's. The question has importance because the early influences on Carlyle's thinking and writing are usually traced to his Calvinistic upbringing, and quite properly. But it should be noted that his interest in mathematics appeared earlier and was from the first stronger than his interest in entering the ministry, which had been his and his parents' expectation when they sent him to the University. His letters are filled with comments and reflections on his mathematical studies. Clearly he reveres geometry for its power both to establish truth and to train the intellect, and it appears that he followed Leslie in preferring synthetic geometry to analytic algebra. One of his real achievements was his solution for the third edition of Leslie's *Elements of Geometry* (1817) of the real roots of any quadratic equation by purely geometrical means, for which Leslie praised him in the text as "an ingenious young mathematician".[21] It is clear too that he sees no antagonism between mathematics and religion or between science and literature.[22] Nor is he yet attracted to idealism. Scottish philosophy and psychology seem barren (he criticizes Dugald Stewart for being "transcendental", Hartley's associational psychology for being "descendental"). Not even history has, by 1818, acquired its appeal for him: reading Gibbon he asks "I wonder what benefit is derived from reading all this stuff: . . . It is vain to tell us that our knowledge of human nature is encreased [by mere historical facts] . . . *Useful* knowledge of that sort is acquired not by reading but by experience" (*CL*, I, 121).

With all his talent and interest in mathematics, however, we must not forget that its attraction for him was practical—he knew it could be useful, could lead to jobs and perhaps to a career. At the same time, he began as early as 1817 to feel some discontentment with problem-solving, which "depends very much upon a certain slight of hand. . . I am not so sure as I used to be that it is the best way of employing one's self—Without doubt it concentrates our Mathematical ideas—and exercises the head; but little knowledge is gained by the process" (*CL*, I, 113). His literary activities gave him more pleasure but offered less support. He read novels, wrote poetry, wrote "literary" letters to his friends; in 1818 he made his first literary attempt with a "flowery sentimental" description of the Yarrow country and sent it to an Edinburgh magazine editor, who did not accept it.[23] He read

Mme. de Staël's *Germany* (*CL*, I, 109) with its introduction to the German philosophers. This book, though it left him cold at first (*CL*, I, 109, 265), may have started to reawaken in his mind some of the earlier, Platonic views of mathematicians which were current in Scotland when he was a student at Edinburgh. John Playfair and, before him, James Beattie, had believed that "the process of abstraction somehow frees mathematical reasoning from the necessity of empirical verification and inductive reasoning". They denied that sensory evidence was needed to justify the basic axioms of mathematics, not only because sensory evidence was untrustworthy but because mathematical evidence was either intuitive or demonstrable by logic.[24] Leslie, though he opposed this Platonizing of mathematical ideas, also opposed the empiricist approach, with his objection to the use of models in teaching geometry, which he called "quackish".

Signs of Carlyle's later attitude towards mathematics are thus already visible. He pressed forward with it, despite a few qualms, as much because it still fascinated him as because it offered a means of support. What he was later to write about Wotton Reinfred (1827) shows that he would not forget the fascination:

> Mathematics and the kindred sciences, at once occupying and satisfying his logical faculty, took much deeper hold of him; nay, by degrees, as he felt his own independent progress, almost alienated him for a long season from all other studies. 'Is not truth', said he, 'the pearl of great price, and where shall we find it but here?' He gloried to track the footsteps of the mighty Newton, and in the thought that he could say to himself: Thou, even thou, are privileged to look from his high eminence, and to behold with thy own eyes the order of that stupendous fabric; thou seest it in light and mystic harmony, which, though all living men denied, thou wouldst not even doubt![25]

This, defictionized, refers to the years between 1816 and 1820 when he was reading Newton and his mathematical and scientific interests were strongest. From the largely mythic accounts we have of his childhood (including his own accounts) we learn that it was his special talent in "figures" that induced his parents to send him to Annan Academy and eventually on to the University. Though he was not really a prodigy, his talent was recognized and encouraged, first by his father, then by relatives (Uncle Frank

Carlyle) and teachers (Mr Morley), until Professor Leslie singled him out for praise in 1810, and again in 1812 with a written certification stating that "Mr. Thomas Carlisle" possessed "talents peculiarly fitted for mathematical investigation".[26] According to a fellow student of Carlyle's he took the *dux* prize at that time "without much effort". (Wilson, *Carlyle*, I, 82.) Indeed he could not fail to recognize his own talents. As a boy he had enjoyed working out for himself mathematical puzzles in the *Belfast and County Almanack*. (Wilson, *Carlyle*, I, 69.) His early letters to Robert Mitchell, and to Hill and Murray, were filled with geometrical discourse. He and Mitchell were particularly fond of sending problems and solutions to one another, both of them reflecting Leslie's notion of mathematics as a discipline of the mind, yet also considering it a kind of diversion. When Mitchell asks Carlyle how it is possible to divide a circle into 360 degrees Carlyle quotes Gauss and Delambre in his demonstration that it cannot be done by plane geometry. (*CL*, I, 82–3.) They debate the perennial question whether an angle can be trisected with a ruler and compass. (*CL*, 1, 7–8, 27–28.) In another letter, out of sheer fun, Carlyle sends Mitchell a theorem and his elaborate demonstration of it done into Latin: "My dialect of that language is, I doubt not, somewhat peculiar—and you may chance to find some difficulty in interpreting it." And he goes on to "rate" his friend:

> Your Theorem about the heptagon does not answer exactly; it is only a very good approximation, as I perceive, and as you may perceive also, by consulting a table of sines and tangents.—I have forgot West's theorem about the circle and curves of the second order.—It is no great matter surely, since I should not be able to demonstrate it tho' I had it. I wish you would send it me notwithstanding.— I hope you have sustained no injury from your excursion to Edinr—I hope too that you spake to Mr. Leslie concerning the books. If you have not procured [me] one, I must request you to lend me yours immediately for a short time, if you can do without it: for one of the boys has begun conics & I have lent him my book—and should like to have another copy of it by me, to consult at home.—You must send me the theorem & book by Mr. Johnson of Hitchill—who I understand is to be at Ruthwell today and who can easily bring them to Annan.—A letter I am expecting with impatience—(*CL*, I, 73–6, 19 April 1816).

The playful manner here does not conceal Carlyle's serious concern with the subject of his ambition to improve his knowledge and skill. Thus he presses Mitchell for a prompt reply, and asks for books and more theorems to try his wits on. At this stage of his life mathematics is more avocation than vocation; it is a game.

The practice of exchanging original problems for solution led in 1814 to what seems to have been his first entry into print, in the small but lively newspaper, the *Dumfries and Galloway Courier*. Since Carlyle plunged *in medias res* it will be necessary to give some of the background. The 7 November 1813 issue of the *Courier* printed a letter addressed to The Editor, signed "ARITHMUS", in which it was proposed to establish a new section in the paper, a sort of Mathematician's Corner, which should complement its already popular "Poet's Corner." Readers were to be invited to send in mathematical or geometrical problems for solution by other readers who, it was hoped, would send in problems of their own and thus create a lively correspondence. The proposal was recommended as "productive of advantage" and likely "to improve the minds of your readers". "ARITHMUS" submitted four problems, and solutions began to appear in the issue of 14 December, from "A Constant Reader" and from "PHILO-MATHES", and in the issue of 21 December from "J.H.", and in the issue of 4 January 1814, from "A.B." "A.B." submitted fresh problems. The practice of anonymity thus begun was broken without warning in the 18 January issue by Messrs W. C. Walsh and W. C. Donald, of Mr White's Academy in Dumfries, who sent in more solutions, and by ALEX. GOLDIE, of Castle-Douglas, a week later. These exchanges were carried on in a vigorous if somewhat humourless way, with little or no comment on either the problems or the solutions and no discussion of the mathematical principles involved. In the 15 February issue some more solutions appeared and two new problems were submitted by "N". At this point Carlyle made his entrance, and the correspondence immediately changed character.

Writing to Carlyle a week later, his college friend, J. E. Hill, asked him "Whom do you intend to take care of the poor fellow's garden until he returns from the destination you appointed him lately—the centre of the earth?" and thus directs us to Carlyle's solutions of "N's" problems in the issue of 22 February.[27] "N's" problems read as follows:

(1) Let AB and BC be the given sides of a rectangle DB; it is possible to divide it into four equal areas, by means of curve lines running from A to C: What is the nature of the curve to be employed for the purpose? No answer to this question has yet been published.

(2) I have in my garden four trees, the third stands in a point equidistant from the first two—the fourth in a point equidistant from the other three—and the first is 20 yards distant from the second, and the third 30 yards from the fourth—to find the distance of all the trees from each other, and likewise the distance from the trees of a point in the garden, where, if I stand, I am equidistant from all the trees?[28]

Reading these in Edinburgh Carlyle at once sat down and dashed off a spirited reply which appeared in the next issue, that of February 22; but it appeared with a fatal misprint which, if it had no larger portent, was at least to stir up a tea-pot tempest. His reply:

To the Editor of the *Dumfries and Galloway Courier*.

Sir—The following are answers to the questions in your last number:

I   The rectangle is capable of being divided into 4 equal parts, by any of the common geometrical curves; though to divide it, we have only to find (by the rules of fluxions) the equation of the curve, whose area is $\frac{3}{4}$ that of the rectangle; to describe two such curves, on the opposite sides, and bisect the space included between them.

Note—The parabola will divide it into three equal parts.

II   Three of the trees are evidently in the circumference of a circle, whose centre is the fourth, and radius 30 yards. The third has one on each side, distant from each other 20 yards; and to find their distance from it, (they are both equal) is the problem—that is: the radius of a circle being 30, to find the chord of half the arc whose chord is 20. By the common rules of plane trigonometry, the result is 10.14 yards. Since, however, only *one* circle can pass through three points, it is evident that, *till the circumference of a circle is made to pass through its centre*, the fourth tree can never be in the circumference of one which passes through the other three; in other words, there can be no point in the garden which is equidistant from all the four.

70

If Mr N. is determined to be equidistant from all his trees, he must go to —— the centre of the earth.

I am, Sir, your &c.

THOMAS CARLYLE

Edinburgh, 18th Feb. 1814.

In the next number (1 March 1814), there appeared the answer to a question submitted earlier by Messrs W. C. Walsh and Donald, and appended to this a sarcastic reply to Carlyle by a reader who for reasons of his own resumed the practice of anonymity. With broad scorn he referred to "the method of Master Thomas Carlyle, of Edinburgh, ((see your last number); viz. the question 'is capable of being' solved 'by any of the common' methods; 'though to' do it 'we have only to find', by 'the rule of fluxions', or by the rule of three, or by the rule of *Thumb*, 'the equation' necessary, and the thing is done."

Irritated by Carlyle's lofty humour this country Jack intended to slay the giant of Edinburgh. His failure to perceive the obvious misprint of "capable" for "incapable", delivered him into Carlyle's unmerciful but still immature hands. The following reply, Carlyle's second contribution, appeared in the March 8 issue:

Sir—Respecting an extremely *acute* 'remark', which dropt from the pen of the right *ingenious*, and (I may say) right *Rule-of-Thumb-ic* 'mathematical' solver, to the question in your last, I think it necessary (since your correspondent, with *laudable modesty*, declines the honour of *fathering* his *jeu d'esprit*, though, haply, the only-begotten of his brain) merely to 'remark' in my turn, that I did not consider a provincial newspaper the proper vehicle for fluxionary investigations, and that 'capable', in my solution, was, by mistake, either in printing or transcribing, inserted instead of '*incapable*', as was evident to any person not blinded by conceit, and whose knowledge of his mother tongue amounts to an acquaintance with *The Adventures of THOMAS HICKATHRIFT*, or *The History of Jack the Giant-Killer*.

Having thus solved your question, and, 'lest he' might have been 'wise in his own conceit', answered 'a fool according to his folly', I beg leave to add, that, should any further *anonymous* attempts at wit appear in your paper against me, I shall regard them 'as the wind that bloweth', and suffer them quietly to 'fleer back' into the '*limbo of vanity*' whence they came—I have the honour to be, &c.

THOMAS CARLYLE

Edinburgh, 4th March, 1814.

Despite the threat, or perhaps because of it, this did not end the matter. Granted, he had sufficient reason to take offence, even allowing for the unperceived misprint, but this torrent of parody and abuse suggests that he took more offence than was given. On the other hand, his prevailing temper is not so much rancour as a boisterous humour that seems to burst exultantly through all bonds of restraint, as if now at last able to engage with someone in words, he gleefully joined combat, using the full battery of eighteenth-century invective and expecting his opponent to reply in kind. This was different from writing letters in private to his friends: he was answering an unknown assailant, and in full view of a small but definite public.

Even if he meant to silence his opponent, however, he should not have left himself vulnerable to counter-attack by referring to that opponent as "blinded by conceit", or to the *Courier* as a "provincial newspaper". The next issue of the *Courier* (March 15) carried another jibe from the same anonymous, and unabashed, critic.

> . . . We are strongly tempted to give another solution of the question by the *new method* (not Carlyleian till sanctioned by the public) first communicated to your scientific readers in your No. for the 22d ult. The method is certainly unrivalled for brevity, simplicity, and universality; rare and precious advantages! But they are unfortunately combined with a serious disadvantage, viz. the result is, at the bottom, universally the same as the question which ought to be answered. At a future opportunity we may, perhaps, give as great publicity to this new method as can be expected by the aid of a provincial newspaper.

How much these contemptuous allusions to Carlyle's vanity and desire for publicity, the bold repudiation of the solution itself, and the writer's persistent anonymity, nettled Carlyle may be guessed. In the same issue of 15 March there was a question he had submitted, to which no solution was ever sent in.[29] The next issue contained no reply from Carlyle to his antagonist, indicating that for the present at least he was abiding by the terms of his threat. All was quiet in the Mathematical Corner, until, in the *March 29* number several items appeared which delivered the *coup de grâce* to the whole correspondence. One of these was Carlyle's solution to a problem that had been submitted by "W.T.". The second was a

letter from "W.T." defending Carlyle and deploring the aggra-
vation of the dispute by the anonymous critic.

> Sir, I hoped, after Mr Carlyle's letter in your paper of the 8th cur-
> rent, that the *new method*, as I now find it called, of solving mathe-
> matical questions, was set at rest, and am sorry to find it revived
> by the solvers of Messrs W. and D's question of the 15th
> inst.

The third item, a note by the Editor himself, reveals the fact
that Carlyle had not, after all, been able to remain silent.

> The renewed attack of Messrs Walsh and Donald on Mr Carlyle,
> has called forth from that gentleman a severe retaliation; but as
> we are unwilling to encourage a *cacoëthes carpendi*, as Mr Carlyle
> happily calls it, or to prolong a controversy which might in the end
> produce irritation, we have taken the liberty of suppressing it.—
> EDITOR.

This put an end to the mathematical correspondence in the
Dumfries Courier for some time. The Editor's assumption that
Carlyle's attackers were Messrs Walsh and Donald does not seem
to have been denied. Whether Carlyle's second rebuttal was more
rhetorical or less, more sharply vituperative or more temperate
and controlled, will never be known. Yet it does not seem to have
displeased the Editor-Minister of Ruthwell; there is in his note a
certain approval of the "severe retaliation" as well as affection for
its writer.[30] No blame is attached to the first rebuttal of 4 March,
only to the repeated attacks by Messrs W. and D. Much of the
trouble he knew had been caused by the fatal misprint, the rest by
their resentment of Carlyle's wit and mathematical prowess. But
only a Carlyle would enter the lists at full gallop and tilt at in-
visible windmills, to convert at one stroke a somewhat staid mathematical correspondence into a slashing polemic, and so end it.
Such a performance, though interesting to watch, could not but be
inappropriate to the quiet pages of the *Courier*. The game had
become a battle.

These letters to the *Courier* no doubt belong under the heading
of juvenilia, and, with their Carlylese, are of more stylistic than
mathematical importance. But they clearly establish his inchoate
ambition, his desire to become known, his sensitiveness to criti-

cism, his sometimes unrestrained truculence, even his difficulty with editors. It is clear too that his mathematical proclivities are geometrical and practical and that he uses Newtonian fluxions and symbols rather than the Cartesian calculus. When the Mathematical Column was revived in November 1816, problems being sent in to the Editor by ALPHA, S. Cowan, and others, Carlyle seems to have wanted to participate, for in his letters to Mitchell, who had become Mr Duncan's mathematical editor, he continued to send problems for nearly another three years.[31] Some of these may have been accepted. As his demonstrations grew more hasty (*CL*, I, 85–6) or careless (*CL*, I, 91, 101) it is evident that his fondness for problem-solving diminished; but at the same time his interest in geometry was broadening under Newton's influence into an interest in mathematics as related to the other sciences. Among his contributions to the *Courier* were two letter-essays on Thunder and Lightning, appropriate subjects, as has been remarked, for the "first published essay" of a writer like Carlyle.[32] He now read the *Principia* with more comprehension, and as his teaching days at Kirkcaldy drew to a close he was freer to consider how mathematics might be more than a game or means of support, might perhaps prove to be the vital part of a liberal education that Leslie had claimed, leading to a deeper understanding of man and society.

But at first it was a means of livelihood. He had earned money as a tutor at least as early as the summer of 1810 when at the age of fourteen he had taught a Major Davidson mathematics at Ecclefechan. With Leslie's recommendation he was nearly always able to eke out his slender resources by tutoring. His first job, as Teacher of Mathematics at Annan Academy in 1814, brought him £70 a year; his second, at the Burgh School, Kirkcaldy, in 1816, £80. When he resigned this position in October, 1818 ("I must cease to be a paedagogue", *CL*, I, 142–3), and went back to Edinburgh to prepare himself for a more attractive career, it was tutoring again, plus his savings, and some other employments, that supported him for the next six years. The Buller tutorship, with its £200 a year, made him financially independent from January 1822 to July 1824, but in 1818 no such windfall was in sight. Irving and Leslie helped him obtain pupils, while he looked, as it seems, in all directions for new opportunities. Though in his parents' eyes he was still supposed to be considering the ministry, he has long before "quitted all thoughts of the church"; and although any literary employment would be welcome he had told Mitchell that "To live by authorship was never my intention" (CL, I, 144). The question remained, what directions were possible? These were his hardest years. It must have been particularly mortifying when his revered Professor Leslie told him that "upon the whole . . . the best plan for *you* seems to be to learn the engineering business, and go to America" (CL, I, 158, 8 Jan., 1819). Though he had no desire to do either he did attend the classes in mineralogy and geology taught by Robert Jameson, Professor of Natural History, but he did not like that gentleman's "most crude theories" and faulted both his accuracy and the organization of his lectures. "Yesterday he explained the [colour] of the atmosphere, upon principles which argued a total ignorance of dioptrics. A knowledge of the external characters of minerals is all that I can hope to obtain from him."[33] Nevertheless he read works by French and German geologists, and then in order to be able to read "the illustrious Werner" in the original began his momentous study of the German language.[34] In February 1819, David Brewster commissioned him to translate a French article on "Some Compounds which depend on very Weak Affinities" by Jacob Berzelius for his *Edinburgh Philosophical Journal*, paying him promptly and honestly for this work, and also for two more scientific papers: a review of Hansteen's book on Magnetism, which was to be Carlyle's first published book review, and a translation of Mohs' German work on Crystallography and Mineralogy.[35] These engaged his scientific concerns, and exercised his power of independent scientific statement. With the Hansteen review he was happily involved in a discussion of the earth's magnetic forces, lines of force (*in*organic filaments), and the laws of controlling magnetic intensity. The experiments which had led Coulomb to the conclusion that the attraction between two particles is always as the square of the distance were, he observed, of doubtful scientific accuracy. Hansteen had now confirmed this conclusion by purely mathematical demonstration; but with perfect self-assurance, he rejects one of Hansteen's findings on the basis of his own knowledge of the parabola. As a whole, the review is a formal, neutral handling of a complex subject. But he concludes that "the whole science is involved in conjecture", and notes wryly that Professor Hansteen draws support for some of his arguments from one of "the sacred numbers of the Indians, Babylonians, Greeks and Egyptians": the number 432, and from the division in Brahminical mythology of the world's duration into four periods of $1 \times 432,000$ years, $2 \times 432,000$, $3 \times 432,000$ and $4 \times 432,000$ years, because these match (with some rounding of figures) Hansteen's own findings of the times taken by each of the four magnetic points to complete its circuit around its pole.[36]

A similar attempt at independent scientific discussion, done at the end of 1819 and meant for the *Edinburgh Review*, was his ill-fated review of what he long after referred to as Pictet's "mechanical *Theory of Gravitation*". Since Jeffrey neither accepted nor returned the manuscript it has been lost for ever, and the actual work Carlyle was reviewing has only recently been identified.[37] At about the same time he seems to have planned to write something on Hevelius's *Selenographia* (1647), and a life of Horrox—which came to nothing. Seeing now that all his skill and training in mathematics were failing to open up a career he attempted to train himself for the Law, but, enrolling in Hume's Scots Law class in the autumn of 1819, though he persevered, he could muster no interest in it, and was mercifully rescued the following March by Brewster's employing him to write the twenty odd *Edinburgh Encyclopedia* articles, which would give him some support and occupy much of his time during the next four years. Only two of the subjects assigned him directly involved mathematicians or scientists, Montucla and Pascal. Most were eighteenth-century historical figures, some were French philosophers (Pascal, Montesquieu, Montaigne), some merely geographical areas. Mungo Park was the only Scot. Brewster did not give him Newton. Yet the M's, N's, and P's served him well enough, for they enabled him to apprentice himself, before a public audience, in the biographical, historical, and journalistic essay, as well as in problems of researching and organizing materials and ideas. His concept of history was still light: it amused and instructed. The "Netherlands" gave him a chance to write history, and he wrote it like Hume and Robertson, an account of great men and celebrated events. In the "Nelson" he could describe his first hero, complete with a sort of conversion. The "Montesquieu" by its distinction of style and thought apparently drew the attention of Francis Jeffrey.[38] The "Montucla" briefly records the career of the French mathematical historian, without revealing anything of Carlyle's own mathematical interests. All the articles show what Lowell called "a certain security of judgement", and occasional flashes of Carlylean phrasing and imagery.

The "Pascal" deserves special attention not only because Pascal was philosopher, mathematician, physicist, and publicist all in one, but because it shows Carlyle's hand. His account of Pascal's life is, as Professor Shine observes, a significant indication of Carlyle's spiritual and intellectual development.[39] In his disapproval of Pascal's *"famous arithmetical machine"*, for example, as "a wonderful but useless proof of its author's ingenuity", we can hardly fail to detect the influence of Leslie: a calculating machine by-passes the mind. Leibnitz's "simpler calculating machine" is also disapproved in passing. And though he suspects as an exaggeration the report that Pascal as a boy had "actually discovered the truth of Euclid's thirty-second proposition" (that the three angles of a triangle are equal to two right angles) without any knowledge of Euclid, yet he describes Pascal's mathematical and scientific achievements with open admiration: the bold proof on the Puy-de-Dome of Toricelli's experiments with the mercury column, the "beautiful" invention of the Arithmetical Triangle which Leibnitz afterwards used in his development of the calculus, the discovery when he was 16 of the "Hexagonal Theorem", and his dramatic demonstration of the mathematics of the cycloid. Such scientific devotion in a devoutly religious man might be questionable, but Carlyle notes with sympathy that Pascal was encouraged to pursue and publish his findings "to show that the highest attainments in a science of strict reasoning were not incompatible with the humblest belief in the principles of religion" (p. 335). He admires Pascal also for continuing his work despite failing health and continual physical pain (cf. Carlyle's dyspepsia). Having recently experienced his own conversion he describes Pascal's conversion to Jansenism without disapproval, as if an attack on Jesuitism were as welcome as one on Atheism. He praises the *Provincial Letters* for their literary quality and formative effect upon the French language (p. 334). And he notes that even after that conversion the "speculations of early life resumed their sway [and] showed that his mathematical powers were diverted, not destroyed" (p. 334). With the quarrels between the Molinists and Jansenists Carlyle does not tarry: "Pascal's work is the main plank, by . . . which some memory of them still floats on the stream of time" (p. 334). But he refuses to deplore Pascal's religious passion or to associate it with insanity. Voltaire, remarking that "after the accident at Neuilly bridge, Pascal's head was deranged, . . . should have remembered, that as the external colouring of our feelings depends on the associations to which we are exposed, and is changed with all their changes, so the appearance of great intellect and lofty purposes, however modified and over clouded, is always entitled to the reverence and approval of every good man" (p. 335). It is a tender portrait. Though he would not express it here, he must have felt a kinship with Pascal; especially now when his intellectual allegiances were shifting and he was becoming more deeply involved in the main issues of Pascal's life, of knowledge and faith, science and religion, the head and the heart, issues that were still unresolved and a source of considerable perplexity to him. This can be seen in a remark following the one quoted above about the compatibility of "a science of strict reasoning" and religious belief (p. 335), that it was a precept for Pascal "that matters of faith are beyond the empire of reason". Well might Carlyle seek a resolution of his own problems redefining reason and relegating science to the lower realm of logic and the understanding.[40] Even when his views were finally matured and set, his mathematical interests, like Pascal's, would be "diverted, not destroyed". There was comfort, curiously, in observing that with all his intellectual attainments Pascal was not always rational; that the same genius that discovered the arithmetical triangle and produced the *Pensées* also made him keep an account of his near-death at Neuilly between the cloth and lining of his coat:

> It should excite not a smile but a sigh, to learn that Pascal believed in the miraculous cure of his niece by a relic at Port Royal; that he reckoned it necessary to appear cold toward his sisters, though he loved them deeply; or that in his latter years, he wore below his shirt an iron girdle studded with sharp points, which he pressed against the skin whenever any evil thought overtook him (p. 335).

While writing these articles for the *Edinburgh Encyclopedia* Carlyle was executing another assignment by Brewster, the translating of Legendre's *Geometry*. This work was, and still is, recognized by mathematicians as a distinguished one, and in Carlyle's translation it would go through many editions in England and America, so that one scholar credits him with an important place in the history of mathematics teaching and another marvels that "the famous Scottish litterateur" should have done it at all.[41] For Carlyle, however, it was an onerous job. He had agreed to undertake it before he knew about the Buller tutorship. Brewster would pay him only £50 for nearly seven months' work, at a time when, with Jane's encouragement, he was trying to devote his efforts to the writing of an original literary work.[42] The matter would not be worth further consideration but for the essay on Proportion which he wrote as the Introductory chapter. Whether Brewster asked him to do this is not known, but since he seems to have written it very rapidly—he later claimed in half a day, "a happy forenoon (Sunday, I fear!),"—it was perhaps his own idea.[43] It was done probably in July 1822, between *Edinburgh Encyclopaedia* articles, and while he was studying hard for a projected history of the Commonwealth. Like the Berzelius and Mohs translations, this one was hack-work and his letters contain frequent complaints, but, curiously, make no mention of the essay on Proportion which he afterwards remembered writing so easily and thought of with pleasure and pride.[44] Yet short though it is, it furnishes valuable clues to the connection between his early mathematical and his later, literary work.

The essay is a model of concision. Two introductory paragraphs explaining the relation of the essentially arithmetical subject of Proportion to geometry are followed by four definitions and some theorems with their corollaries. The doctrine of proportion, he announces in the opening sentence, does not belong exclusively to geometry, since its object is "to point out the relations which subsist among magnitudes in general, when viewed as *measured*, or represented by *numbers*"; it applies also to many other branches of knowledge. Thus, four magnitudes which are in proportion constitute an analogy, and the reasoning which is required to detect and demonstrate proportionality is analogous reasoning (p. xiv). The essay thus lays the groundwork for the extension of 'proportional' reasoning as used in mathematics to the use of analogous reasoning in other subjects. Carlyle takes considerable pains to establish the most difficult proportionalities, as where the terms are incommensurable. Ordinarily, he says, in order to demonstrate that two pairs of magnitudes are proportional, a common measure, or sub-multiple, must be found for each pair. When, however, the members of each pair are incommensurable, that is, have no common measure, the proportionality cannot be demonstrated so simply. This was the very difficulty that Euclid negotiated so "cumbrously" in his Fifth Book that it had to be omitted in most geometry texts. In an elaborate footnote (p. xi) Carlyle proposes a fractional method of obtaining a common measure, dividing successively smaller submultiples of one number of each pair into the other member so as to approximate a common measure, and thus diminishing the discrepancy "below any assigned magnitude". Then, "since the proportion still continues accurate at every successive approximation, we infer that it will, in like manner, continue accurate to the limit which we can approach indefinitely, though never actually reach". He also proposes a geometrical method, which constitutes an equally interesting analogy.[45] This brief foray into the realm of approximation and incommensurabilities assumes a special significance when we consider, among the characteristics of his later thought, his tendency to reason or argue by analogy, making intuitive leaps to find or to establish a condition among one set of terms which will then hold true for an analogous set of terms. Northrop Frye has noted the kinship between literature and mathematics, with their basic units of the metaphor and the equation: metaphor may be seen as a compressed equation, or analogy, the terms of which are either symbols or entities.[46] But in literature their proportional relationships will be more poetic than precise. So in *Sartor Resartus*, if Aprons give protection to the Nürnberg housewife so do the Police protect society; the clothes which cover our bodies wear out, as do the institutions of King and Clergy. The whole of *Sartor*, with its intricate symbolism, is an "infinitely complected" analogy, a working-out of the proportionality of things material and spiritual. It is an extensive example of Carlyle's analogic dialectic executed in large scale and small. Corresponding to the broad parallelism existing between the outer world and the inner are individual parallelisms:

> Thus is the Laystall, especially with its Rags or Clothes-rubbish, the grand Electric Battery, and Fountain-of-motion, from which and to which the Social Activities (like vitreous and resinous Electricities) circulate, in larger or smaller circles, through the mighty, billowy, stormtost Chaos of Life, which they keep alive! [47]

—where the Laystall "is to" (i.e. it circulates) material clothes as social activities "are to" (they animate) life—with Industry and the "electric battery" serving, so to speak, as submultiples in the proportion. The method of analogy may be used in argument, somewhat perilously, as Carlyle knew.[48] But it became a characteristic of his thought. Impatient of logical reasoning, he sought to establish proof by the transference of a truth which, recognized as a truth in one place, must be recognized as true in an analogous place. Yet analogy is not proof: for the "relation which is perceived to exist between two magnitudes of the same kind . . . appears to be a simple idea, and therefore unsusceptible of any good definition" (Legendre, p. xii). Rather, it is persuasion. Impatient also of the kind of sequential, phenomenal thinking that is usually required in narrative fiction, he found himself (no doubt for other reasons as well) unable to complete his *Wotton Reinfred*. What the essay "On Proportion" reveals most clearly is that the same intuitive, analogical thinking that characterized his mathematical demonstrations reappears in his later work. What he wanted in science as in literature, and had a peculiar talent for, was the flash of insight, the sudden perception of significant relation. Each flash was like an act of faith, bringing the discovery of a certitude, of a permanent, spiritual truth.

With the writing of the essay on Proportion, Carlyle brought to an end twelve years of mathematical activity. There is little doubt that by 1822 he considered himself launched on a literary career, though most insecurely and with no clear promise of success. It is not surprising then that he should for at least another ten years leave the mathematical door ajar. When opportunities arrived to apply for teaching positions he would apply. But his intellectual curiosity in mathematics and the sciences as they existed in his time, has all but died. For one thing, it is likely that he had reached his limit as a mathematical thinker. When in 1816 he was reading and attempting to understand Newton's *Principia* (*CL*, I, 79), it was "with considerable perserverance & little success", until he realized that he had too little knowledge of astronomy, whereupon he sent for a copy of Delambre's *Abrégé d'astronomie*, and in the meantime read a number of ancillary works, James Wood's *Elements of Optics*, John Robison's article on optics in the third edition of the *Encyclopaedia Britannica*, and Keill's *Introductio ad Veram Physicam*. Armed with these he read the Delambre when it arrived, with understanding enough, and then, presumably, returned to his study of the *Principia*. In spite of D. A. Wilson's statement that he now "saw with delight the *Principia* 'at his feet' " there is little evidence that he ever wholly mastered this difficult work. The following year, after attempting to read William Wallace's article on Fluxions in the *Britannica* he gave up, because he could not or would not take the time to understand the whole of this Newtonian branch of mathematics. "I wish I had it in my head—," he wrote Mitchell. "But, unless I quit my historical pursuits, it may be doubted whether this will ever happen" (*CL*, I, 112). In 1818 he read but could not understand Lagrange's *Mécanique analytique* (1788), Laplace's *Exposition du système du monde* (1796) and *Mécanique céleste* (1799–1825), and Bossut's *Mécanique* (1810) with its "integrals and differentials".[49] Though he still admired science, and advised Mitchell "you must not leave off Mathematics", he lamented his own lack of comprehension: "To see these truths, my good Robert—to *feel* them as one does the proportion of the sphere & cylinder! 'Tis a consummation devoutly to be wished—but not very likely ever to arrive. Sometimes, indeed . . . I say to myself—away with despondency—hast thou not a soul and a kind of understanding in it? And what more has any analyst of them all? But next morning, alas, when I consider my understanding—how coarse yet feeble it is."[50] After the *Principia* ceased to absorb him he was to advance no further in mathematical thought. He could teach, he could comprehend up to a point, but he could not create. In short, he could not go beyond Leslie's teaching. The mathematics in which he had been trained was in itself a hindrance. Having been taught to avoid analysis, he found it too difficult, and soon came to regard it with distaste on other grounds.

Carlyle does not attribute his loss of interest in mathematics to his own incapacity, or to the geometry-based mathematics he had been taught, but rather to what he regarded as the unphilosophical nature of all mathematical science. As with the solving of geometrical problems, though it exercised the mind and trained one to think, it was narrow and yielded little knowledge. "The worst of it is", he wrote while struggling with Wallace's *Fluxions*, "we are led to his conclusion, as it were thro a narrow lane— often, by its windings shutting from our view the object of our search—and never affording us a glimpse of the surrounding country" (*CL*, I, 112). His growing desire for a comprehensive understanding of man and the universe prompted him to renew his search in history and literature.[51] That he was not yet deeply attracted to history only added to the doubt and misery which darkened this period of his life and which was to culminate in his Leith Walk crisis. Among the complex of causes which brought on this crisis his disillusionment with mathematics must be counted an important one. By 1818 he feared that it would lead neither to the truth nor to the career he needed, and not until the autumn of 1820 would he find an equally absorbing interest in German literature. Nor was he to realize the full promise of the Germans until 1822, when he attained a deeper understanding of Goethe. Carlyle did not simply turn from mathematics to Goethe. There was the agonizingly empty period of his Everlasting No which lasted until his year at Hoddam Hill (1825–1826) and most probably even longer.[52]

Nevertheless he made the plunge early in 1821: "I must live by literature, at all hazards" (*CL*, I, 336) though he could not yet earn a living by it but must spend nearly a year translating the Legendre *Geometry* for Brewster. "Many a time I have wished that, when ruining my health with their poor lean triangles & sines & tangents & fluxions & calculi, I had but been writing any kind of doggerel" (*CL*, II, 116). He is here writing to Jane, whose love of poetry strongly influenced his decision to commit himself to a career of literature when his prospects were still so dim. It would not do to teach Jane mathematics; he must teach her literature, and must therefore be a writer himself. Thus practical circumstances played their part in drawing him away from mathematics. Only for reasons of security did he continue to apply for mathematical teaching positions;[53] only because his literary future was still perilous even in 1833 did he make that last effort to utilize his mathematical skill when he applied for the directorship of the Edinburgh Astronomical Observatory. Though he was qualified for this position, it lay far from his interests and would have entailed a drastic alteration in his career.

Even before he met Jane in June, 1821, a number of literary opportunities had brought encouragement and hope to his old literary ambitions. He reviewed Joanna Baillie's *Metrical Legends of Exalted Characters* for the October issue of Waugh's *New Edinburgh Review*, and wrote "Faustus" for the April 1822 issue. Later in 1822 he seems to have tried his hand at a (now lost) epistolary novel, at a short story, the "Cruthers and Jonson", and some poems. But these were not enough to sustain him either financially or intellectually. During the next five years (1822–1827) he would re-enact what he had done in mathematics, reading widely in order to comprehend, translating to earn money, and writing critical and biographical essays as apprenticeship for the original work he still hoped to do later. But when he attempted a novel, in *Wotton Reinfred*, he had to leave it unfinished at the eighth chapter. Not until he had thoroughly assimilated the Germans (1827–1829) did he find what he had sought in the study and pursuit of mathematics, a *Weltbild*, or philosophic picture of the world which compelled his belief.

To his friend Anna Montagu, after his failure to obtain the chairs of Moral Philosophy at London and St. Andrews, he wrote, "I accordingly came hither [Craigenputtoch]; still bent on 'professing Morals,' in one shape or another, but from a *chair* of my own, and to such audience as I myself could gather round me" (*CL*, IV, 391, 12 Aug. 1828). It was morals, then, that validated and ennobled literature, morals as part of a religious faith. The tradition of Dugald Stewart's course in Moral Philosophy at Edinburgh rose again, joining with Carlyle's religious training, to lead him to the pulpit for which his parents had educated him.

We may now ask what were the consequences of Carlyle's mathematical talent and training. The question cannot be answered precisely, for if we attempt to demonstrate that a mathematician necessarily thinks and writes differently from a physician we become involved in a complex of psychological theories not always amenable to proof. Nor can we define how a man's training in one discipline will determine his ideas or modes of thought after he has adopted another discipline. In Carlyle's case the matter is still more elusive because he was never exclusively preoccupied with mathematics and science. While he was reading Franklin's *Treatise on Electricity* in 1813 he was also deep in Shakespeare. While winning honours in Leslie's mathematics classes he wrote, "Grant me that with a heart of independence, unseduced by the world's smiles, and unbending in its frowns, I may attain to literary fame" (Wilson, *Carlyle*, I, 93). We must remember that the same intellectual habits may arise from diverse disciplines, even from those of science and art. The same needs may be satisfied by them. What had drawn Carlyle to mathematics was intellectual excitement. Each demonstration was an adventure, each problem to be solved a challenge, each solution a conquering of the unknown. When with the Germans he encountered new philosophical questions these too were challenges, problems to be solved, theorems to be fitted into a larger whole. With social and political questions too his mind would seek clear solutions. Though mathematics lacked content he never lost his respect for its power of demonstration. Yet in one way he seriously misjudged it. When he discovered the superiority of Reason over the Understanding, it seemed obvious that mathematics belonged to the latter realm, that in dealing with "visibles" and "mensurables" it must be confined to mere logic. The fact that much mathematical reasoning involves intuition and requires an analogical imagination did not occur to him, even though he used both in his quadratic solution for Leslie's *Geometry*, and in his essay on Proportion for the Legendre. It was the analysts whom he and Leslie deplored who used logic; his own thinking, his perception of analogy and proportion, was an exercise of the very imagination and Reason which he denied to mathematics.

Such an attitude helps to explain Carlyle's increasingly ambivalent opinion of the sciences. He both dislikes and likes them. He will reject them but at the same time retain them as an ideal. After the Legendre translation his references to mathematics grow more critical. In *Wotton Reinfred* science is said to lead only to scepticism and doubt. Poor Wotton, "poring over thy Geometries and Stereometries, thy Fluxions direct and inverse, by the

Newtonian and Leibnitzian method", eventually discovered that "The *Principia* do but enlighten one small forecourt of the mind."[54] By 1829, in "Novalis", Carlyle adduced Leslie's old reprehension of analytical algebra in his own reprehension of "the higher mathematics", which is mechanical because "assisted with visible symbols, with safe *implements* for thinking" (*Works*, XXVII, 51). The same note is struck in "Signs of the Times": "The science of the age, in short, is physical, chemical, physiological; in all shapes mechanical. Our favourite Mathematics, the highly prized exponent of all these other sciences, has also become more and more mechanical" (*Works*, XXVII, 63–64). Yet Masson testifies that "to the end of his life . . . he would talk with great relish about mathematical matters" (Masson, 310). And Tyndall, we remember, said that "he was always in the advance of me, anticipating and enunciating what I was about to say". Mathematics and the physical sciences still claimed place as useful, even necessary, branches of knowledge. Furthermore he now had the example of Goethe, who sometimes said that he took less pride in his poetry than in his work as a scientist, his theory of colours and his discovery of the premaxillary bone. From Goethe and Novalis came authority for Carlyle's mature conviction that science, literature, philosophy, and religion were complementary, all related parts of a whole. If he could not fuse them, but must leave them separate, neither could Goethe. "I conceive mathematics", wrote Goethe, "as the most sublime and useful science so long as they are applied in their proper place; but I cannot commend the misuse of them in matters which do not belong in their sphere, and in which, noble science as they are, they seem to be mere nonsense."[55] In agreement with this position Carlyle believed that the Benthamites were misapplying mathematics in the sphere of morals.

Thus Carlyle believed on the one hand that the mathematical sciences, inherently limited to the logical manipulation of visibles and mensurables, have no value for the moral philosopher; and on the other hand that they are only being misapplied and *made* mechanical by the utilitarians. Science advances by laborious analysis and mechanical gathering of facts; "No Newton, by silent meditation, now discovers the system of the world from the falling of an apple" (*Works*, XXVII, 61–2). Carlyle reserves his respect for a pure science, an ideal mathematics, in which intellection is intuitive, proceeding rather by deduction than induction, and which cannot be corrupted by the mechanists. For this ideal he used, in 1829, the old term "mathesis", meaning the action of learning mathematical science in distinction to exhibiting it. The term connotes mental discipline, silent meditation the mystery of intuition. We may note an analogy with "poesis", the spontaneous 'making' of a poem. Both require genius. Its province is not the "higher mathematics", or even the lower in which he himself had been active, but abstract thought. The ideal mathesis could be found in Euclid, Pascal, Newton, and others who infused their thinking with moral or philosophical significance. To point the contrast, Carlyle now uses the term 'mathematics' pejoratively, to denote any limited or analytical extension of the older mathematical science, requiring a lesser talent. Thus, Novalis is "well-skilled in mathematics, and . . . fond of that science; but his is a far finer species of endowment than any required in mathematics, where the mind, from the very beginning of *Euclid* to the end of *Laplace* is assisted with visible symbols, with safe *implements* for thinking; nay at least in . . . the higher mathematics, has little more than a mechanical superintendence to exercise over these. This power of abstract meditation . . . with Novalis, is a much higher and rarer one; its element is not mathematics, but that *Mathesis*, of which . . . many a Great Calculist has not even a notion" (*Works*, XXVII, 51).

The postulation of a "mathesis" seems to increase and harden his opposition to science. Now all mathematicians are mere Calculists, dealing in counters, and falling short of truth. The *Principia* of Newton has been "swallowed up" in the *Mécanique céleste* of Laplace (*CL*, I, 233), and the *Mécanique* will in its turn be swallowed up because of its machinery. In another passage written at about the same time (1829) he grants them some worth, in an effort to be fair, but with the result that they are once again denounced in order to exalt the ideal. "Without undervaluing the wonderful results which a Lagrange or Laplace educes by means of it, we may remark, that their calculus, differential and integral, is little else than a more cunningly-constructed arithmetical mill;[56] where the factors being put in, are, as it were, ground into the true product, under cover, and without other effort on our part than steady turning of the handle. We have more Mathematics than ever; but less Mathesis" (*Works*, XXVII, 64). He clearly prefers the older mathematics which reached its conclusions the hard way to the newer and more intricate analysis, grinding its arithmetical mill. "Archimedes and Plato", he adds, "could not have read the *Mécanique Céleste*; but neither would the whole French Institute see aught in that saying 'God geometrises!' but a sentimental rodomontade" (*Works*, XXVII, 64). The calculus is calculated; "God geometrises" was intuited. In the right hands, mathematics may still move ahead towards mathesis: he calls Novalis "The German Pascal" (*Works*, XXVII, 53) because "both are mathematicians and naturalists, yet occupy themselves chiefly with Religion". Father Boscovich, the Croation astronomer and mathematician, was able "from merely mathematical considerations" to reach a kind of German Idealism (*Works*, XXVII, 23).

Furthermore he began to see the possibilities of this new Mathesis in his own development. Instead of rejecting science totally and appropriating German transcendentalism he could merge them in a philosophy which should utilize the best of both. After his long studies he had come at last to the point of creation. In February of this year he wrote in his Notebook:

> Has the mind its cycles and seasons like Nature, varying from the fermentation of *werden* to the clearness of *seyn*, and this again and again. . . . In my own case, I have traced two or three such vicissitudes; at present, if I mistake not, there is some such thing at hand for me.[57]

We cannot affirm that the notion of Mathesis was directly related to this new-found "clearness of *seyn*", but he did in the following year commence the writing of his "Thoughts on Clothes" which became *Sartor Resartus*. He did not define the notion but left its brief contexts in "Novalis" and "Signs of the Times" to adumbrate its meaning. Nor does he use the term again. It has served to name the antidote to chop-logic and gerund-grinding and to suggest that "science of the mind" which he had once hoped might arise to complement Newton's great science of "matter" (*CL*, I, 84). It had only partially arisen in such men as Pascal and Novalis, who had left their finest work in the fragmented form of "Thoughts" (*Works*, XXVII, 53). He clung to the hope that it might be rising in Germany, and might yet rise in England also, if the English could be shown the folly of mechanizing all their ways. The deeper signs of the times might not be faith in mechanism but a gradual realization that there is a superior Science of Dynamics, employing "the primary, unmodified forces and energies of man", and dealing with man's infinite rather than merely finite character. Although Carlyle heartily dislikes the Science of Mechanics he does not, despite his objurgations, reject it. Having been carried to excess, it needed to be brought back in balance with that of Dynamics. The two sciences should be complementary. Each is necessary to prevent excess of the other. The balance could be restored by a kind of thinking based on the inward, primary perceptions rather than on logic. Science had not originated in the schools and universities but "in the obscure closets of the Roger Bacons, Keplers, Newtons; in the workshops of the Fausts and the Watts" (*Works*, XXVII, 69). As these "gifted spirits" thought, so must Englishmen think again, in both the inward dynamical province and the outward mechanical. Science must be transcendentalized. It must, like mathematics in Leslie's teaching, become an integral part of the general culture.

After abandoning mathematics and the sciences for a literary career Carlyle retained an *altered* interest in them.[58] He continued to make levies upon them not only for imagery but also for concept. *Sartor Resartus* is studded with figures drawn from his scientific knowledge and mathematics gave him such central concepts as the fraction of life (*Sartor*, 191) and the Hyperbolic-Asymptotic shape of history (*Works*, XXVIII, 176). The very germination of *Sartor* was largely in mathematical terms: man is a living symbol and walks between two eternities and two infinitudes.[59] But the clearest consequence of his long interest and remarkable talent in mathematics seems to have been the analogical habit of mind which we see at work both in *Sartor* and in the earlier essay "On Proportion". It is obvious that many or most of his analogies are couched in symbolic terms and that the pervasive symbolism of *Sartor* can be expressed as a proportion or analogy. The use of symbol and analogy derives from many other sources than mathematics—art, philosophy, myth, anthropology—and there is no doubt that Carlyle's use of them had a diverse provenance; but his ten years of study under Professor Leslie's influence must be

89

counted as one of the most important formative factors in his development. His analogizing imagination was stimulated, his powers of comprehension challenged. Subjected to the rigorous discipline of geometrical and algebraic study, he grew accustomed to reading things in terms of problems to be solved, puzzles to be understood, proportions to be perceived, analogies to be defined. With the final fixing of his interest on literature, his mathematical habits, instead of disappearing, continued in force to determine the special mode of thinking, arguing, and proving, that characterizes the critical and creative writing of his long career.

NOTES

1. On 19 May 1820 Carlyle wrote to a friend, "I have nearly lost all relish for Mathematics, which some years ago I reckoned the loftiest pursuit of the human intellect," *CL*, I, 252. See also *Reminiscences* (Norton); Froude, *Life*, I, 25–6, 130; Wilson, *Carlyle*, I, 258. In his *Carlyle's Early Reading until 1934* (Lexington, Ky, 1953), p. 258, Hill Shine thinks that Newton's *Principia* at least ceased to be an engrossing interest after the Kirkcaldy period (1818). Jacques Cabeau believes that Carlyle's mathematical interests remained strong until 1826–7: *TC, ou le Prométhée enchaîné* (Paris, 1968), pp. 55f.
2. Nora Barlow, ed. *Autobiography of Charles Darwin* (New York, 1958), p. 114.
3. Herbert Spencer, *An Autobiography* (London, 1904), I, 231, *passim* and II, 248–9. But see the anonymous "Herbert Spencer: A Portrait", *Blackwood's Edin. Mag.*, 175 (1904), 110–16 for Carlyle's impact on Spencer.
4. Letter to *The Times*, 4 May 1881, p. 13. Tyndall denies that Carlyle was either incurious or hostile in respect to science and affirms Carlyle's later sympathy with evolution and admiration for Darwin. See also Tyndall's "On Personal Recollections of TC", *New Fragments* (London, 1892). Darwin, though he deplored Carlyle's "garrulity and haranguing at the dinner table", respected his power, his teaching of grand moral truths, and the vividness of his historical descriptions, "more vivid than Macaulay's". *An Autobiography*, p. 113.
5. *Ibid.*, p. 114.
6. A. De Morgan, *A Budget of Paradoxes* (London, 1872), p. 499.
7. H. V. Routh, *Towards the Twentieth Century* (Cambridge, 1937), p. 116.
8. The subject has received scant attention, except from mathematicians. In his *An Introduction to the History of Mathematics* (3rd ed. New York, 1969), pp. 73, 374, 410, Howard Eves credits Carlyle with the

solution of a difficult proposition for Leslie's *Geometry* (1817) and praises him for his translation of the Legendre *Geometry* (1822). Peter A. Wursthorn, in "The Position of TC in the History of Mathematics", *The Mathematical Teacher*, 59 (1966) 755–70, comments on the essay "On Proportion" which he wrote for the Legendre and gives further details of Carlyle's activities as a mathematician and teacher. Norman Gridgeman's "TC, geometer", *New Scientist*, 27 Nov. 1969, pp. 466–7, briefly lauds his mathematical bent at the expense of virtually all his literary work. Jacques Cabeau, *op. cit.*, has written perceptively about Carlyle's mathematical and scientific imagery, and notes the later postulation of "mathesis". See also Maxwell H. Goldberg, "Carlyle, Pictet and Jeffrey", *MLQ*, VII (1946) 291–6; Ian Campbell, "Carlyle, Pictet and Jeffrey Again", *Bibliotheck*, 7 (1974), 1–15, and Samuel Gill Barnes, "Formula for Faith: the Newtonian Pattern in the Transcendentalism of TC", Unpubl. Diss., Univ. of North Carolina, 1953.

9. Froude, *Life*, I, 25–6.

10. For an excellent discussion of this point see George Levine, "*Sartor Resartus* and the Balance of Fiction", *VS*, 8 (1964), 131–60. See also Carlisle Moore, "The Persistence of Carlyle's 'Everlasting No' ", *MP*, 54 (1957), 187–96.

11. Froude, *Life*, I, 26.

12. *The Prelude* (1805–6), lines 58–61.

13. According to Richard Olson, in his "Scottish Philosophy and Mathematics, 1750–1830", *Journal of the History of Ideas*, 32 (1971) 35–37, the Scottish philosopher and mathematician Thomas Reid had come very close to postulating a non-Euclidean Geometry with his "Geometry of Visibles". Carlyle knew Reid's work generally but not this in particular. *CL*, I, 343, 123.

14. In his *The Enchafèd Flood* (New York, 1950) W. H. Auden opens his study of Romantic sea-imagery with Wordsworth's account of his dream of the Ishmael-Bedouin holding the "Stone" and the "Shell", with its imagery of the sea and the desert, and imagery to be found also in Carlyle's voyage-of-life and wasteland images in *Sartor*.

15. Olson, p. 29 n.1.

16. "Because the certainty of mathematical knowledge arises in large measure out of its connection with the primary qualities of matter rather than out of the hypothetical deductive nature of its reasoning alone, it is critical to the Common Sense philosophers that some power of the mind beyond mere reasoning be applied to assure that mathematical reasoning does not stray from its appropriate objects and that it is not extended beyond those circumstances to which it is appropriate. The Common Sense antagonism to algebraic or analytic mathematics arose in part out of this circumstance; for the extreme generality of algebraic symbolism seemed to make it far too easy . . . to fall into error." Olson, pp. 37–8. I am indebted to Olson for his full and convincing discussion of this point.

17. Olson, pp. 40–1.

18. When Carlyle went to the University in 1809, the course had been taken over by Thomas Brown (1778–1820), who, in this respect at least, seems to have taught it as Stewart had done. Carlyle, however, disliked him for "spouting poetry". David Masson, *Edinburgh Sketches* (London, 1892), p. 235.

19. Quoted in Olson, p. 42.

20. John Leslie, *Elements of Geometry and Plane Trigonometry* (Edinburgh 1817, 3rd edition), p. iii.

21. Leslie, p. 340. The solution that appears on pp. 340–1 is not Carlyle's but Pappus's more complex one; Carlyle's appears in the text, on pp. 176–7. Wursthorn calls it "remarkable in its originality, beautiful in its simplicity", *op. cit.*, p. 756. David Masson, who thought that the proposition had been given a geometrical solution before, may have had Pappus of Alexandria's in mind. (*Edinburgh Sketches*, p. 261, n.1.)

22. This is not surprising. Many Scottish ministers combined strong mathematical and scientific interests with their religious thought: e.g. Thomas Chalmers's *Astronomical Discourses* (1817), Edward Irving's early activities in mathematics and chemistry, and Henry Duncan's contributions in geology.

23. *CL*, I, lviii; Wilson, *Carlyle*, I, 155.

24. Olson, pp. 32, 34–5.

25. *Last Words of TC* (London, 1896), p. 22.

26. Wilson, *Carlyle*, I, 76; Wursthorn, p. 758.

27. Unpublished letters (NLS MS, 1764.11) from T. E. Hill to Carlyle, undated, about 24 Feb. 1814, given with the permission of the Librarian of the NLS.

28. All the passages from this mathematical correspondence in the *Courier* are quoted with the permission of the Librarian of the Ewart Public Library, Dumfries, Scotland. See C. R. Sanders' "Editing the Carlyle Letters; Problems and Opportunities", in *Editing Nineteenth Century Texts* (Toronto, 1967), pp. 84–6, and I, 8–9, for briefer accounts.

29. This seems to have been the only problem Carlyle submitted: "A and B are two ships at sea, distant from each other one mile, A east and B west; A sails east by north, at the rate of 7 knots per hour. At what rate per hour must B sail in the direction north-west, so that the locus of their centre of gravity may be a straight line?"

30. According to Wilson, *Carlyle*, I, 99, Carlyle probably did not meet the editor, Henry Duncan, until 24 October 1814, when he was invited to Ruthwell; but he had been made known to Duncan through such common acquaintances as Robert Mitchell and Edward Irving, and Duncan was later to give Carlyle commendatory letters of introduction to David Brewster and Bailie Waugh.—Wilson, *Carlyle*, I, 165.

31. *CL*, I, 91 n. 9, 113. He seems also to have continued working problems, both in the *Courier* and *The Literary and Statistical Magazine for Scotland*.

32. Issues of 6 June and 20 June 1815. See *CL*, I, 59, n. 10 and Wilson, *Carlyle*, I, 88. Though Carlyle called these "purely the effect of *ennui*",

they were inspired by a work he had read in 1813 and still admired, Franklin's *Treatise on Electricity*.

33. Carlyle attended Jameson's classes to the end, 14 April 1819, but wrote afterwards, "I am not calculated for being a mineralogist". *CL*, I, 150, 177.

34. Among those he read were A. J. F. M. Brochant de Villiers and Alexandre Brongniart; he does not mention his countryman James Hutton. *CL*, I, 162, 164, 177. On Carlyle's learning German, see *Correspondence between Goethe and Carlyle*, ed. C. E. Norton (London, 1887), pp. 156–7, and Shine, *Carlyle's Early Reading*, p. 53. For a recent discussion of this question see R. L. Tarr and I. Campbell, "Carlyle's Early Study of German, 1819–1821", *Illinois Quarterly*, 34 (1971), 19–27.

35. Carlyle read the Norwegian Professor Hansteen's work in a German translation; Moh's work was in German. Only two of the planned three parts of Carlyle's translation were published. *CL*, I, 168, 236, 240; David Brewster, ed., *Edinburgh Philosophical Journal*, 2 (1819), 63–7 and 243–53, for the Berzelius; 3 (1820), 124–38 and 4 (1821), 114–24, for the Hansteen; 2 (1820), 154–76, 317–42, and 4 (1821), 56–67, for the Mohs.

36. *Edinburgh Philosophical Journal*, vol. 3, pp. 117–21.

37. *Reminiscences* (Norton), II, 234; Wilson, *Carlyle*, I, 180. The credit for making this discovery goes to Ian Campbell of the University of Edinburgh. The book was, as Carlyle remembered, a French book but it was by Alfred Gautier, and was entitled *Essai Historique sur le Problème des Trois Corps* (Paris, 1817). Carlyle was reviewing, not Gautier's book, presumably, but Pictet's review of the book in the *Bibliothèque Universelle*, Série *Sciences*, V (1817), 253–75, which he edited in *Geneva*. See Campbell "Carlyle, Pictet and Jeffrey Again", *Bibliotheck*, 7 (1974), 1–15.

38. See S. R. Crockett, ed., *Montaigne and Other Essays* (London, 1897), p. xi.

39. Shine, *op. cit.*, p. 95. The "Pascal" appeared in volume 16, part II, pp. 332–5, of the *Edinburgh Encyclopaedia* (Edinburgh, 1830).

40. Hill Shine, *Carlyle's Fusion of Poetry, History, and Religion by 1834* (Chapel Hill, N.C., 1938), pp. 4–13, and *Carlyle's Early Reading*, p. 76.

41. Wursthorn, pp. 764–9; Eves, *op cit.*, p. 374.

42. *CL*, II, 80–1, 99–100. For this reason he asked a friend, then asked his brother, John, for help. John obliged with very acceptable portions of the translation, but it still took valuable time that he wanted for original work.

43. *Reminiscences* (Norton), II, 105–6.

44. Some doubt attached to Carlyle's composition of this essay, which was for a long time thought to have been done by a Scot named Galbraith. The evidence usually cited is Carlyle's own statement in the *Reminiscences*, II, 105–6: "I still remember a happy forenoon (Sunday, I fear!) in which I did a *Fifth Book* (or complete 'Doctrine of Proportion') for that work; complete really, and lucid, and yet one of the *briefest* ever known; it was begun and done that forenoon, and I have (except cor-

recting the press next week) never seen it since, but still feel as if it were right enough and felicitous in its kind! " In an unpublished letter dated 19 June 1869, written apparently to Augustus De Morgan (Univ. of London Library, A.L. 466/2) he wrote that he could not account for "the *Galbraith legend*" but that "I did undoubtedly translate the *Legendre's Geometry*, to which Dr. Brewster gave his name and nothing more." He makes no mention of the essay on Proportion, but quite apart from the *Reminiscences* the internal evidence of style and manner certifies his authorship beyond a doubt. Incidentally, his account in the *Reminiscences* errs in one detail: he calls the essay "*a Fifth Book*" of the *Geometry*, whereas it is the Introduction, occupying pages ix-xvi. Since he never saw the published book, apparently, he may not have known how Brewster finally placed it. Or, he could have been thinking of it as the Fifth Book of Euclid's *Elements*.

45. "If, for example, the first term A were the side of a square, B the second term being its diagonal, and the third term C = A+B the sum or the difference of the former two, there could exist no common measure between any of the terms . . . Nevertheless it is certain that, if C were made the side of a new square, and the diagonal were named D, the two lines C and D would stand related to each other in regard to their length, exactly as the lines A and B stand related to each other in regard to theirs: and though a line, measuring any one of the four, must of necessity be incapable of measuring any of the remaining three . . . yet these four lines are undoubtedly proportional, as truly as if they admitted any given number of common measures . . ." (p. xi).

46. Northrop Frye, *Anatomy of Criticism* (Princeton, 1957), p. 352f.

47. Harrold, *Sartor*, p. 45. Similar passages suggesting a four-way proportion are legion:

> Call one a thief, and he will steal; in an almost similar sense may we not perhaps say, Call one Diogenes Teufelsdröckh, and he will open the Philosopy of Clothes (*Sartor* 88).
> To breed a fresh Soul, is it not like brooding a fresh (celestial) Egg; wherein as yet all is formless, powerless; yet by degrees organic elements and fibres shoot through the watery albumen; and out of vague Sensation grows Thought, grows Fantasy and Force, and we have Philosophies, Dynasties, nay Poetries and Religions! (*Sartor* 88).
> Speech is of Time, Silence is of Eternity. (*Sartor* 219).
> Bees will not work except in darkness; Thought will not work except in Silence; neither will Virtue work except in Secrecy. (*Sartor* 219).

48. Thus Teufelsdröckh recognizes the danger of "sham Metaphors", and the English Editor repeatedly criticizes his "likening and similitudes", and "hyper-metaphorical style of writing, not to say of thinking", (*Sartor*, 73, 287, 293).

49. *CL*, I, 124–8. It may be noted that even Locke could not understand the mathematics of the *Principia*. However it may have been with Car-

lyle that he himself was unable to understand the *Instituzione Analitiche* by Donna Agnesi which he obtained through Leslie (*CL*, I, 138, 140), was unable to solve a difficult mathematical problem that Leslie submitted to him, and made no progress with Biot's *Traité de physique*. (*CL*, I, 158).

50. *CL*, I, 128. Masson wrote, "My recollection is that he used to connect the break-down of his health with his continued wrestlings with Newton's *Principia* even after he had left Kirkaldy for Edinburgh." *Edinburgh Sketches*, p. 282.

51. What he desiderates in mathematics is knowledge of "the grand secrets of Necessity and Freewill, of the Mind's vital or non-vital dependence on Matter, of our mysterious relations to Time and Space, to God, to the Universe". "Signs of the Times", *Works*, xxvii, 64.

52. See Carlisle Moore, "*Sartor Resartus* and the Problem of Carlyle's 'Conversion' ", *PMLA*, 70 (1955), 662–81.

53. From May to September 1820, he inquired through his friend Matthew Allen about a position tutoring a young man, who turned out to be subnormal. Carlyle rejected this in October (*CL*, I, 251–85 *passim*). In 1822 he was offered a Professorship of Mathematics at the Royal Military College at Sandhurst. (*CL*, II, 194, 208, 218, 287.) Though this offered security and comfort he decided by February 1823 to reject it because of his literary aspirations. In 1827 he actively sought to obtain Professorships in Moral Philosophy at the Universities of London (May 1827 to August 1828) and St Andrews (December 1827 to April 1828), which would have involved much mathematics. When these fell through in March or April 1828, he and Jane moved to Craigenputtoch.

54. *Last Words of TC*, pp. 3, 22–3.

55. Quoted in Asa C. Chandler's "Goethe and Science", *Rice Institute Pamphlet*, 19 (1932), p. 132.

56. Compare his disapproval, cited above, of Pascal's "arithmetical machine".

57. *Two Note Books of TC*, ed. C. E. Norton (New York, 1898), p. 132.

58. A further study of the place of Science in Carlyle's work is being completed by the present writer. It was attempted here only to examine his early concern with mathematics and some of the sciences before the writing of *Sartor*.

59. *Two Note Books of TC*, p. 136.

4

Refractions of *Past and Present*

by G. ROBERT STANGE

In spite of the sledgehammered preachments, the brilliant tableaux, the amiable flights of humour, Carlyle is difficult to know. One is in the habit of looking for a definable "position", a reconciliation of opposites, but this atheistical Calvinist will not reconcile the contradictions of his thought or the opposed tendencies of his art; his work is a constant dialectic, an almost reckless play of antithethical forces. The couplings, too numerous to list, can be found in any of his works: a passion for the past confronts journalistic contemporaneity; respect for the plodding accumulation of historical fact somehow lives with the wildest flights of fantastic artistry; contempt for the values of bourgeois society is made to lead to a systematic celebration of Captains of Industry. The whole business can be very irritating—as well as very charming. The clash of opposites produces a continual release of energy, a reassuring sense of life.

The special virtue of *Past and Present* rests, I think, in its accommodation of inherent oppositions to its structure and very language. As an example of Carlyle's historical method it is not as impressive as *The French Revolution*, and as a purely literary work not as affecting and ingenious as *Sartor Resartus*; but as an example of the range of Carlyle's interests, of the intersection of his literary and historical methods, I find it the most appealing— the most central of his works. If we consider it as a special kind of book, it turns out to be three things: an essay in "anti-history", a stylistic *tour de force*, and a tract for the times. To be orderly we must consider the work under these three heads, but it soon becomes clear that in every respect the distinction and power of *Past and Present* are in its exploitation of a stylistic idea.

1

Bracketed by the amateur zeal of the Camden Society (founded in 1838) and the austere precision of Bishop Stubbs' *Constitutional History* (published in 1874), *Past and Present* represents an important stage in the interpretation of the Middle Ages. The celebrated second book, "The Ancient Monk", is in form no more than a highly selective re-telling of *Chronica Jocelini de Brakelonda*, which had been published in 1840 as the thirteenth volume of the Camden Society publications. Detailed studies have been made, both of Carlyle's use of the chronicle and of his historical method.[1] It may not be necessary to repeat that, according to the received opinions of our own day—of the views, let us say, represented by the practice of Sir Lewis Namier—Carlyle was not writing history at all. What has not been sufficiently remarked is the degree to which he himself was aware of and even tended to exploit his anti-historical impulses. His approach to the twelfth century "world" of St Edmundsbury Monastery is resolutely modern; the choice of a medieval subject was, in 1843, very modish, and Carlyle's method was to maintain a double focus on his historical material. "Read it here", he tells his audience, "with ancient yet with modern eyes."[2] There is no attempt at the "objectivity" of more recent historians; we are never "immersed" in the past; neither events, institutions nor persons are given the quiddity of their thirteenth-century existence. There is, in fact, a stubborn avoidance of almost all the qualities of modern historical method, and yet "The Ancient Monk" continues to hold the reader's interest. If it does not give us an insight into the historical past, what—we must ask—does it do?

The answer might be that the finest achievement of Book II is in its expression of a sense of *process*. The modern writer is insistently before us, reading the old chronicle, reacting to it, moralizing on it, extending its meanings. He offers his readers a personal vision, dramatizes for them the way in which a committed, intellectually active man apprehends the materials of his art. Book II lives as a continuing reflection not on historiography, but on the possibility of our knowing the past. This open-ended form, the sense that expression is a process that never is completed, is part of the impulse of Romanticism which infused nineteenth century art. Carlyle's affinities, even when writing history, are with Browning and Dickens rather than with the elder Hallam or Stubbs. The protagonist of Book II is, I would suggest, not Abbot Samson, but Carlyle himself. Our attention is stimulated, our sympathies aroused by the writer's struggle to communicate to us the meaning he has found in Jocelyn's faded chronicle: out of the activity of expressing a historical insight Carlyle draws dramatic tension. This method of involving the reader in the creative process can be seen in the poetry of Browning and G. M. Hopkins. Hopkins, particularly, could make his subject the effort to realize a poetic insight, and by dramatizing the very act of writing poetry give to personal, ostensibly lyrical sensation an air of dramatic action:

> But how shall I . . . make me a room there:
> Reach me a. . . . Fancy, come faster—
> Strike you the sight of it? look at it loom there. . . .[3]

One effect of the dramatic impulse in both poetry and prose is to make the scene the module of construction. And indeed Carlyle as dramaturge often makes his effect by a succession of vivid pictures. This aspect of his writing was commented on from the beginning. Henry James, Sr, for example, remarked that Carlyle was not essentially a man of ideas; picturesqueness, he felt, was "the one key to his intellectual favour"; in order to sympathize he needed "visual contact".[4] And Carlyle himself insisted that it was an "indispensable condition" that the historian "*see* the things transacted, and picture them wholly as if they stood before our eyes".[5]

That Carlyle was faithful to this principle in writing *Past and Present* is affirmed by the most cursory consideration—either of the book itself or of one's recollections of it. Perhaps the most memorable episode of Book II is "The Election", the subject of Chapter VIII. It is worth noting how its climactic episode is conceived:

> What a Hall,—not imaginary in the least, but entirely real and indisputable, though so extremely dim to us; sunk in the deep dis-

tances of Night! The Winchester Manorhouse has fled bodily, like a Dream of the old Night; not Dryasdust himself can shew a wreck of it. House and people, royal and episcopal, lords and varlets, where are they? Why *there*, I say, Seven Centuries off; sunk *so* far in the Night, there they *are*; peep through the blankets of the old Night, and thou wilt see! King Henry himself is visibly there; a vivid, noble-looking man, with grizzled beard, in glittering uncertain costume; with earls round him, and bishops, and dignitaries, in the like. The Hall is large, and has for one thing an altar near it, —chapel and altar adjoining it; but what gilt seats, carved tables, carpeting of rush-cloth, what arras-hangings, and huge fire of logs: — alas, it has Human Life in it; and is not that the grand miracle, in what hangings or costume soever?—(pp. 79–80).

So far the author has given us a static setting, the paragraph that follows brings in the characters; they perform their actions and the scene is concluded as abruptly as if a curtain were lowered.

The literary skill represented by this galaxy of set pieces is stunning, but it is questionable whether they conduce to historical understanding. I think the only way the defender of Carlyle can answer the charge that he was a bad historian is to affirm that he was not a historian at all. He shows, in fact, none of the characteristics that mark serious historians of the most diverse schools. Not being, as James remarked, a man of ideas, he is not at all interested in making ideational patterns out of history; but he is equally unconcerned with either the forms or social effects of institutions. And unlike even the Romantic historians he is not attentive to the interaction of the private and public life—an obliquity which seems at first especially strange in view of the persistence of Carlyle's concept of the hero. However, I think it is the very supremacy of the heroic ideal that annihilates a concern for the complex interpretation of the individual life and the outer, public world. In Carlyle's view the heroic individual *makes* his universe: "The clear-beaming eyesight of Abbot Samson", for example, "is like *Fiat lux* in that inorganic waste whirlpool; penetrates gradually to all nooks, and of the chaos makes a *kosmos* or ordered world!" (p. 92). Elsewhere it is suggested that the "singular shape of a Man" and the "shape of a Time" are the same (p. 126), a view which hardly allows for the study of that web of influences and reactions which some of the more penetrating historians have undertaken. For Carlyle the individuals who are worth writing about exist as discrete beings; all that matters in either past or present is the agon of the individual soul.

Such views, I repeat, make for bad history, but, in Carlyle's case, for intensely effective art. What he is interested in in *Past and Present* is, after all, not the Middle Ages, nor historical method, nor mind or thought, but an image, sensually evoked, of the past.

2

As a work of art *Past and Present* is a triumphant expression of the organic principle, an aesthetic tenet that Carlyle had encountered first in the work of the German critics, and then in the less admired redactions of Coleridge. By the 1830's, however, this notion had become so much a part of Romantic art that its metaphorical foundation was quite forgotten. Coleridge had said, "such as life is, such is the form", and the writers and artists of the new school were not inclined to doubt that in form all genuine art resembled a natural organism—even though such identification would be logically no more valid than the conception of the universe as a machine, or of a poem as an architectonic structure. But from the assumption that the reciprocal connection between art and nature was *real*, that true art was, in fact, *alive*, all other aspects of the organic principle developed. Abstraction, logical pattern, artistic rules are obviously to be contemned. In a truly organic creation there can be no distinction between form and content—an article of faith that led to the more elaborately figurative notion that in a work of art, as in the universe, the smallest part reflects the structure of the whole, and the other way around. A frequent means of illustrating this pleasing relationship was the leaf which repeats in small the structure of the tree. And since art is a natural process, always becoming, never being, it must reflect the dialectic of growth, and incorporate what were called the elementary opposites of existence. Such basic antitheses as the one and the many, odd and even, light and dark, right and left, provided a natural pattern for art.

A reader familiar with Carlyle will have observed that even this brief summary of the organic principle elicits some of his characteristic procedures. For example, a tree was one of the most com-

monly used symbols of natural growth and of the unity of disparate
elements. In *Past and Present* Carlyle heightens this motif and by
recurrent statement makes of the Life-tree Igdrasil the emblem of
his book. It is first mentioned in the peroration of Book I:

> For the Present holds in it both the whole Past and the whole
> Future;—as the LIFE-TREE IGDRASIL, wide-waving, many-toned, has
> its roots down deep in the Death-kingdoms, among the oldest dead
> dust of men, and with its boughs reaches always beyond the stars;
> and in all times and places is one and the same Life-tree! (p. 38).

And again, toward the end of Book II there is an invocation of

> . . . The Life-tree Igdrasil, which waves round thee in this hour,
> whereof thou in this hour art portion, has its roots down deep in
> the oldest Death-Kingdoms; and grows; the Three Nornas, or *Times*,
> Past, Present, Future, watering it from the Sacred Well! (p. 129).

The last mention, almost an exact repetition, comes in the first
chapter of the last book, "Horoscope".

The tree symbol which in poetry has stood for the unification
of body, soul and spirit (*viz.* Tennyson's "Hesperides" and Yeats's
"Among School Children") represents for Carlyle the unity of time
and natural order. Since the three *Nornas* are also the tenses by
which language is organized, syntax embodies the essential condition of being; the written work is made of living stuff, and like
the life-tree has its roots among the dead dust of the past, grows
in the present and reaches to the stars of the future ("Horoscope").

The whole book, as its title suggests, is based on a pattern of
oppositions. The two experienced aspects of time, the known
present and the past that the writer makes known to us, determine the ordering of the sections—a formal arrangement which
suggests the penetration of the present by the values of the past,
an act of realization which might bring about a better future. The
large antithesis of the title is played out in a series of variations:
smaller contrasts between law and anarchy, man and phantasm,
heaven and hell, valetism and heroism, idleness and work, facts
and semblances, jargon and genuine speech. Individual phrases and
sentences tend to incorporate contraries: "Brief brawling Day,
with its noisy phantasms, its poor paper-crowns tinsel-gilt, is gone;
and divine everlasting Night, with her star-diadems, with her
silences and her veracities, is come!" (p. 156). Such continual

101

oppositions are the mechanics of Carlyle's style; we move through his writing from one "wondrous Dualism" (p. 44) to another. The technique seems at first to resemble eighteenth-century antithetical prose, but the effect of Carlyle's method is altogether different. A writer like Gibbon, for example, holds the two elements of his sentences in a witty and pleasing balance. Each sentence—it is not extreme to say—is an image of reason, the syntax weighs the pro and the con, leads the well-conducted mind by normal, rational procedures to the truth. As aesthetic structures Gibbon's antithetical periods are analogous to the ordered symmetries of eighteenth-century architecture. But in Carlyle's writing there is no symmetry; the play of contraries is varied and dynamic, rudely jolting us into some new awareness. Often one element of an opposition is meant to annihilate the other: "It is very strange, the degree to which these truisms are forgotten in our days; how, in the ever-whirling chaos of Formulas, we have quietly lost sight of Fact" (p. 176). Or: "Observe, too, that this is all a modern affair; belongs not to the old heroic times, but to these dastard new times" (p. 156). Elsewhere the oppositions are fused: "O Mr. Bull, I look in that surly face of thine with a mixture of pity and laughter, yet also with wonder and veneration" (p. 160). Most characteristically, however, Carlyle's phrases seem designed to show how one term of an antithesis contains its opposite: "The cloudy-browed, thick-soled, opaque Practicality, with no logic utterance, in silence mainly, with here and there a low grunt or growl, has in him what transcends all logic—utterance: A Congruity with the Unuttered" (p. 159). The puns here are clever, but they lead to an illuminating paradox; the "cloudy-browed, thick-soled" Man of Practice is "dumb" in the proper Carlylean way, but he may have his head in the very heavens and be more durable of soul than his opposite number, the Man of Theory. The resolution of this sentence does not yield that pleasure in paradox that is a grace of Augustan prose; there is instead a rather solemn affirmation— opacity and silence are ultimately the only clear speech; the gross and earthy are the ethereal—statements such as this are closer to parable than they are to wit writing. Again and again one discovers that Carlyle's sentences re-enact the movement of discovery through transcendence.

Whereas the antithetical periods of Gibbon and other Augustan writers are discrete, each figuring a well-balanced world view, Carlyle's are part of a larger analogical structure. The sentence mirrors the chapter, the chapter the book. The architectural parallel to this style would be the Gothic of Abbot Samson's day, the aesthetic of which Carlyle could have found in Goethe's famous panegyric of Abbot Erwin, architect of Strasbourg Cathedral.

The image of the world projected by Carlyle's prose is of continual becoming, of ideas and things always being born out of their opposites. The sense of experience that Carlyle's writing leaves us with is suggested by Vico's term, "the coincidence of contraries". In shaping a work like *Past and Present* Carlyle would want his antitheses to be dictated by nature rather than by what seemed to him the mechanical rationalism of Augustan prose. It was his task to find a "living" form in which the relation between contraries is as that of the trunk of a tree to its flower, or of life to the death from which it has sprung.

The prose-texture of the non-historical sections of *Past and Present* has the density of good poetry. In a brief essay it is impossible to perform the kind of sentence by sentence analysis that such writing demands, yet by looking at the skeleton of imagery in a representative chapter it might be possible to suggest what rewards further study could bring. "Phenomena" is the first chapter of the third book, "The Modern Worker". The title picks up a minor but persistent motif in the first and second books, and Carlyle here prepares to work out the various implications of the word. It derives—we are meant to know—from the Greek verb which means "appear" or "show". In philosophical usage phenomena are objects known through the senses rather than through thought or intuition, and phenomenalism is the theory that there is no knowledge or existence outside the phenomenal world. In science phenomenology is the description of objects without interpretation, explanation or evaluation. In ordinary usage a phenomenon is simply any observable fact or event. As one or another meaning of the word is developed, all its connotations remain present as overtones.

After an abrupt, Browningesque beginning, the text of the chapter is set forth in the second paragraph: "We have quietly closed our eyes to the eternal Substance of things, and opened them only to the Shows and Shams of things." The author then goes on to present, with phenomenological detachment, three appearances or shows, all occurring in the present but belonging to different epochs of history; each example is a procession which has lost all meaning, and in the conclusion all three are whirled together into one phantasmagoric rush toward the devouring gulf. Earlier in his book Carlyle had given a preliminary statement of this theme:

> What sight is more pathetic than that of poor multitudes of persons met to gaze at King's Progresses, Lord Mayors' Shows, and other gilt-gingerbread phenomena of the worshipful sort, in these times; each so eager to worship; each with a dim fatal sense of disappointment, finding that he cannot rightly here! (p. 55)

More ominously, and more than once, he had alluded to the destination of these processions: "We are rushing swiftly on the road to destruction; every hour bringing us nearer, until it be, in some measure, done" (p. 30). The streets over which these emblematic progresses proceed are both the "broad way" of the New Testament and a "life road" advancing "incessantly" toward "the firm-land's end" (p. 143).

The first of the "Phantasms riding with huge clatter along the streets, from end to end of our existence" (p. 137) is the rheumatic Pope, who, finding it laborious to kneel in his car in the procession on Corpus-Christi Day, has had constructed a "stuffed rump" or cloaked figure inside which he can sit with his hands and head extended, and so bless the Roman population.[7] The construction in which the "poor amphibious Pope" sits is merely a prop for what Carlyle calls "the Scenic Theory of Worship" and this bit of tourist lore comes to image the decay of the living, medieval Catholicism extolled in Book II. The Pope's frankness and wholeheartedness, which the author claims to admire, are employed in "Worshipping by stage-machinery; as if there were now, and could again be, in Nature no other" (p. 139).

The next degraded symbol, or "Phantasm walking the streets", appears in London rather than Rome, and resumes in one ludicrous image the inanity of a decadent aristocracy:

> The Champion of England, cased in iron or tin, rides into Westminster Hall, 'being lifted into his saddle with little assistance,' and there asks, If in the four quarters of the world, under the cope

104

of Heaven, is any man or demon that dare question the right of this King? Under the cope of Heaven no man makes intelligible answer, —as several men ought already to have done. Does not this Champion too know the world; that it is a huge Imposture, and bottomless Inanity, thatched over with bright cloth and other ingenious tissues? Him let us leave there, questioning all men and demons (pp. 140–1).

The final phenomenon is an empty symbol of the bourgeois world, the "great Hat seven-feet high, which now perambulates London streets" advertising the products of a hatter in the Strand. Carlyle's comment on this achievement of English Puffery can stand as a final judgment on the social utility of modern advertising:

> The Hatter in the Strand of London, instead of making better felt-hats than another, mounts a huge lath-and-plaster Hat, seven-feet high, upon wheels; sends a man to drive it through the streets; hoping to be saved *thereby*. He has not attempted to *make* better hats, as he was appointed by the Universe to do, and as with this ingenuity of his he could very probably have done; but his whole industry is turned to *persuade* us that he has made such (p. 141).

The three symbols of passing phenomena bring into focus a cluster of allusions that have appeared in earlier sections of *Past and Present*; but further, their congruity with each other enhances their meaning. Each example, available to any reader of the daily press, represents with factual precision a great ruling institution, two of which are beyond reconstruction, a third which may yet regain its value by honest work. All involve the use of an integument or artificial covering, a schema which—as *Sartor Resartus* sufficiently demonstrates—expresses a view not only of appearance and reality, but of truth and falsehood, and ultimately of the transcendental as opposed to the phenomenal world. Each artifice moves to the plaudits of the crowd, and each is hollow. But the most characteristic trick of Carlyle's humour is the fact that, though the symbols display themselves in the streets around us, they seem to belong to a mad, surreal world. In the conclusion to "Phenomena" the Pope, the Champion of England and the great Hat are swept up, along with other "unveracities", in a phantasmagoric procession that resembles some vision of Hieronymus Bosch. This is no longer merely a crowd-pleasing progress through the streets of Rome or

London, but a whole population advancing "toward the *firm-land's end*". The overtones now evoke the rush of the Gadarene swine, the frenzied procession of the lemmings:

> . . . the seven-feet Hat, and all things upwards to the very Champion cased in tin, begin to reel and flounder,—in Manchester Insurrections, Chartisms, Sliding-scales; the Law of Gravitation not forgetting to act. You advance incessantly towards the land's end; you are, literally enough, 'consuming the way.' Step after step, Twenty-seven Million unconscious men;—till you are *at* the land's end: till there is not Faithfulness enough among you any more; and the next step now is lifted *not* over land, but into air, over ocean-deeps and roaring abysses:—unless perhaps the Law of Gravitation have forgotten to act? (p. 144).

Even the kind of superficial account of Carlyle's prose that I have given suggests that, though his attitudes are essentially "Victorian", he belongs to a distinctive tradition. His literary structures are conceived in a very different way from those of Newman and Arnold, or even from those of his disciple Ruskin. A prose so densely allusive, organized according to an elaborate scheme of interwoven symbols, fiercely magnifying for satiric purposes the impedimenta of everyday life, finds itself on a line which extends—in English literature—from Swift to Joyce. If *A Tale of a Tub* is one of the ancestors of *Past and Present*, *Ulysses* is certainly its legitimate heir.

3

Considered as a social tract *Past and Present* turns out to have had an unexpectedly large influence. It has been used by thinkers on both the left and the right, and ultimately it appears to have succeeded by the force of its style, rather than by the weight of its social facts or the cogency of its arguments. The aspect of the book's influence which has been least commented on is its effect outside England. Within a year after its publication in April 1843, *Past and Present* had been treated to a review by Emerson and an extensive interpretation in German by Friedrich Engels.

It would be hard to conceive anything more perfervid than Emerson's essay in the *Dial*. For him the book is not only a "new poem", an "Iliad of English woes", but, "In its first aspect it is a political tract, and since Burke, since Milton, we have had nothing to compare with it."[8] Emerson seems determined to make the book all things to all men: "Every reader shall carry away something."[9] And though he comments on the disproportion of Carlyle's picture, "the habitual exaggeration of the tone",[10] he concludes that Carlyle's is the first style to express the richness of the modern world, the only "magnificent" style of his time.

Emerson's conceit that *Past and Present* was Carlyle's "poem" on England, and the *French Revolution* his poem on France became received opinion in the United States. As far as Carlylean attitudes were applied to a developing industrial society, they were derived from *Past and Present*. The great vision of Bury St Edmunds and of medieval organicism seems to have interested American readers only as "literature", but the social myth of Captains of Industry may be said to have found its natural home in the United States. In other quarters, particularly in the vague traditions of populist thought, the denunciation of a system in which the "cash-payment nexus" was the sole bond of human society became a part of the everyday vocabulary. It is worth noting, however, that this influence is purely rhetorical. Carlyle imposed in the most powerful way an attitude, a general receptiveness; he most emphatically did not communicate a connected set of ideas, or—much less—a system of thought. His singularity in this respect is felt if one compares his influence in America with that of John Mill, or even Ruskin. To his journal Emerson confided a remark about *Past and Present* which he kept out of his review; he observed that what Carlyle was "doing now for England & Europe" was "rhetoricizing the conspicuous objects".[11] It is a shrewd and quite complete definition.

Engels' admiration for Carlyle is less well known than Emerson's, but he may have spread the fame of *Past and Present* wider than any other commentator. His article, *"Die Lage Englands*; 'Past and Present' by Thomas Carlyle," was written in January 1844 and published immediately in the short-lived *Deutsch-Französische Jahrbücher* which Marx had initiated in Paris.[12] The essay, which has never been translated into English, is extraordinarily interesting; it is not only the first product of Engels' association with Marx, but—as its title suggests—is a kind of preliminary sketch for Engels' own book, *Die Lage der arbeitenden Klasses in*

England, which was published in Leipzig in 1845, but did not reach the English public until 1892.[13] One of the commentators on Marxist thought says that the young Engels "saw the English industrial situation . . . through the eyes of Thomas Carlyle".[14] In the light of Engels' first-hand experience of the factory system in Manchester and his close association with working-class people in England, the claim is hyperbolic; but it seems fair to regard Engels' book as one of the most important results of Carlyle's influence on other writers.

The degree of respect Engels shows for Carlyle's social views, and the warmth of his admiration for what he calls this "wonderfully beautiful" book come as a surprise from a writer whose political astringency and polemical fierceness are famous. It is revealing of Engels' own character that he begins his discussion by emphasizing the living, human quality of Carlyle's writing. Of all the books and pamphlets that have appeared in recent years, he finds Carlyle's the only one that strikes a humane note or expresses an essentially humanitarian point of view.[15] Carlyle is identified for Engels' continental readers as an interpreter of German literature, and is then placed politically—in a way that Disraeli might have appreciated—as being by origin a Tory, a party to which he always stands closer than he does to the Whigs. "So much is certain," Engels bitterly adds, "a Whig could never have written a book that was half so human as *Past and Present.*"[16]

Though Engels tells his readers that he is simply going to proceed in an orderly way through the four parts of Carlyle's book, and then begins with long quotations from the first chapter, he manages to create the impression that the book is purely a social tract. He skips, for example, from the middle of the first book to the second chapter of the third, ignoring the whole medieval section. It is not, I think, that Engels wishes to conceal Carlyle's medievalism, or his religiosity, and to re-make him into a socialist critic, but rather that he is eager to give his readers the *usable* Carlyle, to translate a devastating vision of English industrial society. Addressing himself to the reactionary elements of Carlyle's thought, he points out that what Carlyle means by "atheism" is not disbelief in a personal God, but "disbelief in an inner essence of being (*Wesenhaftigkeit*), in the infinity of the universe, disbelief in inner reason (*Vernunft*), a despair of the human spirit and of truth". His struggle is not against disbelief in the revelations of the Bible, but against that "most terrible of unbeliefs, unbelief in the Bible of World-history".[17] Though Engels' interpretation errs in making Carlyle sound rationalist and humanistic, it seems to me to be closer to the truth than the views of those commentators who have insisted on Carlyle's theological bent, and evoked his vision of God. Nietzsche's remark that Carlyle was "an English atheist who made it a point of honour not to be one" has the virtue of avoiding by paradox both extremes of misinterpretation, but Engels' enthusiastic praise of the "humane" Carlyle affirms a side of the man that we may too often overlook.

Carlyle's yearning for an "Aristocracy of Talent" and his belief in Hero-worship are simply brushed aside by Engels as he moves into an extended interpretation of Carlyle as a pantheist, and indeed a *German* pantheist.[18] He relates his views to those of Goethe and accurately places him as "mehr schellingisch als hegelisch".[19] Having located Carlyle on ground where Engels feels at home he is then able to employ against him his own newly-forged ideological weapons. He attacks Carlyle and the whole tribe of German pantheists for their belief that a new religion could reconstitute a decaying society and a universe that has been deprived of meaning. Engels draws his arguments from the writings of Feuerbach, whose *Grundsätze der Philosophie der Zukunft* had been published in 1843, and of Bruno Bauer, both of whom he and Marx were shortly to attack with zeal.

Engels' discussion is, of course, an oversimplification, since it ignores the Calvinistic bases of Carlyle's views and implies that by taking a proper turn here and there he would emerge as a rational social critic. However, if the young Engels did not manage to penetrate in his definitions to the paradoxical heart of Carlyle's *Weltanschauung* where the forms of Calvinist belief, German metaphysics and a fierce social indignation play out their continual dialectic, he at least discussed Carlyle's work with a seriousness and sophistication that is not found anywhere else in the forties and fifties. There was not, to my knowledge, any British writer who considered Carlyle's work in so wide a philosophical context, and gave it such serious and informed attention.

But what is most admirable in Engels' essay is his reminder to us that as a social tract *Past and Present* is not merely an occasional pamphlet, but still an active, usable document, drawing on many currents of thought and belief. Engels need not have relied on Carlyle for his information about the condition of England. As his subsequent book shows, he had collected a great deal of data on his own, and by 1843 several writers had described "the perilous state of the land". The English book which has sometimes been associated with *Past and Present*, R. B. Seeley's *The Perils of the Nation; An Appeal to the Legislature, the Clergy, and the Higher and Middle Classes* (London, 1843), demonstrates how necessary literary art may be even to the communication of social statistics. Seeley's four-hundred-odd pages are marked by knowledge and deep (Evangelical) earnestness. His view of England is as dark as Carlyle's; for him England is "one vast mass of superficial splendour, covering a body of festering misery and discontent . . . however capital may have prospered, *the nation*, in a most important point, *has declined and decayed*".[20] Seeley quotes remarks made in the Commons by Buller and Lord Ashley (later Lord Shaftesbury), he refers to reports of the Commissioners of Enquiry and passes on a great deal of useful information about conditions of housing and sanitary regulations. But all of Seeley's shocking facts do not, somehow, startle or move us. His concern and obvious rectitude conduce finally to a kind of nagging dullness. Engels sums it all up when he insists that only Carlyle's book strikes the "menschliche Saiten". It is not just the note of humanity, it is the note of life. And it is this resonance, rather than the scope of his political views or the adequacy of his social documentation that gives Carlyle's tract for his times an indestructible energy.

NOTES

1. Grace J. Calder, *The Writing of "Past and Present"* (New Haven, 1949) contains a great deal of valuable information. A. M. D. Hughes' edition of the work (Oxford, 1918) has an informative introduction and full annotation.
2. *Past and Present, Works*, X, 107, hereafter page references bracketed in text.

3. "The Wreck of the Deutschland", stanza 28.
4. See 'Some Personal Recollections of Carlyle", *The Literary Remains of Henry James*, ed. William James (Boston, 1885), pp. 429 and 425. A more extended study of this aspect of Carlyle is C. R. Sanders, "The Victorian Rembrandt: Carlyle's Portraits of His Contemporaries", *Bulletin of the John Rylands Library*, 39 (1957) 521–57.
5. *Letters of TC to John Stuart Mill and Robert Browning*, ed. A. Carlyle, (London, 1923), p. 83.
6. Goethe's essay, "Von deutscher Baukunst", was published in 1773 under the auspices of Herder, and is the most important early statement of the spiritual beauties of "Gothic" architecture—a term which Goethe consciously rescued from disrepute. See *Gedenkausgabe der Werke, Briefe und Gespräche*, ed. Ernst Beutler, 24 vols. (Zurich, 1949–50), *Schriften zur Kunst*, XIII, 16–26.
7. A number of travellers to Rome seem to have commented on this ingenious contrivance. Henry Crabb Robinson saw a Corpus Christi procession in 1830 and described with some wonder the artful chair by which the Pope "acts kneeling". *Diary, Reminiscences and Correspondence of Henry Crabb Robinson*, ed. T. Sadler (London, 1869), II, 469–70.
8. *"Past and Present"* in *Natural History of the Intellect*, in *The Complete Works of Ralph Waldo Emerson*, ed. Edward W. Emerson (Boston and New York, 1904), XII, 379. The original essay appeared in the *Dial*, 4 (July, 1843), 96–102.
9. *Natural History*, p. 380.
10. *Natural History*, p. 386.
11. *Journals and Miscellaneous Notebooks of Ralph Waldo Emerson*, ed. W. H. Gilman and J. E. Parsons (Cambridge, Mass., 1970), VIII, 408.
12. See Karl Marx-Friedrich Engels, *Werke* (Berlin, 1957), 525–49.
13. *The Condition of the Working Classes in England in 1844* (London, 1892) is a translation of a new continental edition published in Stuttgart in the same year.
14. Peter Demetz, *Marx, Engels and the Poets* (Chicago, 1967), p. 37.
15. *Werke*, p. 525.
16. *Werke*, p. 528.
17. *Werke*, p. 539.
18. *Werke*, p. 542.
19. *Werke*, p. 543. A much fuller discussion of Engels and Carlyle is to be found in Steven Marcus's *Engels, Manchester and the Working Class* (New York, 1974), pp. 102–12.
20. Seeley, pp. xvii, xxxviii–ix.

5

Stern Hebrews Who Laugh: Further Thoughts on Carlyle and Dickens*

by GEORGE H. FORD

My subtitle, "Further Thoughts", relates to my having published a dozen pages on this topic, many years ago, a topic that has more recently gained prominence by its being extensively treated in books by Michael Goldberg and William Oddie, both appearing in 1972.[1] One of my friends, after reading these two full-length books on Carlyle and Dickens, complimented me by saying that it had been my good fortune not to have said too much on the topic. His compliment—if it was a compliment—haunts me now with a sense that it might have been well to follow Carlyle's gospel of silence and to say no more. I am, nevertheless, prompted to risk a return to the topic, or at least a phase of it, for Carlyle himself serves as a model of how hard to abide by is his gospel of silence.

Another comment on my previous discussion, less complimentary but more relevant, is by William Oddie who begins his book, *Dickens and Carlyle*, with a complaint about "the procedure adopted in one widely cited account of the relationship, by a scholar rightly held in some esteem". We learn later that this misguided scholar (however esteemed) is George Ford who made the mistake of remarking, in print, that the influence of Carlyle on the style of Dickens' later novels is "easily seen". Mr Oddie's objection, I now realize, is basically sound. The influence is *not*

* In its original form this essay was presented as a paper at a Modern Language Association conference in New York, December, 1974.

"easily seen". Furthermore the relationship between the two styles may perhaps not be a matter of influence. To "see" the influence, if it is there, would call for a lot of close work by stylistic experts, and although something will be said about style in what follows, my discussion will usually be of a more general nature and will deal with the question of stylistic affinities, which is more manageable than the question of direct influence. Moreover, this approach has the advantage of not involving us very much with priorities as such; instead it can be related to the question of affinities in general.

What were these affinities, and lack of affinities, that characterize this remarkable relationship? That from the time of his first meeting with Carlyle in 1840 Dickens was powerfully attracted by him is simply a fact for which we have plenty of documentation. Many of my undergraduates are bewildered by the story of this relationship; they find it incredible. And even older readers, as Edward Alexander remarks, are "embarrassed" by Carlyle's impact on an age of literature to which, nowadays, they otherwise feel well-disposed.[2] Yet the Victorian age and its literature will never be adequately understood without our trying to appreciate how that powerful magnet attracted everyone into its field in the 1840s, including those who later moved away from its field when it became too intense for them. In 1866, when Carlyle blew his whistle to assemble his team in defence of Governor Eyre (to which Dickens, of course, responded), it is most instructive to remember that the leaders of the opposing team, Mill and Huxley, had earlier been profoundly affected by Carlyle.[3] The commonplace I want to establish is that such writers as Ruskin or Browning or Arnold were attracted variously, and what we need to discriminate about Dickens is what areas of the magnetism attracted him and what parts, if any, repelled him. Their relationship was one of elective affinities, certainly, but also one of selective affinities.

In this regard we might ask what these two men talked about during the several times they met over a period of thirty years. I wish someone with the skills of a Walter Savage Landor or a Richard Howard could recreate such imaginary conversations for us, but I propose, instead, to consider what topics they probably did *not* talk about. The chief of these, it seems to me, would have been the art of the novel, or even, in much depth, Dickens' own novels.

Their first encounter gives a clue relating to my guess here. In 1837, Carlyle read *Pickwick* and described it in a letter: "thinner wash, with perceptible vestige of a flavour in it here and there was never offered to the human palate".[4] And in the following year, in his essay on Scott, he made another disparaging reference to *Pickwick*.[5] Three years later, when he met Dickens in person and generally liked him, one wonders whether he observed the amenities by complimenting the young novelist and perhaps making some allusion to the trial scene in *Pickwick*—a scene that in later life he was to enjoy with open-stopped hilarity. This was the procedure he was later to follow when *David Copperfield* was being published, and he delighted Dickens, when they met, by likening himself to that lone lorn creetur, Mrs Gummidge. What he privately thought about *David Copperfield* was disclosed in a letter recently published by Charles Sanders. In 1849, after disposing of Thackeray's *Pendennis* as "nonsense" Carlyle turns his pen on *Copperfield*:

> Dickens again is said to be flourishing beyond example with his present series of funambulisms [*Copperfield*, that is, is a rope-dance]:—I read one No of it (I am quite fallen behind) last night; innocent waterest of twaddle with a *suspicion* of geniality.[6]

Now I am not trying here to make Carlyle into a hypocrite; we all do this every day, as Molière's blunt speaker, Alceste, painfully discovered. What I am interested in speculating about, instead, is whether Carlyle ever told Dickens face to face about that thin wash and the rope-dancing. Despite his proverbial bluntness, I do not suppose that he did so. What he might have done, as he did with Meredith, was to recommend that Boz should turn to writing history instead of novels. "Man," he told Meredith, "ye suld write heestory! Ye hae a heestorian in ye!"[7] But that is not the same as saying, to Dickens' face, that *Dombey and Son* is a mere rope-dancing stunt, as Carlyle describes it in a fierce letter of 1847:

> Oh for a thousand sharp sickles in as many strong right hands . . .
> I poor devil have but one rough sickle, and a hand that will soon
> be weary . . . Dickens writes a *Dombey and Son*, Thackeray a

Vanity Fair; not *reapers* they, either of them! In fact the business
of the rope-dancing goes to a great height.[8]

William Oddie concludes, in fact, that Dickens "never saw this
side of Carlyle's feelings about him".[9]

Here I must part company. If Dickens did not know of Carlyle's
contemptuous evaluation of specific novels of his, he must surely
have known what the Master thought about novels in general.
With Carlyle's early essays on History and Biography, or on Sir
Walter Scott, Dickens is likely to have been familiar; in his library
at Gad's Hill there were three different editions of the *Critical
and Miscellaneous Essays* (1840, 1857, 1869–70). But even if
Carlyle's early writings had been overlooked, Dickens could hardly
have missed the *Latter-Day Pamphlets* (a copy of the 1850 edition
was also in his library at Gad's Hill). And for a novelist as passionately dedicated to his craft as Dickens was, how would he have
responded to the following passage from the pamphlet on "Jesuitism", with its fantastic blast against fiction and story-telling and
Fine Arts that serve "to fib and dance":

> The Fine Arts . . . are to understand that they are sent hither
> not to fib and dance, but to speak and work; and . . . that God
> Almighty's *Facts* . . . are the one pabulum which will yield them
> any nourishment. . . . Fiction, I think, or idle falsity of any kind,
> was never tolerable, except in a world [of the indolent]. . . . Given
> an idle potentate, monster of opulence, gluttonous bloated Nawaub,
> of black colour or of white,—naturally he will have prating story-
> tellers to amuse his half-sleeping hours of rumination; if from his
> deep gross stomach . . . they can elicit any transient glow of in-
> terest, tragic or comic, especially any wrinkle of momentary
> laughter, however idle, great shall be their reward. Wits, story-
> tellers, ballad-singers, especially dancing-girls who understand their
> trade, are in much request with such a gluttonous half-sleeping . . .
> Monster of Opulence. A bevy of supple dancing-girls who with due
> mixture . . . of lascivious fire, will represent to him . . . the Loves
> of Vishnu, Loves of Adonis, Death of Psyche, Barber of Seville, or
> whatever nonsense there may be, according to time or country:
> these are the kind of artists fit for such an unfortunate stuffed
> stupefied Nawaub, in his hours of rumination. . . . Luxurious Europe,
> in its reading publics . . . is wholly one big ugly Nawaub of that
> kind; who has converted all the Fine Arts into after-dinner amuse-
> ments.[10]

Now it might be said that the personal relationship of Dickens and Carlyle resembles that established between Boswell and Johnson, and that if Boswell learned to listen to Johnson's expressions of prejudice against Scotland, then surely Dickens could listen patiently to hair-raising diatribes such as this in which, in effect, Carlyle implies that the novelist's role is close to that of a whore as well as a liar. I cannot myself imagine that Dickens' response would be only a wry smile and a shrug.

It seems he responded in two ways, one that is clearly recognizable, and the other purely a matter of speculation. First, that if the writer cannot be an historian and is stuck with being a mere novelist, he can redeem some of the drawbacks of the rope-dancing profession by providing what Scott, in Carlyle's view, had failed to provide: [11] novels with a purpose (as Robert Colby calls them) in which a traditional story combines with social criticism and prophecy. From the time of his writing *The Chimes* in 1844, Dickens seems to have been aware of what was expected of him under the stern eyes of his great task-master. In many respects the role was thoroughly congenial to him. He had tasted power with his creation of Little Nell; he tasted power again, of a different order, with his creation of a Jarndyce and Jarndyce case, or a Circumlocution Office (which Carlyle admired) or a Coketown. And the task was made even more congenial because his view of the ills of society corresponded at so many points with Carlyle's view. It is remarkable how often the two writers draw from the same store of images to characterize corruption. Consider, for example, the stunning opening paragraph of *Bleak House*:

> As much mud in the streets, as if the waters had but newly retired from the face of the earth, and it would not be wonderful to meet a Megalosaurus, forty feet long or so, waddling like an elephantine lizard up Holborn Hill.

It may be noted that William Oddie prints a passage from this same paragraph of *Bleak House* in order to demonstrate that it has no similarities to Carlyle.[12] But let us look at a sentence from one of Carlyle's pamphlets, published in 1850, a year before Dickens began writing *Bleak House*. Carlyle is speaking of problems facing America:

116

New Spiritual Pythons, plently of them; enormous Megatherions, as ugly as were ever born of mud, loom huge and hideous out of the twilight Future in America.[13]

And in these same two works, as elsewhere, it is noteworthy how both writers resort to the image of fire as a cleansing agent. Carlyle cites a wit who commented: "That there was but one reform for the Foreign Office,—to set a live coal under it."[14] A year later Dickens concludes his chapter on Chancery iniquities by voicing the hope that the whole might be "burnt away in a great funeral pyre". Parenthetically, I should mention that similarities of this kind are, of course, most clearly in evidence in comparisons between *The French Revolution* and *A Tale of Two Cities*, but because this topic has been masterfully covered in Michael Goldberg's book and in William Oddie's, I am looking to other texts. Visions of an apocalyptic burning, as we might expect, are more prevalent in Carlyle. Of conditions in 1850 he speaks, characteristically, of "a bottomless volcano or universal powder-mine of most inflammable mutinous chaotic elements, separated from us by a thin earth-rind".[15] Dickens' scene of the fiery death of Krook, a year or so later, is one way of conveying the same sense. But the most recurrent image that they share is of contemporary society as a plague-infested "cess-pool", as Carlyle calls it. "British industrial existence", he writes, "seems fast becoming one huge poison-swamp of reeking pestilence physical and moral."[16] In *Bleak House*, as Michael Steig's article demonstrated, the dominant vision is an excremental one.[17] The same would apply to *Our Mutual Friend*, as a recent article by Avrom Fleishman indicates, although Fleishman's title, "The City and the River",[18] is less startling than Steig's. And it can surely be said that in *Little Dorrit*, again we are re-introduced to a cess-pool. Dickens' gruesome account of London, in that novel, with the Thames as a "deadly sewer" and its gutters reeking with "foul smells"[19] is in the same excremental vein. Tite Barnacle of the Circumlocution Office has a little house on a "hideous little street of . . . stables, and dung-hills".[20] Carlyle, earlier, had likened government offices to an Augean stable which he devoutly hoped Sir Robert Peel might clean away. Peel, he says, might go into that stable of King Augias, which appals human hearts, so rich is it, high-piled with the droppings of two-hundred years; and Hercules-like to load a thousand night-wagons from it, and . . . swash and shovel at it, and never leave it till the antique pavement . . . show itself clean again! [21]

All this indicates how congenial the role was for Dickens and why the younger writer can report to his mentor, in a letter of 1863: "I am always reading you faithfully and trying to go your way."[22] But was it really so congenial as all this seems to indicate? For, after all, even when the rope-dancer aspires to social criticism, he is still a rope-dancer. Perhaps in that letter of 1863 there is an undertone of discontent: "I am always reading you faithfully and *trying to go* your way." Did Dickens never protest that the role of "stern Hebrew", in which Carlyle wanted all writers to be cast, was not one to which he cared to be restricted? Tennyson, we know, spoke his mind about Carlyle when he remarked:

> About poetry or art Carlyle knew nothing. I would never have taken his word about either; but as an honest man, yes—on any subject in the world.[23]

My guess is that Dickens would have shared Tennyson's verdict, although, so far as I know, there is not a hint of formal evidence from reports of conversations or from letters so far published. Is it possible that his disaffection from parts of the stern Hebrew creed surfaced in his novels rather than in his correspondence?

The speculative trial balloon I'm launching here derives from my having been struck, some years ago, by the similarity between Carlyle's comment on Dickens and one of Mr Bounderby's re-curring speeches in *Hard Times*. Dickens, Carlyle said, "thought men ought to be buttered up, and the world made soft and accommodating for them, and all sorts of fellows have turkey for their Christmas dinner".[24] This comment sounds curiously like Mr Bounderby's saying: "There's not a Hand in this town, Sir, . . . but has one ultimate object in life. That object is, to be fed on turtlesoup and venison with a gold spoon",[25] and perhaps this speech represents an impish expression of an area of disagreement between the two writers. A similar impishness is evident in a suppressed passage of *The Chimes*, which Michael Slater reprints in his edition of *The Christmas Books*.[26] Here Dickens has fun with Carlyle's well-known passage about Gurth's brass-collar in *Past and Present*. These, however, are minor. What I have been wondering about is something larger-scaled in their contrasting attitudes towards rope-dancing and how these might bear on *Hard Times*. It seems odd indeed that a novel dedicated to Thomas Carlyle should have as its chief reference point of virtue a circus. "People mutht be a amuthed [Thquire]. They can't be alwayth a learning, nor yet can't be alwayth a working . . ." says Mr Sleary, and perhaps that message is addressed not merely to the Utilitarian Gradgrind but to the Puritan Carlyle. And again when Dickens wrote to Charles Knight on this point he might have addressed his outburst to Carlyle:

> I earnestly entreat your attention to the point (I have been working upon it, weeks past, in *Hard Times*) . . . The English are . . . the hardest-worked people on whom the sun shines. Be content if, in their wretched intervals of pleasure, they read for amusement and do no worse. They are born at the oar, and they live and die at it. Good God, what would we have of them.[27]

If my guess here has any shred of validity, it may account for the curiously defensive tone that Dickens adopts when he writes to Carlyle about this novel. He seems almost to be trying to reassure him: "I know it contains nothing in which you do not think with me, for no man knows your books better than I."[28] And it may be significant that we have no record of Carlyle's response to *Hard Times*, as was pointed out by Richard Dunn in his article on the dedication for *Hard Times*.[29] All that we do have as record is a recently discovered letter from Jane Carlyle, hitherto unpublished, in which she comments upon the dedication (this letter, written to a friend, is undated):

> By the way, Dickens is going to dedicate *Hard Times* to Mr. C.! Moreover, he has invited us to spend a week with him at Boulogne. And that would be better than sitting in a pool of water in one's back-court—But, of course, we shan't go.[30]

The exclamation point here is a tantalizing item which could be interpreted in a variety of ways.

Dickens' feeling of disaffection may surface again in a more unexpected place in some of the awesome speeches of Mrs Clennam in *Little Dorrit*. Like Carlyle when he is wearing his Calvinist clothes and speaking of the rope-dancers, Mrs Clennam speaks of "those accursed snares which are called the arts". Might Carlyle, as he was reading this passage, pause and wonder whether his disciple was here kicking over the traces and off dancing with a rope again as he had done in *Hard Times?*

The comparison to Mrs Clennam is, of course, on further re-flection, an absurd one, for Mrs Clennam never laughs. What is distinctive about Carlyle's Hebraic role is its admixture of colour-ful jocularity.

And it is this mixture, it seems to me, that is at the centre of the shared relationship of these two writers. In a short essay of 1852, *The Opera,* Carlyle offers a vivid example of the mixture. Once more he is out to attack the arts, but this time his attention is centred on the performance of an opera at the Haymarket, the frivolity of which he contrasts with the stern virtues of the Psalms of David. At the end, however, he offers a correction to the impression his essay may have developed. He is not, he says, recommending that England try to imitate the "fanatic Hebrews". His ideal, rather, is "Populations of stern faces, stern as any Hebrew, but capable withal of bursting into inextinguishable laughter on occasion."[31]

The saving clause about laughter is a crucial one, and the essay itself, in its grotesquely funny account of an opera, embodies the principle. Here is an example, his description of ballet dancers:

> The very ballet-girls, with their muslin saucers round them, were perhaps little short of miraculous, whirling and spinning there in strange mad vortexes, and then suddenly fixing themselves motion-less, each upon her left or right great toe, with the other leg stretched out at an angle of ninety degrees,—as if you had suddenly pricked into the floor, by one of their points, . . . a multitudinous cohort of mad restlessly jumping and clipping scissors, and so bid-den them rest, with opened blades, and stand still in the Devil's name![32]

Too many solemn readers of Carlyle forget what a funny writer he is, as G. B. Tennyson has reminded us.[33] As he himself noted in a letter to Mill: "I have under all my gloom, a genuine feeling of the *ludicrous*; and could have been the merriest of men, had I not been the sickliest and saddest."[34]

Surely here was one of the chief affinities between the two men and the two writers. If Landor were to have done one of his imaginary conversations, he would have to have left a lot of space on his pages for the shared *ho, ho, ho's*. If there were some topics to be skirted, there were plenty of others where mutual laughter could be shared, such as the misuse of statistics by the Utilitarians; laissez-faire; the indolence of the dandy; Parliamentary elections, oratory, and bungling; Charles II, and what Carlyle called, in *The Nigger Question*, "Exeter-Hallery and other tragic Tomfoolery".[35] The "vast blockheadism" they detected in the prosperous world of Mid-Victorian England provided them with a fun house. Their most obvious affinity, as I suggested earlier, is their shared vision of a sick society ("Merdle's complaint") and its attendant features of muddy corruption and foggy incompetence. The further affinity is their shared capacity to find the spectacle a field for laughter and colourful evocation. Consider, for example, Carlyle's treatment of the Second Reform Bill, a subject about which he feels passionate indignation. Yet in the midst of his apocalyptic prophecies, in *Shooting Niagara*, he indulges, as well, in what (as he says) the Germans call "mischief-joy". He finds a "secret satisfaction" that it is Disraeli who puts through the Bill:

> that he they call 'Dizzy' is to do it. . . . A superlative Hebrew Conjuror, spell-binding all the great Lords, great Parties, great Interests of England, to his hand in this manner, and leading them by the nose, like helpless mesmerized somnambulant cattle, to such issue, —did the world ever see a *flebile ludibrium* of such magnitude before?[36]

Now to labour a commonplace, this is totally unlike the way Mill writes, or Newman writes, or Mrs Gaskell writes. There is an element of "banter" here, as Carlyle himself called it,[37] which, combined with highly colourful language, constitutes the trademark of his writings, and of Dickens' also.

Of course, not all of Carlyle's writings or Dickens' writings are in this vein. When Dickens employs what we might call his soft style, jocularity and banter are absent.[38] Joyce, in *Ulysses*, points up this contrast in his stunning imitations of the two writers. Carlyle, whom Joyce obviously enjoys, is represented by a passage full of life and fun, but Dickens, whom Joyce disliked, is represented by a treacly imitation of the death of Dora Copperfield ("O Doady, loved one of old, faithful lifemate now it may never be again, that faroff time of the roses").[39] Trollope also played up the difference in *The Warden* by styling Dickens as Mr Popular Sentiment and Carlyle as Dr Pessimist Anticant. Trollope rightly treats them as a team of outsiders mutually at odds with the dominant temper of the 1850's, but his epithets also point to differences. It is when Carlyle and Dickens converge on anticant and corruption that their literary affinities become most discernible.

Finally, on the score of similarities, there is a witty essay by Sylvère Monod, recently published, on *Hard Times*, in which he asks the question, partly in jest: Who else, besides Dickens, could have written *Hard Times*? And he concludes, of course, that only Dickens could have written it.[40] Obviously I am not suggesting that Carlyle could have written it[41] (indeed, I have ventured to stress how un-Carlyle like is its circus theme), but I am suggesting that the manner of no other writer is as close to Dickens' hard style, in *Hard Times* and elsewhere, as is that of Carlyle.

Supplementary Note: Carlyle's Letter on the Death of Dickens

Two sentences from a letter written by Carlyle in July 1870, on the occasion of Dickens' death, have often been cited by critics and biographers (see, e.g. Goldberg, p. 18). These sentences were first published by D. A. Wilson in *Carlyle in Old Age* (London 1934), p. 209. Apparently they must have been derived from an extract in a sale catalogue rather than from a complete copy of the letter itself.

The original letter, now in the Berg Collection of the New York Public Library, has been hitherto unpublished. It was located and transcribed for me by K. J. Fielding, as was the previously unpublished letter from Georgina Hogarth that prompted Carlyle to write. I am grateful to him for his generosity, and also to the Custodians of the Berg Collection for their kind permission to publish these two documents.

Something needs to be said about the circumstances under which the letters were written. According to the terms of Dickens' will, his sister-in-law, Georgina Hogarth, was to receive "all the little familiar objects from my writing-table and my room, and she will know what to do with those things". Soon after his death, Georgina began writing to various persons offering them mementos of their friendship with Dickens. Her letter to Carlyle was addressed to him in Dumfries where he had gone for a summer holiday, having left London in late June, subsequent to Dickens' funeral on 14 June.

The most noteworthy aspects of Georgina's letter and Carlyle's reply is the indication that the two men had not been meeting "very often" in Dickens' later years, and also, once again, the stress Carlyle makes on the qualities of Dickens the man rather than on the "talent" of the writer.

Both letters are written on mourning paper. The envelope for Georgina's is not postmarked, and her letter was presumably transmitted to Carlyle by Forster, co-executor of Dickens' estate.

The "two poor girls" referred to were Dickens' daughters: Mary Dickens and Kate (Mrs. Charles Allston Collins).

Gad's Hill
Monday—June 27th:

My dear Mr. Carlyle—

I have the charge under my dearest Brother-in-law's Will of distributing the "familiar objects" belonging to him amongst the friends who loved him. I had best tell you how very few the objects are, in proportion—and that I am obliged to offer the merest trifles to many.—But Mr. Forster assures me that I may venture to offer you one of the walking sticks which he constantly used—and that you will value it as a Memorial of your lost friend.—You did not meet very often of late years—but there was *no one* for whom he had a higher reverence and admiration besides a sincere personal affection than for yourself.—I hope you will not think it an impertinence in me to express this to you.—The two poor girls join me in sending respectful love to you—and I am always dear Mr. Carlyle

Most sincerely yours
Georgina Hogarth

The Hill, Dumfries, 4 july
1870

Dear Miss Hogarth,

I accept with a mournful gratitude, and many sad and tender

123

feelings, that little Memorial of the loved Friend who has suddenly departed,—gone the way wh*h* is that of us also, and "of all the Earth," from the beginning of things! —

It is almost thirty years since my acquaintance with him began; and on my side I may say every new meeting ripened it into more and more clear discern*t* (quite apart from his unique *talent*) of his rare and great worth as a brother man. A most correct, precise, clear-sighted, quietly decisive, just and loving man;—till at length he had grown to such recogniti*n* with me as I have rarely had for any man of my time. This I can tell you three, for it is true, and will be welcome to you: to others less concerned I had as soon *not* speak on such a subject.

Poor Mrs Collins: poor Miss Dickens,—deep, deep is my pity for them, dear young souls; but what word can I say that will not awaken new tears! God bless you, all three,—I will say that and no more.

Yrs with many thanks & sympathies

T. Carlyle.

NOTES

1. See George Ford, *Dickens and His Readers* (Princeton, 1955), pp. 88–92 etc.; Michael Goldberg, *Carlyle and Dickens* (Athens, Georgia, 1972); William Oddie, *Dickens and Carlyle* (London, 1972).
2. Alexander, "TC and D. H. Lawrence: A Parallel", *University of Toronto Quarterly* (*UTQ*), 37 (1968), p. 248.
3. See, e.g., George Ford, "The Governor Eyre Case in England", *UTQ*, 18 (1948), 219–33, and also *Dickens and His Readers*, p. 91n. As further instance of the pervasive nature of Carlyle's influence, see N. John Hall, "Trollope and Carlyle", *NCF*, 26 (1972), pp. 197–205.
4. NLS MS, 531.7.
5. "Sir Walter Scott" (1838), *Works*, XXIX, 26.
6. C. R. Sanders, 'The Carlyles and Thackeray", in *Nineteenth-Century Literary Perspectives*, ed. Clyde de L. Ryals with the assistance of John Clubbe (Durham, N.C., 1974), p. 180.
7. See Ford, *Dickens and His Readers*, p. 89n.
8. Quoted by Oddie, p. 23.
9. Oddie, p. 21.
10. "Jesuitism" (1850), *Works*, XX, 322, 327–9.
11. On the Waverley Novels Carlyle comments: "Not profitable for doctrine, for reproof, for edification", *Works*, XXIX, 76.
12. Oddie, p. 37.
13. *LDP* (1850), *Works*, XX, 21. See also Goldberg, p. 61. For another

example of Carlyle-like passages in *Bleak House* see G. B. Tennyson's
review of Oddie in *Dickens Studies Newsletter* (March, 1974), p. 27.
14. *Works*, XX, 111.
15. *Works*, XX, 7.
16. *Works*, XX, 27.
17. Steig, "Dickens' Excremental Vision", *VS*, 13 (1970), 339–54.
18. Fleishman, "The City and the River: Dickens's Symbolic Landscape",
Studies in the Later Dickens, ed. Jean-Claude Amelric (Montpellier,
1973), pp. 111–32.
19. *Little Dorrit*, book 1, ch. 3.
20. *Little Dorrit*, book 1, ch. 10. Another example of the two writers'
drawing from the same stores of images is their satirical references to
varnish. In *Dorrit* (book 2, ch. 2) Mrs General "varnished the surface
of every object that came under consideration. The more cracked it
was, the more Mrs General varnished it." Ten years later, referring to
the rottenness of English institutions, Carlyle comments: "Varnish,
varnish; if a thing have grown so rotten that it yawns palpable, . . .
bring out a new pot of varnish . . . and lay it on handsomely. Don't
spare varnish. . . . Varnish alone is cheap and safe."—"Shooting
Niagara: and After?" (1867), *Works*, XXX, 20.—I do not know whether
Carlyle may have used the image of varnish in earlier writings.
21. *LDP*, *Works*, XX, 91–2.
22. *The Letters of Charles Dickens*, ed. W. Dexter (London, 1938), III, 348.
Cf. note 28.
23. Hallam Tennyson, *Alfred Lord Tennyson, A Memoir* (London, 1897),
II, 335.
24. Quoted by Ford, *Dickens and His Readers*, p. 91n.—Carlyle's attitude
towards the Christmas feasting he witnessed in London was sometimes
censorious and sometimes simply bewildered. In 1843, however, his
distaste was overcome, for that season, by reading *A Christmas Carol*.
As Thackeray reported, in *Fraser's*: "A Scotch philosopher, who
nationally does not keep Christmas Day, on reading the book, sent out
for a turkey, and asked two friends to dine—this is a fact! " See Philip
Collins, *Dickens, The Critical Heritage* (London, 1971), p. 149. As
Collins notes, Jane Carlyle was "overwhelmed" by her husband's "un-
wonted access of Christmas feeling . . . especially as she did not know
how to stuff a turkey".
25. *Hard Times*, book 2, ch. 2.
26. *The Christmas Books*, ed. M. Slater (Harmondsworth, Mddx., 1971),
I, Appendix A. Slater's discussion of the passages is in his "Carlyle and
Jerrold" in *Dickens Centennial Essays*, ed. Ada Nisbet and Blake Nevius
(Berkeley, 1971), pp. 191–2. Slater remarks: "In this case . . . he
[Dickens] was not the 'pushover for Carlyle's bullying, sensational intellectual tone' that Angus Wilson finds him always to have been."
See also a reviewer in *Fraser's* (1850) who contended that Dickens was
generally a critic of Carlyle rather than a disciple, and who commented:
"We even remember a passage in *Dombey and Son* which looks like

an overt declaration of war against the great priest of Hero-worship" (Collins, *Dickens, The Critical Heritage*, p. 248).

27. *The Letters of Dickens*, II, 548. See also Sheila M. Smith, "John Overs to Charles Dickens: A Working-Man's Letter and its Implications", *VS*, 18 (1974), 194–217. One of Overs' grievances about the lot of the working-man in the 1840's was the frustration of his wish to "enjoy myself on God's holyday". 'The horrible blasphemy of Parliament and the Saints", he notes, forbids such indulgence. "We tell you you must not, and shall not rest and be happy" (p. 207).

28. *Letters of Dickens*, II, 567.

29. R. J. Dunn, "Dickens, Carlyle, and the *Hard Times* Dedication", *Dickens Studies Newsletter*, 2 (1971), 90–2.

30. For locating and transcribing this letter, and also for information previously cited concerning Dickens' library at Gad's Hill, I am indebted to K. J. Fielding.

31. "The Opera" (1852), *Works*, XXIX, 402–3. See also Teufelsdröckh's laughter in *Sartor*, ed. Harrold, pp. 32–4.

32. *Works*, XXIX, 399.

33. See G. B. Tennyson, *Sartor Called Resartus* (Princeton, 1965), pp. 273–83.

34. NLS MS, 618.29.

35. "The Nigger Question" (1849), *Works*, XXIX, 367. The foibles of American life could be added to this list. Carlyle's response to the satire of "Yankeedoodledodom" in *Martin Chuzzlewit* was "loud assent, loud cachinnatory approval!" (*The Letters of Charles Dickens*, Pilgrim Edition [London, 1974], III, 542n). About *American Notes* he had also responded enthusiastically and wrote to Dickens telling him so (*ibid.*, pp. 356–7). His approval of *American Notes* may have been reinforced by Dickens' kindly reference to him (this passage seems to have been generally overlooked in discussions of the two writers). In praise of the Transcendentalists ("followers of my friend Mr. Carlyle") Dickens notes their "good healthful hearty disgust of Cant, and an aptitude to detect her in all the million varieties of her everlasting wardrobe".

36. "Shooting Niagara: and After?" (1867), *Works*, XXX, 11.

37. From a letter of 26 March 1842, quoted by Oddie, p. 26.

38. Concerning his hard public-style prose see George Ford, "Dickens and the Voices of Time", in *Dickens Centennial Essays*, ed. Nisbet and Nevius, pp. 50–5.

39. *Ulysses* (New York, 1936), p. 413.

40. See Monod, "*Hard Times*: An Undickensian Novel?" in Amelric, pp. 71–92.

41. Concerning Carlyle's problems as a writer of fiction, see George Levine, *The Boundaries of Fiction: Carlyle, Macaulay, Newman* (Princeton, 1968).

6

Carlyle and Arnold: The Religious Issue

by DAVID J. DeLAURA

1

Carlyle's later religious position, after 1834 and his more or less decisive move away from German transcendentalism, has never been fully detailed. Part of the reason lies in his failure to clarify his thought in the area, and part in a deliberate course of concealment as his theological position left him permanently outside the confines of even a broadly defined Christian orthodoxy. The usual view is that the implications of Carlyle's social and religious opinions were left ambiguous with the publication of *Cromwell*, and that only with the *Latter-Day Pamphlets* (1850) and *The Life of John Sterling* (1851) was the extremity of his views apparent. "The Negro Question", published in December 1849 and the precursor of the *Pamphlets*, gave, as Froude says, "universal offence. Many of his old admirers drew back after this, and 'walked no more with him'." (*Life*, IV, 26). But the actual story, which can only be sketched here, is more complicated.

A full account of the almost meteoric rise and fall of Carlyle's reputation between the publication of *The French Revolution* in 1837 and 1850, a period when many distressed young men were drinking deeply at the Carlylean well, would throw a good deal of light on the central issues of the troubled forties. Even among those who knew him personally and never failed to acknowledge his genius, doubts about the effect of Carlyle's teaching began very early. In 1844 Elizabeth Barrett, not yet Mrs Browning, shrewdly noted the equivocalness of his oracles in just such sensitive areas as religion and politics: ". . . the prophet of the Circle hath displayed a cloven tongue!—and peradventure the sincerity of his mode of expression in several works may at times have been questionable." But she thought that *Past and Present* (1843) had settled most doubts, and before most others she saw that no sect was to have Carlyle. She also saw that the apparent identification of Right and Might "has enabled any despot to show some sort of reasoning for any violent act". Miss Barrett was one of the first of many to indict Carlyle for a tone of dissatisfaction, "unhopefulness", and melancholy, and an "unfair method" of diminishing man "by comparison with space and time, and the miraculous round of things".[1] The next year, George Gilfillan was even friendlier to Carlyle's creedless religiosity, and praised him for giving in *Sartor* "the spiritual history of many thinking and sincere men of the time". But he repeated Elizabeth Barrett's charge that the "great moral fault" in *Heroes and Hero-Worship* (1841) is that Carlyle "idolizes energy and earnestness in themselves, and apart from the motives in which they move, and the ends to which they point". And in speaking of "Chartism" (1839) and *Past and Present*, he formulated what was to become the most frequent accusation against Carlyle in the coming years, that he has no remedy for "our political and social disease". "Does a difficulty occur? He shows every ordinary mode of solution to be false, but does not supply the true. . . . Or is it that he is only endowed with an energy of destruction and is rather a tornado to overturn, than an architect to build?"[2]

Nowhere was he more intensely read than among the Arnold-Clough circle at Oxford; but even there the growing doubts are manifest. As early as September 1847, Tom Arnold, Matthew's younger brother, wrote that Carlyle "is much to be pitied; having a philosophy that teaches him to be discontented with the life of other men, without shewing him how to attain to a higher".[3] Despite the public silence, Carlyle's darkening mood after 1845 was becoming well known among the wide range of literary and intellectual types with whom he associated in Cheyne Row, at the Ashburtons', and elsewhere. It was the revolutionary events in France, beginning in February 1848, that roused him from his morose lethargy, first to a high-prophetic welcome, and finally to the inevitable contemptuous rejection as the revolution sputtered out by the summer. For a moment he carried others with him, including Matthew Arnold and George Eliot.[4] But it was the Irish crisis that precipitated Carlyle's decisive swing toward the extremer authoritarianism of his later years. The four Irish articles of that spring, too little known even to Carlyle scholars, were immediately recognised as far more radical and inflammatory than Carlyle's previous recommendations of repressive force. Even Fonblanque and Ritoul, the sympathetic editors of the *Examiner* and the *Spectator*, where the articles appeared, insisted on trimming Carlyle's sails.[5] These essays alone would have provided plenty of basis for Arnold's judgment in September 1849, well before the "Nigger Question" in December, that Carlyle was a "moral desperado" (*LC*, p. 111).[6] But a month *before* the first of these new articles appeared, a slightly malicious Emerson reported on an evening party that included Thackeray, Samuel Wilberforce, and Charles Buller. "Carlyle declaimed a little in the style of that raven prophet who cried, 'Woe to Jerusalem,' just before its fall. But Carlyle finds little reception even in this company, where some were his warm friends. All his methods included a good deal of killing, and he does not see his way very clearly or far."[7] Emerson carried home a revealing vignette of the young men, "especially those holding liberal opinions", who "press to see him": "He treats them with contempt; they profess freedom and he stands for slavery; they praise republics and he likes the Russian Czar; they admire Cobden and free trade and he is a protectionist . . . they praise moral suasion, he goes for murder, money, capital punishment, and other pretty abominations of English law."[8]

The Irish articles provoked something between disgust and dismay. Mill answered the first one sternly, and Carlyle's friend Edward FitzGerald said, he "raves and foams, but has nothing to propose".[9] There can no longer, then, be any surprise that the Clough who had burlesqued Carlyle's style in the letter of 19 May beginning "Ichabod, Ichabod, the glory is departed" (*CC*, I, 207), should have asked the departing Emerson on the Liverpool docks in July: "What shall we do without you? Think where we are. Carlyle has led us all out into the desert, and has left us there."[10] It is not surprising, either, that J. A. Froude, not yet the singular disciple of Carlyle he was to become, included in his autobiographical account in *The Nemesis of Faith* (published February 1849) of his wrestling-free from Tractarianism a more direct attack on Carlyle: ". . . of all these modern writers, there is not one who will boldly up and meet the question which lies the nearest . . . to our hearts. Carlyle! Carlyle only raises questions he cannot answer, and seems best contented if he can make the rest of us as discontented as himself."[11] Young men like Arnold, Clough, and Froude would also have heard a report from William E. Forster, Carlyle's companion on the Irish tour in the summer of 1849, who "was shocked at the almost exultation of Carlyle at the wretchedness of the people".[12]

Well before the autumn of 1849, then, Carlyle was already in the isolation he was to endure for the rest of his life, and which he describes in a pathetic journal entry for November 11: "In dissent from all the world; in black contradiction, deep as the bases of my life, to all the philanthropic, emancipatory, constitutional, and other anarchic revolutionary jargon, with which the world, so far as I can conceive, is now full" (Froude, *Life*, IV, 22). "The Nigger Question" and *Latter-Day Pamphlets* turned away almost all of "liberal" opinion, and most notably rent beyond repair the already strained friendship with Mill.[13] And yet, though most of Carlyle's social and political prescriptions were almost overnight and forever rejected by all sane Englishmen, it should not be forgotten that a quite amazing range of even Victorian freethinkers, including Mill, continued to speak of him with something like affection, almost as if the later diatribes did not count.[14]

2

Arnold's well-known description of Carlyle in 1883 as one of the four "voices" at Oxford in the forties could almost have described the change in his reputation between 1843 and 1850: "There was the puissant voice of Carlyle; so sorely trained, over-used, and mis-used since, but then fresh, comparatively sound, and reaching our hearts with true, pathetic eloquence" (*DA*, pp. 142–3). The poetry, the blazing genius, the largeness of moral and historical vision—all these affected the sensitive young of all persuasions. The decline of Carlyle's reputation as a political and social thinker is the major subject of the evidence gathered above; but the reasons for the darkening of Carlyle's social vision from the mid-forties until the *Pamphlets* is not precisely the topic I want to deal with here.[15] It is somewhat harder to isolate Carlyle's decline as a specifically religious teacher, and the stages by which his position became known. Alert readers like Elizabeth Barrett saw his coming separation from all parties, and indeed from all brands of even liberal Christianity.[16] But many Anglicans, Dissenters, and Catholics had hoped, especially after *Past and Present* and *Cromwell*, that he was an ally. They were proved entirely mistaken.[17] The vitriol Carlyle poured over the religious world in "Jesuitism" (August 1850) could be seen simply as part of the vomiting-up mood of the *Pamphlets*; the religious issue as such was not quite directly engaged. But *Sterling*, his last meaningful public religious statement, separated Carlyle from every variety of contemporary religious thought. The new Broad Church party under the leadership of F. D. Maurice and Kingsley were especially offended to find Carlyle rejecting the Coleridgean defence of the Church, "that, by an intellectual legerdemain, uncertainties could be converted into certainties", and endorsing Sterling's discovery that "the Highgate philosophy was 'bottled moonshine' " (Froude, *Life*. IV, 69, 73). As Froude puts it, "From all that section of Illuminati who had hitherto believed themselves his admirers, he had cut himself off for ever, and, as a teacher, he was left without disciples, save a poor handful who had longed for such an utterance from him" (*Life*, IV, 75).

Gilfillan, this time reviewing *Sterling*, saw that Carlyle had openly revealed "the foregone conclusion, . . . long ago reached," that "he loves Christianity as little as he does its clergy". But, anticipating the modern difficulty in describing Carlyle's religious position, Gilfillan saw that Carlyle was even then "never so explicit as he should be" and that his religious opinions were "uncertain, vague, indefinite, perhaps not fully formed". He saw that the general public "are still in the dark as to his religious sentiments", and some still call him a Christian and even a "Puritan". Hurrying Carlyle off the stage perhaps a trifle prematurely, Gilfillan insists that Carlyle's "giant shadow is passing swiftly from off the face of the public mind. . . . It is *too late*. The gospel of negation has had its day, and served its generation, and must now give place to a better and nobler evangel."[18] At any rate, James Martineau was probably right in saying, in 1856, that although in a general way still influential, Carlyle's "specific action on the *religion* of the age . . . already belongs in a great measure to the past".[19]

This " 'Latter-Day Pamphlet' time", as Carlyle called it,[20] when he was revealing his final position in almost all matters, coincided exactly with the period of greatest spiritual struggle for the young Oxonians of Arnold's generation—the years of Clough's resignation of his Oriel fellowship, of Froude's *Nemesis*, and of Arnold's "Empedocles on Etna". These were obviously the "doubts and miseries" to which Arnold bitterly alluded in 1881: "It was very well for Mr. Carlyle to bid us have recourse, in our doubts and miseries, to earnestness and reality, and veracity and the everlasting yea, and generalities of that kind; Mr. Carlyle was a man of genius."[21] This, for the vague and useless *positive* side of Carlyle's message. Like others, Arnold chose the *Pamphlets* as the symbol of Carlyle's "furious" defects of tone and manner (*CPW*, III, 275). *Sterling* presented that younger generation with a different order of challenge. George Brimley, though hostile in saying Carlyle "has no right . . . to weaken or destroy a faith which he cannot or will not replace with a loftier", saw the importance of the book: "This life of Sterling will be useful to the class whose beliefs have given way before Mr. Carlyle's destroying energies; because it furnishes hints, not to be mistaken though not obtrusive, as to the extent to which they must be prepared to go if they would really be his disciples."[22] The years 1848–51 were an important turning point in English intellectual and spiritual life, and the series of shocks given by Carlyle to the intellectual community in these years helped to distinguish, harden, and spell out the implications of the tangled lines of earlier Victorian thought. After the convulsions of the Hungry Forties—Tractarian agonies, Chartist agitations, and revolutions across the face of Europe—England settled down in the fifties to a period of "opulence and peace".[23] To use a facetious shorthand, a whole generation married in the years around 1850, and adopted that Victorian panacea for spiritual doubt, domesticity—Arnold, Clough, Tom Arnold, Froude, as well as such non-Oxonians as Tennyson and Kingsley. More importantly for present purposes, it seems not to have been noted that, Arnold excepted, all the men of his circle—Clough, Tom Arnold, Froude, J. C. Shairp,[24] J. D. Coleridge—drew back from the Carlylean precipice and adopted by the early fifties one or another variety of Christianity, however liberal, or (in Clough's case) a near-Christian theism. It is Arnold's own remarkable independence of viewpoint (despite his own marriage, the inspectorship, and a quick decline in his poetic career) that allowed him to work out his own position more slowly, and to profit variously from Carlyle's example.

3

It may startle even to suggest that the Arnold who in 1857 called Carlyle "part man—of genius—part fanatic—and part tom-fool", and who two years later scornfully rejected "that regular Carlylean strain which we all know by heart and which the clear-headed among us have so utter a contempt for",[25] was in any positive way indebted to Carlyle's religious views. Moreover, Carlyle's name is almost entirely absent from Arnold's four major books of religious criticism published between 1870 and 1876. Still, as Mrs Tillotson and I have shown, both his poetry and his social views of the sixties are saturated with Carlylean phrasing, imagery, and ideas.[26] A likeness, if not debt, between the two even in religious views has occasionally been noted. Basil Willey has it that "Carlyle's position resembles that of Arnold in *Literature and Dogma*; it is so differently stated as to be hardly recognizable as similar, yet essentially it is so".[27] And one of Arnold's best-equipped clerical reviewers, J. Llewelyn Davies, reviewing *Literature and Dogma*, noted that although Carlyle was "in many respects unlike our preacher of mildness and sweet reasonableness", nevertheless his "conception of God and Christ" and his "feeling towards the Bible" are like Arnold's:

> As disciples of Goethe, they are both emancipated from *anthropomorphic* theology, but they have in common a profound reverence for righteousness and for the Old Testament which they did not learn from Goethe. To Mr. Carlyle as well as to Mr. Arnold, "God" is the enduring and awful power which makes for righteousness; and which causes that no unrighteousness shall prosper. The language of each about the religion of Christ is modelled mainly upon the type of Goethe's, and is more sympathetic towards it than

133

the ordinary tone of modern Liberalism. How far they would agree in their estimate of what Christ was, and in their judgment as to what he really said and what character he assumed, could only be conjectured, as Mr. Carlyle has thought it best to be silent on these questions.[28]

One of the best of Arnold's critics, R. H. Hutton, also pointed out that Arnold's lifelong presuppositions were exactly those of the 1840's, the period of Carlyle's greatest influence, when "certain premature scientific assumptions, . . . in vogue before the limits in which the uniformity of nature had been verified, had been at all carefully defined". Arnold belongs

> rather to the stoical than to the religious school—the school which magnifies self-dependence, and regards serene calm, not passionate worship, as the highest type of the moral life. And he was at Oxford too early, I think, for a full understanding of the limits within which alone the scientific conception of life can be said to be true. A little later, men came to see that scientific methods are really quite inapplicable to the sphere of moral truth, that the scientific assumption that whatever is true can be verified is, in the sense of the word 'verification' which science applies, a very serious blunder, and that such verification as we can get of moral truth is of a very different though I will not scruple to say no less satisfactory, kind from that which we expect to get of scientific truth. Mr. Arnold seems to have imbibed the prejudices of the scientific season of blossom, when the uniformity of nature first became a kind of gospel, . . . when Emerson's and Carlyle's imaginative scepticism first took hold of cultivated Englishmen. . . .

He finds Arnold's "immovable prejudices" revealed in his view that "miracles do not happen" or that "you can verify the secret of self-renunciation, the secret of Jesus, in the same sense in which you can verify the law of gravitation, one of the most astounding, and, I think, false assumptions of our day".[29]

Though hostile, Hutton is essentially correct. What we need to spell out is why Carlyle, more than Emerson or (as Davies saw) Goethe, remained a relevant influence, if not model, during Arnold's later "theological" period. First, Carlyle was both "religious" and independent. Arnold always proudly valued his own independence from all parties (he was a liberal of the future and his church the religion of the future); even his religion of the seventies is

134

markedly original, in its intellectual radicalism combined with deep piety, and it falls outside the categories of the period. From his undergraduate days on, he keeps his distance from any variety of Christian orthodoxy, and even from any of the species of liberal and broad theology sponsored by such apparently natural allies as Jowett and Stanley and Maurice. For the lonely and eccentric Christian explorer like F. W. Newman or Colenso he can maintain an unpleasantly jeering and snobbish contempt. Most important, he is never tempted to join forces with the loose coalition of freethinkers of a newer generation who, following Mill especially, had put theological struggles behind them for good: Leslie Stephen, John Morley, Huxley. He is particularly Carlylean in sensing that the new "humanist" religions—in the wake of Saint-Simon, or Comte, or Feuerbach—had a dubious future.[30]

Both men were, in an important sense, both "religious" and "conservative" (*CPW*, VII, 398). They were doing the essential work of the nineteenth century—indeed of the modern world—in testing to see how much that was essential in the inherited religious consciousness could legitimately survive the collapse of the old institutions and of classical metaphysics. Despite Arnold's early interest in Eastern religions and Carlyle's flirtations with the German Idealists, both remained intellectually and emotionally what the categorizers call "ethical monotheists". They are also alike in the broad pattern of their spiritual careers: each gave up a childhood orthodoxy in the face of the apparently unanswerable rationalist arguments against a "personal" divinity, but each gradually assembled a "reconceived" Biblical religion. Both were "modernists" before that position became widely available in the pragmatist intellectual climate of the latter nineteenth century, and indeed Arnold's greater success in defining his position made him an important influence on the movement. Carlyle's "prophetic" character lay in his highly developed sense, which more and more religious people including the orthodox came to have, that some permanent change was overtaking man's religious consciousness, but that the whole traditional scheme of religious feelings and values could somehow be preserved—as Pater was to say, "the same, but different".[31] The central residue was the assertion of a shadowy providentialism, operative less and less in individual acts and lives than in some broad historical perspective. Carlyle passed on to Arnold a very Goethean fastidiousness about discussing the attributes of a "personal" God ("Wer darf Ihn nennen?"), although Carlyle would have conceded no future for even the redefined Christian Church that Arnold eventually sponsored.

Carlyle's "curious blending of stoicism, Hebraism, and transcendentalism", of which Harrold speaks,[32] left traces in Arnold's writings, but to these Arnold, though even more uncertain about divinity, added softer and more traditionally devotional elements. Carlyle, the "born Calvinist" whose faith had been shipwrecked by his reading in Gibbon, Hume, and the French Philosophes, went to the Germans, "seeking to reconstruct . . . a belief in the transcendent sovereignty of Right and in a world of immanent divine law". Though his career is unified by insistence on "the conception of moral right as the only reality, of the duty of obedience and 'self-annihilation', of the religious nature of work, of the organic unity of all things, and of the reality of heroes", by 1843 Carlyle's God was less the Divine Idea than "the Jehovah of eternal law and wrath".[33]

Arnold and his contemporaries would have had great difficulty in charting this change and simplification in Carlyle's religious thinking, partly because between 1837 and 1843 works of every period of his career became suddenly available, and because Carlyle's theological position remained inchoate and intellectually unclarified in any event. Nevertheless Arnold was particularly well situated to see that Carlyle had failed to make that Exodus from Houndsditch which he so urgently called for in the *Pamphlets* and *Sterling*.[34] Negatively, and as a programme for his own then highly tentative religious position, Arnold would not have disapproved of the attempt to remove from religion "this ghastly phantasm of Christianity", "Semitic forms now lying putrescent, dead and still unburied" (*LDP*, p. 68). Even in the seventies Arnold would have agreed that most of Christian theology had been a "broken-winged, self-strangled, monstrous . . . mass of incoherent incredibilities" (*LDP*, p. 289). Carlyle's programme would be acceptable, if not its tone: "The Jew old-clothes having now grown fairly pestilential, a poisonous incumbrance in the path of men, burn them up with revolutionary fire . . . but you shall not quit the place till you have gathered from their ashes what of gold or other enduring metal was sewed upon them, or woven in the tissue of them" (*LDP*, p. 330). Arnold's own less strenuous version of the Exodus was his approval in the sixties of the idea (endorsed by Teutonic sages like Humboldt, Bunsen, and Schleiermacher) of a Christianity stripped of its "alien Semitic" features and brought into line with "the opener, more flexible Indo-European genius".[35] In the forties and early fifties, while marking off his distance from all other positions and undergoing his own Exodus from Hounds-ditch, Arnold would have responded to Carlyle's image of the "tragic pilgrimage" required now of the honest man, "in defiance of pain and terror, to press resolutely across said deserts ["the howling deserts of Infidelity"] to the new firm lands of Faith be-yond" (*JS*, pp. 96, 60).[36]

But all this was negative if necessary, a stern preliminary to a more positive spiritual assertion. Here Arnold would have seen that the social dead end of the *Pamphlets* embodied a more general spiritual failure that also extended to *Sterling*. Carlisle Moore sug-gests that Carlyle felt, "but never admitted to himself openly, that there was a sort of second Everlasting Yea to struggle toward, a further faith and a more practical wisdom". It is "as if he felt there was a divine wisdom possible for him which he needed greater effort to find expression for".[37] It was probably not so much the intellectual deficiencies of Carlyle's vague theism that Arnold stepped back from, as a more fundamental failure in tone, spiritual "tact"—in short, love. At the very least, the "moral atmosphere" Arnold was "snuffing after" in September 1849 seems sufficiently different from the ferocities of Carlyle in these years. As Arnold says in the Yale MS, probably in the late forties: "I can-not conceal from myself the objection which really wounds and perplexes me from the religious side is that the service of reason is freezing to feeling, chilling to the religious mood. And feeling and the religious mood are eternally the deepest being of man, the ground of all joy and greatness for him."[38] And by 1853 he can say: "I would have others—most others stick to the old religious dogmas because I sincerely feel that this *warmth* is the great bless-ing, and this frigidity the great curse—and on the old religious road they have still the best chance of getting the one and avoid-ing the other" (*LC*, p. 143).[39]

Behind this is the larger and long-recognized "happiness" issue

that divided Arnold from Carlyle when Arnold came to formulate
in the seventies his view that "Happiness is our being's end and
aim", and that happiness is "the witness and sanction" of right
conduct (*CPW*, VI, 195, 192).[40] But it is obvious that even before
1850 Arnold had rejected Carlyle as a model for his own slowly
developing religious thought. The pose of austere but elevated
aesthetic detachment experimented with in "Resignation" had
obviously broken down by the time of Arnold's poems of dis-
tress in 1849 and 1850: "Empedocles", "Tristram and Iseult",
"Obermann", and the Marguerite poems. Arnold had indeed in-
corporated "whole pages" of the argument of *Sartor Resartus* into
the "sermon" of "Empedocles",[41] but even the minimalist doctrine,

> I say: Fear not! Life still
> Leaves human effort scope.
> But, since life teams with ill,
> Nurse no extravagant hope;
> Because thou must not dream, thou need'st not then despair!
>
> (I, ii, 422–6)

is obviously brought into question by Empedocles' (and implicitly
Arnold's) inability to live in accordance with it. Carlyle is certainly one of the "masters of the mind" in "Stanzas from the
Grande Chartreuse" (begun 1851), "At whose behest I long ago/
So much unlearnt, so much resigned . . ." (ll. 73–5). But there is
surely a rebuke in the words Arnold used (in the first text, 1855)
to describe the high but bleak ethical stance enjoined on him by
his post-Christian teachers:

> For rigorous teachers seized my youth,
> And prun'd its faith and quench'd its fire,
> Showed me the pale cold star of Truth (ll. 67–9).

There may even be a reference to Carlyle in the faint vision of a
future age, "More fortunate, alas! than we,/Which without hard-
ness will be sage . . ." (ll. 158–9). Arnold's prescription in
October 1852 of a poetry that should become "a complete magis-
ter vitae", "including . . . religion with poetry" (*LC*, p. 124), and
the call in the Preface of 1853 for a poetry that should "inspirit and
rejoice" (*CPW*, I, 2), though he was not yet prepared to supply

138

such a poetry himself, are indications of a steady movement away from Carlyle and, in the last analysis, from the grimmer limitations imposed by modern naturalism.[42]

One way in which Carlyle did help Arnold in these years was in explaining the significance of the career of John Sterling. An important event for Carlyle and his public was J. C. Hare's publication in 1848 of Sterling's *Essays and Tales*, with a Life of the Author running to over 200 pages. Sterling, who had died in 1844 at the age of thirty-eight, had because of bad health and theological difficulties left a clerical calling for a career in editing and the writing of fiction and poetry. Hare implicitly presented the life, strongly influenced by the scepticism of Carlyle, as a tragedy of spiritual defeat. Beyond the inherent interest of the "emblematic" history (*JS*, p. 268) of this man, a "failure" after the brilliant promise of his youth at Cambridge, Hare's two volumes for the first time gave evidence of the extremity of Carlyle's later religious views, hitherto veiled from the public, but now frankly revealed in his correspondence with Sterling from the time of their meeting in 1834. Except for Hare's volumes, Carlyle might not have revealed so fully in "Jesuitism" and *Sterling* the depth of his religious frustration and alienation. His own life of Sterling is conceived as a corrective to Hare's account, and stresses the ambiguous "heroism" of his disciple's struggle to put off the Hebrew old-clothes of clericalism and theology. This was done primarily in justice, as Carlyle conceived it, to Sterling, attempting to rescue him from even liberal theologizers like Hare. In the process, Carlyle undoubtedly exaggerated Sterling's later scepticism and his rejection of religious interests.[43] But in presenting the unpublished letters that passed between himself and Sterling, Carlyle revealed much of his own position for the first time. The accidental timing of Hare's publication gave Carlyle the occasion for going as far as he ever was able in mapping out the Exodus from Houndsditch.

Arnold would have seen himself in Sterling, to some extent, and would have received sympathetically Carlyle's view that Sterling had saved his soul by removing himself from the "putridity, artificial gas and quaking bog" of contemporary theology (*JS*, p. 266). Arnold's own mood on the subject was not very different at the time. As he said of a book by F. W. Newman in May 1850, "It is a display of the theological mind, which I am accustomed to regard as a suffetation. . . . One would think to read him that enquiries into articles, biblical inspiration, etc., etc., were as much the natural functions of a man as to eat and copulate" (*LC*, p. 115). But Arnold would also have seen Clough in Sterling and may well have borrowed Carlyle's imagery and tone in describing the career of that later spiritual shipwreck. Arnold complained to Clough in 1853, "you would never take up your assiette [in life] as something determined final and unchangeable for you and proceed to work away on the basis of that" (*LC*, p. 130). We are told in "Thyrsis", rather vindictively, that Clough "could not rest"; he could not wait the passing of contemporary storms: "he is dead" (ll. 41, 49–50). Clough is the "cuckoo", a "Too quick despairer", a "light comet" (ll. 57, 61, 71). Even in conceding that he and Clough shared a "quest", Arnold insists on Clough's enfeebled and troubled state; too aware of the "storms" and contentions of present controversy, his muse "failed" (ll. 211, 214–15, 49, 224, 226). Carlyle, too, had presented Sterling as a creature of "impetuous velocity", "headlong alacrity", "rashness and impatience", who unsuccessfully sought guidance among the welter of modern "Professors of political, ecclesiastical, philosophical, commercial, general and particular Legerdemain". Though "high-strung", his was a "light and volatile" and "too-hasty soul", wanting in "due strength" (*JS*, pp. 84, 91, 234–5). Whatever the ties between the two portraits, Arnold sought to stabilize himself as neither Sterling nor Clough could. Independent, proud, and aloof, Arnold knew, above all, how to wait. His religious position was to be worked out very gradually, especially from 1862–63, when he turned his fuller attention to the religious situation.

4

Arnold's theology of the seventies was worked out in the context of surprisingly wide reading in theology and Biblical criticism.[44] Still, despite all his tergiversations with regard to Carlyle as a spiritual model, a good number of Carlyle's characteristic doctrines and habits of mind are detectable in Arnold's later religious writings, and they need detailing. Above all, there is the

140

shared reluctance to "name" or define the divinity. As Sterling said of *Sartor* in the notable letter of 29 May 1835: "What we find everywhere, with an abundant use of the name God, is the conception of a formless Infinite . . .; of a high inscrutable Necessity, which it is the chief wisdom and virtue to submit to, which is the mysterious impersonal base of all Existence" (*JS*, p. 116). Harrold sees this as predictive of the nineteenth century's increasingly vague formulas like Arnold's *"the enduring power, not ourselves, which makes for righteousness"*.[45] Sterling's charge that Carlyle did not acknowledge a "Living *Personal* God", a charge Arnold sustained in the seventies and firmly refused to repent of, was part of the nineteenth century's terror of Spinoza and "Pantheism", a line of thinking mediated to both Carlyle and Arnold by Goethe. Carlyle and Arnold were the true agnostics of the century, who refused to speculate on the nature of God; the label "agnostic" as applied by Huxley or Stephen to themselves was really a fig leaf for their atheism.[46] The result in both cases is a reliance on expressions like "the Eternal" and "the Eternal Power" to bridge the gap between a Spinozism they intellectually could not surrender and a deepening of the religious consciousness (especially in Arnold) they saw as emotionally necessary.[47] It also led to a self-protective jettisoning of the entire apparatus of theological speculation and dogma. Carlyle's contemptuous rejection of "Evidences, Counter-Evidences, Theologies and Rumours of Theologies" as a "world of rotten straw" and "wretched dead mediaeval monkeries and extinct traditions" (*JS*, pp. 125–26, 140–1), is not so far in tone from Arnold's analogizing of the Holy Trinity to the three Lord Shaftesburys (*CPW*, VI, 575–8), which gave so much offence.[48] Both men also resolutely put aside even "the larger hope" of personal immortality, that residual dogma of liberal Victorian religionists like Tennyson.[49]

Arnold's "natural experimental truth" of Christianity, which separated the "old forms" from their "essential contents" (*LECR*, pp. 174, 177), is in effect a more patient and more successful working out of the implications of Carlyle's "natural supernaturalism". Carlyle was as certain as Arnold that, in the traditional sense of the term, *"miracles do not happen"* (*CPW*, VI, 146; see VII, 368), and their discussion of miracles actually uses the same imagery.[50] In both, the playing off of "fact" and "reality" against "formula" and "symbol" (*LDP*, pp. 293–4) springs from the century's rationalist impulse to get behind all variable historical cultures to a permanent and universalistic (but finally fairly Christian) moral residue. But Arnold is, ultimately, less iconoclastic than Carlyle, or than some of Arnold's recent commentators would have him. The "old forms of Christian worship", "thrown out at a dimly-grasped truth", put in "approximative" language and now surrounded by "tender and profound sentiment", will survive as "poetry", a needful body of images and sentiments (*LECR*, pp. 177–8).[51] Arnold's new Christian is not nearly so naked as Carlyle's pilgrim in the desert. But both insisted that "a new religion" was a chimera: "you already have it," Carlyle declares, "have always had it!" (*LDP*, p. 333).[52] What was changed was the basis of proof for the older system of values, now that historical and metaphysical defences were failing it. Rationalism and an almost mystical iconoclasm join in Carlyle's call:

> A man's 'religion' consists not of the many things he is in doubt of and tries to believe, but of the few he is assured of, and has no need of effort for believing. His religion, whatever it may be, is a discerned fact, and coherent system of discerned facts to him; he stands fronting the worlds and the eternities upon it: to *doubt* of it is not permissible at all! He must verify or expel his doubts, convert them into certainty of Yes or No; or they will be the death of his religion (*LDP*, p. 313).

There is a very similar tone in Arnold's insistence that "Religion must be built on ideas about which there is no puzzle", and his doctrine that "the natural victoriousness of virtue, even in this world," rests on a "boundless certitude" based on "plain grounds of reason", rather than on Bishop Butler's alleged "imperfect evidence" of "probabilities" and "prudence" (*LECR*, pp. 294, 300–5; *CPW*, VI, 267–8).

Arnold's natural religion was to be "verified" not only in individual experience, but in "the whole history of the world to this day", which is "perpetually establishing the pre-eminence of righteousness". History is thus an "immense experimental proof" of the "necessity" of Christianity, "which the whole course of the world has steadily accumulated" (*CPW*, VI, 392, 397, 400). This important and often overlooked aspect of Arnold's religious thought, first developed in the concluding chapters of *Literature and Dogma* (1873), is perhaps his most explicit borrowing from Carlyle. "Is not God's Universe", Carlyle asks in *Sartor*, "a Symbol of the Godlike; is not Immensity a Temple; is not Man's History, and Men's History, a perpetual Evangel?" (*SR*, pp. 253–4). He comes closest to Arnold's point of view in *Past and Present*: "When a nation is unhappy, the old Prophet was right and not wrong in saying it: Ye have forgotten God, ye have quitted the ways of God, or ye would not have been unhappy" (*PP*, p. 28). They even coincide in the analogy they use for their Spinozistic deity operating in history. That "the great Soul of the World is just and not unjust", says Carlyle, "is not a figure of speech; this is a fact. The fact of Gravitation known to all animals, is not surer than this inner Fact . . ." (*PP*, p. 229). That there is "an eternal not ourselves that makes for righteousness", echoes Arnold, "is really a law of nature, collected from experience, just as much as the law of gravitation is" (*CPW*, VII, 191). There is a difference: Arnold is usually not very specific in his modern examples supporting his morality of history (except perhaps for the French defeat of 1871), whereas Carlyle is wildly elated, and soon depressed, by every revolutionary event up to at least 1848. Arnold would of course have been unreceptive to the associated view that Mights "forever will in this universe in the long run" mean Rights (*PP*, 191); and he might not have been surprised if he heard Carlyle's "cry of pain" to Froude about God's activities in history: "He does nothing" (*Life*, IV, 260). Both Arnold and Carlyle had a yearning for a City of God on earth, almost a theocracy; but of course Carlyle's vision of the "Drill-Sergeant" duke or earl doing the work of God by creating within his own domain a "superlative private Field-regiment" aiding Parliament in "warring-down" Anarchy ("Shooting Niagara", *CME*, XXX, 41, 43) is rather different in its implications from Arnold's final prophecy of the Kingdom of God as "an immense renovation and transformation of things" on earth, through the "dissolution" of the old order—"dissolution peaceful if we have virtue enough, violent if we are vicious, but still dissolution".[53]

The coincidences of attitude in religious and moral matters could be extended. Notably, there is Carlyle's view that literature is "the haven of expatriated spiritualisms" and that "the Fine Arts be if not religion, yet indissolubly united to it, dependent on it, vitally blended with it as body is with soul" (*LDP*, pp. 168, 319) —a view in a general way consonant with Arnold's more absolute prediction that "most of what passes with us for religion and philosophy will be replaced by poetry".[54] Even closer, perhaps, if not more pleasant, are Carlyle's screech against "a strange new religion, named of Universal Love", "a *new* astonishing Phallus-worship, with universal Balzac-Sand melodies and litanies" (*LDP*, pp. 80–1), and Arnold's protest against the Goddess Lubricity, who reigns at Paris, whose ideal is "the free development of our senses all round", and whose newer prophets are Hugo, Zola, and Renan.[55]

5

But, as I have suggested, Carlyle was less a source of particular doctrines than an influence, an ambience, almost a stain that Arnold never washed out of his thinking—as well as a positive model in his iconoclasm, and a negative one in his failure to march quite through the desert. Carlyle's later theism is simpler, if less articulated, than Arnold's: Carlyle is not the "English atheist, who made it a point of honour not to be one," that Nietzsche wittily called him, nor was his faith quite the "inextinguishable" flame that Basil Willey finds it.[56] The shrillness of his later appeals to a Calvinistic taskmaster God, though entirely sincere, and the frenzy with which he would smash all religious "forms", suggest to me a growing and terrifying doubt concerning the availability of the older varieties of transcendence, even as a vague force operating in history. Doubt and affirmation continue strong, and unresolved, to the end.

Arnold learned to live more serenely with his impalpable and gently affirmed divinity. A chief means for securing this serenity, and the centre of his theology, was his richly developed Christology. Carlyle, who insisted on a God of terror and fear, would have disdained Arnold's deity, stripped of such rough attributes. Carlyle's system, in Arnold's eyes, virtually came down to this: *I suffer, therefore I am.*[57] Both Carlyle and Arnold were attracted to Novalis's doctrine of Annihilation of Self (*Selbsttödtung*) and Goethe's recommendation of Renunciation (*Ent-*

sagen) (*Sartor*, pp. 186, 191; *LPD*, p. 303), and both sought to deepen them into something more authentically religious. But Arnold's "natural law of rule and suppression" brings not only Carlyle's pain and suffering, but joy and peace by "attachment" to Jesus, through his "method" of inwardness, his "secret" of self-renouncement, and his "temper" of mildness and sweetness.[58]

What Arnold had, and Carlyle lacked, was an authentic doctrine of conversion. Carlyle's own "conversion" in the twenties was rudimentary in content,[59] and like Evangelical conversion, had an underdeveloped sense of the ensuing spiritual life. As Willey says, in Carlyle's conversion "there is no contrition, no reliance upon grace or redeeming love, but on the contrary, much proud and passionate self-assertion. The emotion that follows release is hatred and defiance of the Devil, rather than love and gratitude towards God."[60] Although Arnold's doctrine of conversion also lacked to a large extent a traditional sense of sin and submission, he had an implicit theory of grace and he knew that religion must be located in the "central" or "buried" self, which by the seventies had become the "real" or "best" self. Arnold knew that the sense of the holy is deeply intertwined with man's possession of his own interiority. In contrast, Carlyle fled from and feared his own interior self and the chaos he would encounter there. He was right (and in this like Arnold and the Tractarians) in asserting that the self-preoccupation of a "morbid" Methodism ("'Am I right? Am I wrong? Shall I be saved? Shall I not be damned?'") was "but a new phasis of *Egoism*, stretched out into the Infinite" (*PP*, p. 117; see *CPW*, VI, 35–6). But there is something else revealed in a remark he made to Espinasse about his own avoidance of self-examination: "I never troubled myself . . . about my faults, it was only not struggling enough."[61] In Arnold's terms, Carlyle was not a "still, considerate mind", nor did he qualify for membership among the "children of the second birth" (*LC*, p. 110). The chasm that Carlyle fixes, in "Characteristics" (1831), between "the Voluntary and Conscious" and "the Involuntary and Unconscious" (*CME*, XXVIII, 10) is wider than the gap between Arnold's ordinary self and best self. In insisting that even in "the Moral sphere" not only is "self-contemplation" a "symptom of disease" and a form of "self-seeking", but "unconsciousness" is evidence of "wholeness" (*ibid.*, pp. 7–8), Carlyle was in effect renouncing that legitimate quest for self-knowledge and self-possession that is central in Arnold's career.[62]

Despite a strong mystical bent of his own,[63] Arnold refused to slip the leash of "ordinary" consciousness, however expanded and elevated. This is the limitation of his religious vision, but also a source of its continuing appeal. Carlyle predicted that spiritual seekers must face two centuries of "foul agnostic welter through the Stygian seas of mud" before they "pursue their *human* pilgrimage"; he would have viewed Arnold's serious concern with the residual value of the emotion, art, worship, and ethics of historical religion as a premature regression to the "superstitious terror" and "pestilential" old-clothes of mankind's now outgrown past (*LDP*, pp. 329–30). Carlyle's "naked" religiousness has its attractions, but very few followers. Arnold's position is logically vulnerable, and flawed by its shortsighted dependence on what proved to be orthodox Christianity's continually diminishing hold on the educated community. But it remains close to the implicit religious position of a large number of "humanistically" oriented people in the West who have not simply broken with man's religious past. In the nineteenth century England produced at least three men of original theological and religious genius—Coleridge, Newman, and F. D. Maurice. Outside of orthodoxy altogether, Arnold joins them in having created single-handedly one of the permanently available modern religious positions. For all his reservations about Carlyle's tone and temper, Arnold acknowledged to the end that the "scope and upshot of his teaching are true" (*DA*, p. 196). In working out his own religious views. Arnold was continuing not only his father's work, but curiously and problematically, Carlyle's too.

NOTES

The following additional abbreviations are used:

CME: *Critical and Miscellaneous Essays, Works,* XXVI–XXX.
JS: *The Life of John Sterling, Works,* XI.
PP: *Past and Present, Works,* X.
CC: *The Correspondence of Arthur Hugh Clough,* ed. Frederick L. Mulhauser (Oxford, 1957).

CPW: *Complete Prose Works of Matthew Arnold*, ed. R. H. Super (Ann Arbor, 1960–).

DA: Matthew Arnold, *Discourses in America* (New York, 1924).

LC: *Letters of Matthew Arnold to Arthur Hugh Clough*, ed. Howard Foster Lowry (London and New York, 1932).

LECR: Matthew Arnold, *Last Essays on Church and Religion, in St Paul & Protestantism and Last Essays on Church and Religion*, 2 vols in one (New York, 1833).

NL: *New Letters of TC*, ed. A. Carlyle, 2 vols (London, 1904).

1. R. H. Horne, *A New Spirit of the Age* (London, 1844), II, 270–3, 276. *Dyer*, p. 371, lists the essay as "largely Elizabeth Barrett's composition".

2. George Gilfillan, *A Gallery of Literary Portraits* (Edinburgh, 1845), pp. 124, 134, 136–7. J. B. Mozley, in a review of *Cromwell* in April 1846 (*Essays Historical and Theological* [London, 1878], pp. 229–37), delivered a strong blow against the doctrine of Might and Right, and Carlyle's emphasis on the "grandeval element of Power", "beyond the sphere and limits of morality".

3. *New Zealand Letters of Thomas Arnold the Younger* . . . (Auckland and London, 1967), p. 7.

4. I have explored Arnold's mood in the spring of 1848, and how he differed from both Carlyle and Clough, in "Matthew Arnold and the Nightmare of History", in *Victorian Poetry* (London, 1972). And see *The George Eliot Letters*, ed. Gordon S. Haight (New Haven, 1954), I, 252–3.

5. See *Life*, III, 437. The articles are collected in *Rescued Essays of TC*, ed. Percy Newberry (London, 1892).

6. In "Arnold and Carlyle", *PMLA*, 79 (March 1964), 104–5, I puzzled over the apparently sharp change in Arnold's views between March 1848 and September 1849. The evidence presented here suggests that the later view was long preparing in the minds of Carlyle's acquaintances, and that Arnold's mood of March 1848 was one of only temporary elation.

7. James Elliot Cabot, *A Memoir of Ralph Waldo Emerson* (Boston and New York, 1899), II, 530–1.

8. And so on through suppression of freedom of the press and "stringent government". See "Carlyle", in *The Complete Works of Ralph Waldo Emerson* (Boston and New York, 1883, 1904), X, 491–2; written in 1881, but incorporating a letter written shortly after the 1848 visit.

9. See Mill, in the *Examiner*, 13 May 1848, p. 107; and *Letters of Edward Fitzgerald* (London, 1910), I, 239, 4 May 1848. After listening to Carlyle dismiss the notion of immortality in Tennyson's presence, in May 1846, Fitzgerald reported: "Carlyle gets more wild, savage and unreasonable every day; and I do believe will turn mad." Wilson, *Carlyle*, III, 325–7. Tennyson, a good friend of Carlyle's, told Elizabeth Rundle in 1848: "You would like him for one day, but then get tired

of him; so vehement and destructive." See Sir Charles Tennyson, *Alfred Tennyson* (New York, 1949), p. 231.

10. Cited in Katherine Chorley, *Arthur Hugh Clough: The Uncommitted Mind* (Oxford, 1962), p. 132. In some versions, "the wilderness".

11. *The Nemesis of Faith*, ed. Moncure D. Conway (London, 1903), p. 23. For Carlyle's amusing reaction to the book ("a wretched mortal's vomiting up all his interior crudities, dubitations, and spiritual, agonising bellyaches, into the view of the public, and howling tragically") see *NL*, II, 59.

12. Ellis Yarnall, *Wordsworth and the Coleridges* (New York, 1899), p. 253. Forster became Matthew Arnold's brother-in-law in the summer of 1850.

13. See Mill's article, signed "D", in *Fraser's*, 41 (Jan. 1850), 25–31; and Edward Alexander, "Mill's Marginal Notes on Carlyle's 'Hudson's Statue' ", *ELN*, 7 (December, 1969), 120–3. David Masson, in the *North British Review* (Nov. 1850), exactly caught the gathering mood: "For some years . . . a reaction has been in process against Mr Carlyle and his doctrines—a reaction, the elements of which were in existence before, but have only recently come together and assumed something like declared organization." See *TC, The Critical Heritage*, ed. J. P. Seigel (London, 1971), item 28, pp. 335–6.

14. See Mill's *Autobiography and Other Writings*, ed. Jack Stillinger (Boston, 1969), pp. 105–6; *Essays of George Eliot*, ed. Thomas Pinney (London, 1968), pp. 212–5; Leonard Huxley, *Life and Letters of Thomas Henry Huxley* (London and New York, 1903), I, 318, II, 172; Leslie Stephen, "Carlyle's Ethics", in *Hours in a Library* (London, 1899), III, 305, and *Some Early Impressions* (London, 1924), pp. 53–4, 105–9—the last explaining why undergraduates in the fifties turned for religious guidance from Carlyle to Maurice. As Stephen said in 1881 (Seigel, p. 485), "The character had a power quite independent of the special doctrines asserted."

15. The best account of both the personal and the public reasons for the tone of the *Pamphlets* is given in Chapters I and II of Evan A. Reiff's 1937 Iowa Dissertation, "Studies in Carlyle's *Latter-Day Pamphlets*".

16. The hostile William Sewell, in the *Quarterly* (Sept. 1840), had found "no profession of a definite Christianity" in Carlyle, and instead "a new profession of Pantheism". The equally High Church William Thomson, in the *Christian Remembrancer* (Aug. 1843), accused Carlyle of "an infidelity that dares not speak out", and says of *Heroes*, "*It is not a Christian Book.*" See Seigel, items 11 and 13. Kathleen Tillotson, in "Matthew Arnold and Carlyle" (*Mid-Victorian Studies* [London, 1965], p. 225 and n.), cites a phrase from the *British Quarterly Review*, 10 (Aug. 1849), 1–45, acknowledging Carlyle's standing as a critic, and by calling the article "strikingly representative of the contemporary view of Carlyle", implies that the article is favourable to Carlyle. In fact, with the exception of one paragraph from which she quotes (p. 42), the article is an elaborate attack on Carlyle's "onesidedness and exaggera-

ation" in all matters, and especially the "mischief" his religious views have done. In her fascinating study, *Novels of the Eighteen-Forties* (London, 1956), p. 152, Mrs Tillotson claims that, so pervasive was Carlyle's influence in the forties that, "even when such acceptance was shaken by *Latter-Day Pamphlets* at the end of the decade, Carlyle's power over men's minds did not wane". And citing Saintsbury (*Corrected Impressions*, 1895), misleadingly in my judgment, she declares, "Only towards the close of the century did it become usual to measure Carlyle by the content of his teaching. . . ." As the evidence of the present article suggests, her general view of the history of Carlyle's "influence" and reputation at mid-century requires numerous and careful qualifications.

17. On 26 Jan. 1850, early in the writing of the *Pamphlets*, Carlyle wrote (*NL*, II, 86–7): "All the twaddling *sects* of the country, from Swedenborgians to Jesuits, have for the last ten years been laying claim to 'T. Carlyle,' each for itself; and now they will find that the said 'T.' belongs to a sect of his own, which is worthy of instant damnation."

18. G. Gilfillan, *A Third Gallery of Portraits* (Edinburgh, 1854), pp. 313–27; originally in *Eclectic Review*, 7 (Nov. 1851), 717–29. The same assessment of Carlyle's total detachment from Christianity, even an "antichristian" spirit, was made by John Tulloch (*North British Review*, Feb. 1852), and the High Church *Christian Observer and Advocate* (April 1852); see Seigel, items 33 and 34.

19. "Personal Influence on Present Theology", in *Essays, Reviews and Addresses* (London, 1890), I, 266. No one seems to have made anything of Kingsley's remarkable letter of 5 April 1857, disclaiming adherence to Carlyle's "theology or quasi-theology", and declaring his "eternities" and "abysses" to be nothing to him but "clouds and wind put in the place of a personal God": see J. H. Rigg, *Modern Anglican Theology*, 1st ed. 1859 (3rd ed. London, Wesleyan Conference Office, 1880), p. 391, see also pp. 4–6, 116, 381–2, 414. Kingsley's three letters to Rigg—printed as two and with significant omissions—occur in *Charles Kingsley, His Letters and Memories of His Life*, ed. by His Wife, 2nd ed. (London, 1877), II, 22–3; the letters were further shortened, or even deleted, in later abridgements. In Nov. 1856 Kingsley expressed his wrath and disgust with Carlyle's "present phase, moral & intellectual"—though he later resumed friendly relations. See R. B. Martin, *The Dust of Combat, A Life of Charles Kingsley* (London, 1959), pp. 198–9.

20. *Reminiscences* (Froude), p. 449.

21. *Mixed Essays and Irish Essays and Others* (New York, 1904), p. 33.

22. George Brimley, "Carlyle's Life of Sterling", in *Essays* (1st ed. 1858; 3rd ed., London, 1882), pp. 247–9. Originally in *Spectator*, 24 (25 Oct. 1851), 1023–4.

23. See G. Kitson Clark, *The Making of Victorian England* (New York, 1967), p. 32.

24. Froude is an exception only in becoming an open "disciple" of Carlyle's. What his rationalistic Protestantism owes to Carlyle, apart from the notion of the Bible of History, is a different question, not much illuminated in W. H. Dunn, *James Anthony Froude, A Biography* (Oxford, 1961) I, 72–4, 97, 111–12, 201–2. J. C. Shairp, an unduly neglected minor critic, was to become Professor of Poetry at Oxford (1877–85). His withdrawal from Carlyle can be gathered from W. A. Knight, *Principal Shairp and His Friends* (London, 1888). Just what of Carlyle's message Clough retained after the forties needs further clarification. The fullest discussion is in Michael Timko, *Innocent Victorians* (Athens, Ohio, 1966).

25. R. B. Lowe, "Two Arnold Letters", *MP*, 52 (May 1855), 264; and *LC*, p. 151.

26. See nn. 6 and 16.

27. *Nineteenth Century Studies: Coleridge to Matthew Arnold* (London, 1955), p. 113.

28. "Mr Matthew Arnold's New Religion of the Bible", *Contemporary Review*, 21 (May 1873), 850–1.

29. *Essays on Some of the Modern Guides to English Thought in Matters of Faith* (London and New York, 1888), pp. 131–3.

30. "Progress", a poem of the early fifties, implies respect for some permanent relevance in "the old faiths" and a contempt for "the pride of life" of those moderns who are indifferent to "the fire within" and the need to *"be born again"*.

31. Not until Froude's *Life* appeared in the eighties would Arnold have been able to see even fragments of "Spiritual Optics", written in Nov. 1852, Carlyle's final and unsuccessful attempt to clarify his natural supernaturalism. The complete text is for the first time presented in Murray Baumgarten, "Carlyle and 'Spiritual Optics'", *VS*, 11 (June 1968,) 503–22. In the "overturning" of the spiritual world, involving a new series of divineness "in man himself", "nothing that was divine, sublime, demonic, beautiful, or terrible is the least abolished for us". The ancient Jews were essentially right about Godhood, Providence, Judgment Day, the Eternal Soul of Right—even if they misattributed this scheme to the 'Great Jehovah and Creator" (Baumgarten, pp. 514, 516, 517). Unfortunately, Baumgarten treats the MS as a problem in rhetoric, without reference to its substance or significance, and thus fails to note that most of Carlyle's position here would have been evident to the alert reader of Carlyle's published prose of the period.

32. "The Mystical Element in Carlyle (1827–1834)", *MP*, 29 (May 1932), p. 463.

33. *Carlyle and German Thought, 1819–1834* (New Haven, 1934), pp. 235–7.

34. See Harrold, *Carlyle and German Thought*, p. 336: ". . . he never parted wholly from some of the thought-forms of dogmatic Christianity: he never made the 'exodus from Houndsditch.' Though the author of *Sartor Resartus*, he never adequately re-tailored his convictions. His failure to do so contributed one of the major elements in the 'Victorian compromise.'"

150

35. *CPW*, III, 301. See my *Hebrew and Hellene in Victorian England: Newman, Arnold, and Pater* (Austin, 1969), p. 172.

36. The pilgrimage Carlyle outlines is to be done in "darkness" and in "the raging gulf-currents": "Some arrive; a glorious few: many must be lost,—go down upon the floating wreck which they took for land" (*JS*, pp. 96–7). Is there a hint of this in the portrait of "the pale master" on the "spar-strewn deck" struck by the "tempest" in "A Summer Night" (published 1852)?

> And the sterner comes the roar
> Of sea and wind, and through the deepening gloom
> Fainter and fainter wreck and helmsman loom,
> And he too disappears, and comes no more.
>
> (Lines 70–3).

Or a hint of the pilgrimage in "Rugby Chapel": "Friends, who set forth at our side, / Falter, are lost in the storm. / We, we only are left!" (Lines 102–4, and see 117–8)?

37. "The Persistence of Carlyle's 'Everlasting Yea'", *MP*, 54 (Feb. 1957), 196.

38. Cited in *The Poems of Matthew Arnold*, ed. Kenneth Allott (London, 1965), p. 262.

39. Even in the late forties Carlyle knew that the Exodus, "alas! is *impossible* as yet, tho it is the gist of all writings and wise books, I sometimes think—the goal to be wisely aimed at as the first for all of us. . . . But they that come out hitherto come in a state of brutal nakedness, scandalous mutation; and impartial bystanders say sorrowfully, 'Return rather, it is even better to return.'" Wilson, *Carlyle*, III, 409. Also, as Francis Espinasse reports (*Literary Recollections and Sketches* [London, 1893], p. 196), "in spite of all the harsh things that he wrote concerning the creed of orthodoxy, he recognised its hold on human nature, and said to me once, 'it will be a long time before they give it up'".

40. See *PMLA*, 79 (1964), 126–7.

41. C. B. Tinker and H. F. Lowry, *The Poetry of Matthew Arnold: A Commentary* (London, 1940), p. 300. All quotations of Arnold's poetry are from *The Poetical Works of Matthew Arnold*, ed. C. B. Tinker and H. F. Lowry (London, 1950).

42. The shift in Arnold's poetry and poetics is summarized with admirable lucidity by K. Allott, in "A Background for 'Empedocles on Etna'", *Essays and Studies*, NS 21 (1968), 80–100.

43. Good comments on the dialectic of the two books are given by William Blackburn, in "Carlyle and the Composition of *The Life of John Sterling*", *SP*, 44 (October 1947), 672–87. That Sterling's religious concerns continued strong to the end of his life is evident in Anne Kimball Tuell's excellent *John Sterling: A Representative Victorian* (New York, 1941). Though in my judgment he exaggerates in reading *Sterling*

as a "complete reversal" of the premises of *Sartor* and in totally "interiorizing" Carlyle's religious position in the book, Albert LaValley, *Carlyle and the Idea of the Modern* (New Haven and London, 1968), chapter 6, gives the book the most brilliant and searching treatment it has ever received.

44. The best account of Arnold's religious position and its sources is given in William Robbins's *The Ethical Idealism of Matthew Arnold* (London, 1959). His passing references to Carlyle (pp. 58, 123, 167) suggest no direct influence, only a general feeling for "the moral purposiveness of life".

45. Harrold, *Sartor*, p. 307. That Carlyle did not include his own evasive reply of June 4 (now in *Letters of TC to John Stuart Mill, John Sterling and Robert Browning*, ed. A. Carlyle [London, 1923], pp. 191–4) is indicative of his radical mood in 1851.

46. See Walter E. Houghton, "The Rhetoric of T. H. Huxley", *Univ. of Toronto Quarterly*, 18 (January 1949), 159–75.

47. For a fascinating discussion of Coleridge's inability (one I think he shared with Carlyle and Arnold) to relinquish either the "I am" of orthodox Christianity or the "it is" of Spinoza, see Thomas MacFarlane, *Coleridge and the Pantheist Tradition* (Oxford, 1969).

48. Arnold would have approved the sentence in Carlyle's reply to Sterling in June 1835: " 'Personal,' 'impersonal,' One, Three, what meaning can any mortal (after all) attach to them in reference to such an object?" (*Letters of TC*, p. 193).

49. See Carlyle to Tennyson in 1846: Wilson, *Carlyle*, III, 325–7; *CPW*, V, 171; VI, 232, 291, 403–4.

50. See the parallel passages on floating iron brought together by R. H. Super, in *The Time Spirit of Matthew Arnold* (Ann Arbor, 1970), pp. 70–1.

51. If Arnold read the letters of Sterling to his cousin William Coningham, first published in 1848, he saw a more "Christian" variant of the Carlylean discrimination predictive of his own later tone and vocabulary. In *Twelve Letters* (2nd ed. London, 1851), p. 14, Sterling contrasts "the moral and devotional side of Christianity" ("full of truth and goodness") with the present creed, and advocates "the combination of lax latitudinarianism as to the history of religion with earnest elevation of faith and feeling as to its eternal ideas". Morse Peckham's discussion of Carlyle's separation of the principle of "belief" from all particular "beliefs" (*Victorian Revolutionaries* [New York, 1970], chapter II) applies largely to Arnold, though Arnold saw more "permanent" values in the Judaeo-Christian experience.

52. See Arnold's scorn for reconstructed "religions of the future": *CPW*, III, 279–80.

53. *LECR*, p. 327; and "A Comment on Christmas", *Contemporary Review*, 47 (April, 1885), 472. John Holloway is suggestive on the difference in tone, though he underplays the seriousness and even danger of Arnold's later views: "All the apocalyptic quality of Carlyle's historical deter-

minism is gone; the trend of events is governed not by some ever-ready and apocalyptic hand, but by a gentle Platonic harmony between virtue, reason, and reality. The course of history is not grand, simple and mysterious, but neat and orderly, now one thing and now another, according to time and place." *The Victorian Sage* (1953; rpt. Hamden, Conn., 1962), p. 205.

54. *Essays in Criticism, Second Series* (London, 1896), p. 3. The link was mentioned in passing by Mrs Tillotson (*Mid-Victorian Studies*), p. 230; I have touched on the same idea in *PMLA*, 79, 117n., where I failed to note her earlier raising of the issue. The topic has received its most detailed treatment in Lawrence J. Starzyk, "Arnold and Carlyle" (*Criticism*, 12 [Fall, 1970], 281–300), which errs in my judgment by simplifying and overstating the identification of the two realms, especially in Carlyle. I have pursued the theme in "The Future of Poetry: A Context for Arnold and Carlyle", forthcoming in a Festschrift for Professor C. R. Sanders, ed. J. Clubbe (Duke Univ. Press).

55. See *CPW*, VI, 390–2; "Numbers", *DA*, pp. 49–62; "A Comment on Christmas", p. 470. Tennyson's "Locksley Hall Sixty Years After", with its "troughs of Zolaism", came later, in 1886.

56. From *The Twilight of the Gods: The Complete Works of Friedrich Nietzsche*, ed. Oscar Levy (Edinburgh, 1909–13), XVI, 70; Willey, p. 113. The best balanced modern presentation of Carlyle's theism can be found in the final chapter of G. B. Tennyson's *"Sartor" Called "Resartus"* (Princeton, 1965). I agree that Carlyle's conversion was not mere "glorification of his ego" (p. 325) and that in an important sense "his orientation remained basically Christian", but Tennyson tends to pull Carlyle to a more traditional position than the evidence warrants, even in the matter of the immortality of the soul (p. 328). On the imaginative ambience of Carlyle's theology, as well as his pride and contempt for ordinary mortals, R. H. Hutton, *Modern Guides* (n. 30, above), chapter I, remains of great value.

57. See A. O. J. Cockshut, *The Unbelievers: English Agnostic Thought, 1840–1890* (London, 1964), p. 133: "Carlyle valued unhappiness, because it seemed to show that *we don't fit*. It was better, he thought, to be a torn and bleeding animal body doomed to destruction between two wheels. Then, at least, one was alive."

58. *CPW*, VI, 295, 310, 299. And see "A Comment on Christmas", p. 472, where the annulment of self is made the condition of a broader "happiness in the common good".

59. See Harrold, "The Mystical Element" (n. 33, above), p. 463: "His 'purgation' amounted only to a Calvinistic rejection of worldly ease, and his 'illumination' never went further than 'a flash of rudimentary vision' into the 'otherness of natural things'. . . ." The long and complex process of Carlyle's "conversion" is studied in Carlisle Moore, "*Sartor Resartus* and the Problem of Carlyle's Conversion", *PMLA*, 70 (Sep. 1955), 662–81.

60. Willey, p. 115. C. R. Sanders, "The Question of Carlyle's 'Conversion' ",

Victorian Newsletter, No. 10 (Autumn 1956), p. 11, probably too strongly, places Carlyle's conversion in "a rebellious spirit and a determination to emancipate himself from all that would shackle his own ego". See also Cockshut, *The Unbelievers*, p. 135.

61. *Literary Recollections* (n. 39, above), pp. 196–7.

62. James Martineau saw some of this in 1856. Carlyle's rejection of "reflective thought", he says, is a rejection of "inwardness", and a "tragic paradox", springing "from a deep sense of the hatefulness of self-worship, and the barrenness of mere self-formation" (*Essays, Reviews and Addresses*, I, 269–70). And yet I agree with Mrs Tillotson (*Mid-Victorian Studies*, p. 238) that the fundamental image and point of Arnold's "The Buried Life" (published 1852) may have a source in Carlyle's words: "Of our Thinking, we might say, it is but the mere upper surface that we shape into articulate Thoughts;—underneath the region of argument and conscious discourse, lies the region of meditation; here, in its quiet mysterious depths, dwells what vital force is in us" (*CME*, XVIII, 4–5).

63. Arnold's rich contrast of the "voluntary, rational, and human world, of righteousness, moral choice, effort" and "the necessary, mystical, and divine world, of influence, sympathy, emotion" (*CPW*, III, 36–8) uses terms parallel to Carlyle's but though the second "element" stretches beyond "our own undertanding and will" it too is none the less part of our "consciousness".

7

Latter-Day Pamphlets: The Near Failure of Form and Vision

by JULES P. SEIGEL

Even serious readers of Victorian literature are apt to pass quickly over Carlyle's *Latter-Day Pamphlets*, briefly noting his attacks against the dogmas of progress, sacred nineteenth century institutions and minority groups, noting the aggressive and abusive tone and the seemingly chaotic structure of the work.[1] Often the *Pamphlets* are dismissed and perhaps, in the minds of many sensitive and otherwise sympathetic readers, for good reasons. Coming to the *Latter-Day Pamphlets* after two world wars, and the unbelievable Nazi holocaust, Carlyle's attacks against Jamaican blacks sitting idle, up to their ears in pumpkins, and Irish paupers too lazy to work, weary us. His strident talk of beneficent whips and leather along the backs of the unemployed in these times when all forms of individual life seem threatened set us on edge.[2] Yet we have no choice but to agree that the bloom held out by the promises of nineteenth century democracy has wilted, that the dogmas of democracy are upheld only by sacrifices, and that bureaucracy, democracy's offspring, has succeeded at producing as many evils as it has benefits. And Carlyle's criticism of the machinery and methodology of nineteenth century democracy in the *Pamphlets* has a bitter, cutting tone matched by no other prophetic voices of his time.

What actually were the reasons for such vitriolic outbursts, for this fierce and unbalanced work which, as David Masson said, brought the general antipathy towards Carlyle to a crisis and made him "unpopular with at least one half of the kingdom"? One explanation was that the Sage of Chelsea had taken to whisky; another, suggested by William B. Aytoun, was that the work was a product of a "diseased imagination".[3] Yet the *Pamphlets* do not, as Albert J. LaValley has shown, "represent a complete volte-face from his earlier political and social writings. They may be frightening in both what they say and how they say it, but they are still an outgrowth of Carlyle's earlier social writings" (pp. 279–80). One recognizes not only familiar language but also familiar themes: there is the continuing search for heroes, the call for action and not words (the need for silence), the necessity of work and redemption, attacks against the immorality of the economics of the day, against selfish beaverism and huckstering, against the foolishness of parliamentary reform rather than reform of the self, and against the hypocrisy of organized religion. His cutting satire in the *Pamphlets* lays bare evils still recognizable in the modern world, such as consumerism and the special rhetorics—bureaucratic and private—which exert unbelievable control over the people. Everything is, in Carlyle's words, either "Fit for the market; not fit" (p. 181). In his general exposure of the immorality of rhetoric—simply *lying*, as he puts it—he points to the corrosive effects it has in a modern democracy: "Words will not express what mischiefs the misuse of words has done, and is doing, in these heavy laden generations"[4] (p. 181). These familiar Carlylisms are expressed in his harshest and most direct style.

Yet his vision is intensified and his anxiety heightened. The language is violent as Carlyle agitates, urges and threatens. His voice becomes one of desperation as he strikes out trying to put down simultaneously all his disjointed and painful observations.[5] It is precisely this formlessness, a stylistic neurosis, that characterizes the *Pamphlets*. The familiar themes and images, however unsystematically presented, seem mainly held together by the urgency of the writer's voice, painfully haranguing, relentlessly arguing his readers into accepting his prophetic message. It is obvious that Carlyle's many personae (Jefferson Brick, Crabbe, Prime Minister, Benevolent Man, Future, and others) all have the same voice—authoritative, satirical, and aggressive. His is a sensibility marked by frustration; often grotesque, consistently angry. As George Levine has suggested, Carlyle has "identified himself with his creation, and Carlylese becomes the staple mode of expression at the same time as its sustaining tensions and its implicit faith in the possibilities of this world have broken down".[6]

Levine argues that the earlier works of Carlyle could survive artistic analysis, but he questions whether analysis could do anything for the inartistic *Latter-Day Pamphlets*. For him the *Pamphlets* are triumphs of negativism, unrelieved by the flexibility of the earlier and more obviously coherent works. Levine has noted this shift: "A style whose essence is the expression of a complicated vision of a dualistic universe and of the constant movement of all things in time from one pole to the other now becomes the vehicle for a proliferating and grotesque vision of evil in the world and of a diminishing and increasingly abstract vision of the ideals necessary to banish that evil" (p. 122). What has happened is that the "vision of the world is unrelievedly bleak and disillusioned. . . . Carlyle . . . is responding wildly and incoherently—and ineffectually—to all the aspects of his society which repel him" (pp 122–3). Fragmentation and splintering replace a sustained artistic and structural tension.

Carlyle's earlier fears of democracy were intensified by the outbreak of the revolutions of 1848, harbingers of inevitable democracy. These fears were then exaggerated by his growing awareness of the misery of Ireland. Together they represented the most fearful elements of an expanding democracy—an uncontrolled population without work, without direction, bereft of leadership, lost in social chaos and anarchy. It was the confusion and complexity of democracy which Carlyle now envisioned as a reality. Its great convulsions would inevitably destroy his essential vision of nature as a hierarchical structure—a simplistic and neatly ordered society and universe. To his Calvinistic sensibility democracy was also noisy and dirty—personally obnoxious:

> A world no longer habitable for quiet persons: a world which in these sad days is bursting into street-barricades, and pretty rapidly turning-out its "Honoured Men," as intrusive dogs are turned out, with a kettle tied to their tail. To Kings, Kaisers, Spiritual Papas and Holy Fathers, there is universal "*Apage!* Depart thou; go thou to the — Father of thee!" in a huge world-voice of mob-musketry and sooty execration, uglier than any ever heard before (p. 260).

F

157

The *Latter-Day Pamphlets* register a series of traumatic and fearful responses to a modern democratic culture. All the corollaries of democracy—decision by universal ballot, in particular, never a true way of electing the "best"—the greater distribution of "wealth", and the doctrines of progress, all become magnified and grotesquely distorted by an imagination which is able on the one hand to see the disease and corruption inherent in the political and economic systems themselves, but, on the other, is unable to dissociate that which it created itself from its own particular disoriented vision.

Carlyle's anxiety about Ireland was intensified by his visit there during July and August of 1849. Yet even before this he was well aware of the sick and starving Irish immigrants crowding their way into the industrial centres of Great Britain, where the population was already rising at an extraordinary rate. It is estimated that during these years "about a million of the Irish died and about a million fled overseas".[7] Carlyle clearly foresaw that such changes needed government, and that there were few countries like the United States, which at the present time "can do *without* governing,—every man being at least able to live, and move-off into the wilderness, let Congress jargon as it will . . . with mud soil enough and fierce sun enough in the Mississippi Valley alone to grow Indian corn for all the extant Posterity of Adam at this time;—what other country ever stood in such a case?" (p. 227). Neither crowded England nor starving Ireland was in such an enviable condition. Carlyle, in this mood of heightened anxiety, could practically hear the firing of muskets along Cheyne Row. His response was grim, calling for regimentation, to bring the "Captainless under due captaincy" (p. 36).

His aggressive stance in the face of advancing democracy and growing poverty, disease, and population derives more from his fear of the multiple unknowns inherent in these social phenomena than from any particular plan to stem the movements; though Carlyle does offer such concrete proposals in the *Latter-Day Pamphlets* as organized work forces or agricultural regiments to reclaim waste lands. Yet the *Pamphlets* are mainly his painfully-recorded responses; an answer to the crisis, and a search for some sort of artistic form to his response. In a strange way, Carlyle is both the prophet and the prophecy.

As early as two full years before the publication of the first pamphlet, Carlyle was struggling to embody his scattered and troubled thoughts into some kind of form. In a letter to his mother (26 Jan. 1848) he writes that as

> soon as my cold is quite gone, I have one or two bits of jobs that I must fall to. Not of much moment; but they will keep me going; a *big* job lies deep in the background, not yet shaped into any form, but likely to be heavy enough when it comes! (NLS).

The big job which would not shape itself was a source of anguish for Carlyle throughout 1848, 1849, and into much of 1850, as shown by many painful references in his letters. Froude tells us that Carlyle's journal contains virtually nothing for the four years preceding the February 1848 revolutions on the continent. But there was a flurry of activity early that February when Carlyle notes "a scheme of books" to be done: "Exodus from Houndsditch", "Ireland: Spiritual Sketches", "The Scavenger Age", and "Life of John Sterling". Only the life of Sterling made its way into a book.[8] It was, then, the revolutions of 24 February on the continent, and particularly in Paris, that began to harden Carlyle's thinking. His journal for 5 March announces a new scheme, the germ of the *Latter-Day Pamphlets*.

> Scheme of volume: *Democracy*. What one might have to say on it? (1) Inevitable now in all countries: regarded vulgarly as *the* solution. Reason why it cannot be so; something farther and ultimate. (2) Terrible disadvantage of the Talking Necessity; much to be said here. What this comes from. Properly an insincere character of mind. (3) Follows *deducible* out of that! *Howardism*. Regard every Abolition Principle man as your enemy, ye reformers. Let them insist not that punishment be abolished, but that it fall on the right heads. (4) *Fictions*, under which head come Cants, Phantasms, alas! Law, Gospel, Royalty itself. (5) Labour question. Necessity of government. Notion of voting to all is delirium. Only the vote of the wise is called for, an advantage ever to the voter himself. Rapid and inevitable progress of anarchy. Want of bearing *rule* in all private departments of life. Melancholy remedy: "Change as often as you like." (6) Though men insincere, not all equally so. A great choice. How to know a sincere man. Be sincere yourself. Career open to talent. This actually is the conclusion of the whole matter.
>
> Six things. It would make a volume. Shall I begin it? I am sick, lazy, and dispirited.[9]

159

Soon after (26 Mar.) Carlyle confesses to his sister Jean that he is thinking seriously of "some kind of Book,—poor wretch!—but the times with me too are not without their difficulties!" (NLS).

The revolutions held Carlyle's attention fast during these weeks. In a letter to Thomas Erskine (24 Mar. 1848), he sees them as a "spectacle of history", as "this immense explosion of Democracy", and as a time to be joyful yet a time for sadness. There is joy inasmuch as mortals "long towards justice and veracity", but sadness that "all the world, in its protest against False Government should find no remedy but that of rushing into No Government or anarchy (kinglessness)", which Carlyle takes this "republican universal suffragism to inevitably be". For Carlyle, violence is an almost inevitable corollary of universal democracy. In the same letter he remarks that an "abundance of *fighting* (probably enough in all kinds) one does see in store for them; and long years and generations of weltering confusion, miserable to contemplate, before anything can be *settled* again. Hardly since the invasion of the wild Teutons and wreck of the old Roman Empire has there been so strange a Europe, all turned topsy turvey, as we now see. What was at the top has come or is rapidly coming to the *bottom*, where indeed, such was its intrinsic quality, it deserved this long while past to be."[10] But the stable hierarchical order of Carlyle's reality is being threatened. The fearful posture of this letter foreshadows the familiar, anxious tone of the *Latter-Day Pamphlets*.

Because he was deeply disturbed, his whole psychological orientation threatened, he seems continually to refer to his desire to speak out and to write, but finds that his "heart is as if half-dead, and has no wish to speak any more, but to lie *silent*, if so might be, till it sank into the Divine silence, and were then at rest. Courage, however!"[11] Three days later, and after referring to a pleasant dinner with Sir Robert Peel, Carlyle once again records in his journal his response to the violence of the revolutions:

N.B.—This night with Peel was the night in which Berlin city executed its last terrible battle (19th of March to Sunday Morning the 20th, five o'clock). While we sate there the streets of Berlin were all blazing with grapeshot and the war of enraged men. What is to become of all that? I have a book to write about it. Alas![12]

160

So, too, his journal entry for 5 April 1848 shows the unsettling combination of the times weighing heavily upon him and his anguishing over some kind of literary commentary: "The future for all countries fills me with a kind of horror. I have been scribbling, scribble, scribble—alas! it will be long before that makes a book. Persist however."[13]

Frustrated at his inability to decide what shape his response should take, Carlyle tried his hand at a series of articles.[14] They were troublesome to him, and he was well aware of the public outcry they would arouse. Yet he still wished to write a book as he says in his letter to his mother:

> I have a good many "Articles" still lying in me; and indeed I have been thinking of late seriously, whether I should not set up some little bit *Paper* of my own, and publish them there. But that is a little precarious . . . and I do not like it much. On the other hand, there is no Newspaper that can stand my articles; no *single* Newspaper that they would not blow the bottom out of in a short while! For example, the *Examiner* should have had all these three articles put together as one: but then poor little Lord John Russell is a pet of theirs, and I could not put them on doing such a thing; so had to cut the Articles in *three*. . . . At most, if nothing else will do, I can write the things in a *Book*; and really that is perhaps the *best* way, in other respects too, after all. (19 May 1848, NLS).

A year later (writing to his sister, 18 June 1849) he is still distressed over his inability to execute some singular composition and complains that all things have been "lying in a *fallow*, ill-conducted, unprofitable and ungainly state with me for one, which has impeded the discharge of a great many duties! My book has stood at a dead-lock, this long while. . . ." He complains further that his "*inner-man* (meaning both soul and *stomach* by that term) has been in a bad way" (NLS). It is interesting to see that even during the actual writing of the *Pamphlets*, he was still searching for the book. To his mother, he writes (11 May 1850):

> My last Pamphlet got on very badly,—there was so much bustling &c and my own bad nerves and liver were so put about. I do not yet know for certain how many more I shall have to write. I think sometimes of making out the dozen; but *ten* seem likelier for the present; nay something (a *cowardly* something) whispers occasionally. "If the thing grow *too* hot, you may finish with *eight*," which

is only one more now! What I have farther to say must grow into a *Book* in that case. But I think *ten* is the likelier. We must try to do and choose what is wisest for us! (NLS).

Yet Carlyle had lost his former hope of regeneration of the self in the face of social fragmentation. Throughout the *Pamphlets* there are points where Carlyle reasserts his earlier faith, but they appear sporadically and outside the consistent tone of accusation. The follies of democratic bureaucracy he dwells on continually irritated him. Prompted by a vision of a diseased society, Carlyle's stance becomes largely responsive and captious rather than synthetic and creative. The obnoxious elements he sees in society grate sharply on his senses, as shown by the imagery of excrement and slime. There is also recurring imagery of economics ("spiritual banknotes", "gold bullion of human culture", "nature keeps silently a most exact Savings-Bank") which jostles against imagery of technology (of railroad miracles: "The distances of London to Aberdeen, to Ostend, to Vienna, are still infinitely inadequate to me! Will you teach me the winged flight through Immensity, up to the Throne dark with excess of bright!" (p. 277)). Every image is charged with the sense of a newly-emerging society, and with its overwhelming presence.

Carlyle found himself faced with a problem of epic dimension; its scope was nothing less than the known world; and he felt himself called upon to prophesy about it passionately. It was a subject of the immediate present, a subject yet of cosmic proportion, and a subject beyond the scope of biography or past history—both genres already familiar to Carlyle. In a way he was attempting to write a latter-day epic, but given his anxiety during these months and his anger and confusion, what finally emerges is a series of long pamphlets which participate in several literary styles, prophetic, satiric, and epic. Most obvious in tone is the voice of the Biblical prophet, condemning and exhorting.[15] This voice, however, fuses with that of the satirist, viciously and brutally laying bare to the bone with directness and often times with embarrassing incisiveness. It is a voice which may be compared to that of Eldridge Cleaver's in *Soul on Ice*, a work which, like the *Pamphlets*, engages in angry satire and the most acute name calling.[16]

Yet, still interesting, in certain ways, is the use Carlyle makes

162

of the traditional epic. The *Pamphlets* are clearly a continuation of the epic theme of democracy which was so brilliantly and coherently handled in *The French Revolution*.[17] As most readers notice there seems more coherence in the *Pamphlets* in terms of texture (imagery and theme) and tone than there is in terms of any formal structure, such as that of the epic. Yet there is also an attempt, either consciously or unconsciously, to superimpose, if nothing else, the sense of being epic. It may even be of significance that Carlyle made it clear that he wanted to write twelve pamphlets, one for each month of the year, but also the number of books that one finds in such secondary epics as the *Aeneid* and *Paradise Lost*.[18]

Carlyle's personae have long, set speeches resembling those of the epic, and yet they are all in the same voice—that of Carlyle himself. The *Pamphlets*, in imagery and tone, collectively resemble a descent into hell itself, though it is the hell of a democratically-oriented society. It is both reminiscent of the epic and yet almost a burlesque, for if the times had called for a mythic hero of the calibre of Hercules, his modern counterpart has to be Robert Peel. Carlyle's language, too, is not like the high style of the epic; rather it is usually a satiric, biting, and oracular tone. Yet one might say that Carlyle's audience is at one moment invited to feel awe by the grim rehearsal of what he sees as the universal moral and social decadence of the present, and then to respond to his ridicule. Finally, in the broad political sweep of the *Pamphlets*, he is not unlike a modern epicist.

> The subject of all epic poetry might thus be said to be politics, but a politics not limited to society, a politics embracing the natural and the fabulous worlds, embracing even the moral or spiritual worlds they sometimes shadow forth, and involving ultimately the divine. The implications expand to suggest, if not frankly to assert, a cosmic power struggle.[19]

In the opening lines of *Paradise Lost*, Milton announces the theme of his epic through the classic epic question and answer:

> Say first, for Heav'n hides nothing from thy view,
> Nor the deep Tract of Hell, say first what cause
> Mov'd our Grand Parents in that happy State,
> Favour'd of Heav'n so highly, to fall off

From their Creator, and transgress his Will
For one restraint, Lords of the World besides?
Who first seduc'd them to that fowl revolt?
Th' infernal Serpent; he it was, whose guile, . . . (I, 27–34)

In the first *Pamphlet* Carlyle rhetorically asks his modern epic question, indeed more prosaically, but clearly—in form and tone —similar:

What *is* Democracy; this huge inevitable Product of the Destinies, which is everywhere the portion of our Europe in these latter days? There lies the question for us. Whence comes it, this universal big black Democracy; whither tends it; what is the meaning of it? A meaning it must have, or it would not be here. If we can find the right meaning of it, we may, wisely submitting or wisely resisting and controlling, still hope to live in the midst of it; if we cannot find the right meaning, if we find only the wrong meaning or no meaning in it, to live will not be possible! (pp. 9–10).

For Milton the symbolic act of man's disobedience brought death to man and the loss of Eden. It is a personal sin which each man must subdue in order to regain paradise and overcome a hell which in Christian terms is individualized. So, too, Carlyle sees Democracy as demonic, symbolic of potential death, a force which once unleashed, it will "behove us to solve or die" (p. 9). He presents a myth of social degradation and alienation, and not chiefly religious alienation and personal death as in *Sartor*. He appeals for heroes:

Who will begin the long steep journey with us; who of living statesmen will snatch the standard, and say, like a hero on the forlorn-hope for his country, Forward! Or is there none; no one that can and dare? And our lot too, then, is Anarchy by barricade or ballot-box, and Social Death?—We will not think so (p. 169).

Societal death is seen throughout in the images of asphyxiation, the absence of lungs; his is a culture, as Carlyle puts it, slowly wheezing to death.

Carlyle's prophesying of a political apocalypse is also somewhat epical. The *Latter-Day Pamphlets* contain a sense of inevitable change; ultimate chaos seems always at hand. The whole world— from England, and the continent, to America—is on the brink of disaster. As Thomas Greene notes, the epic poet must attempt to "clear away an area he can apprehend, if not dominate, and commonly this area expands to fill the epic universe, to cover the known world and reach heaven and hell. Epic characteristically refuses to be hemmed in, in time as well as space; it raids the unknown and colonizes it. It is the imagination's manifesto, proclaiming the range of its grasp, or else it is the dream of the will, indulging its fantasies of power" (p. 10).

Although, then, there is no tightly structured development throughout the pages of the *Latter-Day Pamphlets* of the epic theme of Democracy, its presence is everywhere, affecting the actions of all the characters and all the institutions. Democracy has arrived and has been announced to the world in message after message; it is as if "all the populations of the world were rising or had risen into incendiary madness" (p. 153). In another metaphor Democracy is seen as some vital force rising from the bowels of the earth and forcing itself upon the political and social realities of the mid-nineteenth century world. Or, again, it is a bottomless volcano or "universal powder-mine of most inflammable mutinous chaotic elements, separated from us by a thin earth rind" (p. 7) and is fanned into anarchy by "students, young men of letters, advocates, editors, hot inexperienced enthusiasts, or fierce and justly bankrupt desperadoes" (p. 7).[20] Democracy is the "grand, alarming, imminent and indisputable Reality" (p. 9) and its problems must be solved or the world will die. No force seems at all able to drive it back to its elemental depths.

Society, indeed the Victorian world, is the scene of a cosmic night battle. Democracy, on the one hand, is a reality and will not retreat, and the laws of nature, on the other hand, are inflexible and hierarchical, as Carlyle sees them. What we have is a confrontation out of which Carlyle, in the overview of the *Latter-Day Pamphlets*, is unable to imagine a resynthesis along the lines of *Sartor Resartus*, *Past and Present*, or, for that matter, *The French Revolution*. This, it seems, is another basic reason that the *Pamphlets* appear so incohesive, disconcerting, and uneven. Carlyle, too, feels himself led towards personal disillusionment and self-destruction. Democracy is the devil, so to speak; it represents the present confusion, the complexity of modern life in confrontation with nature; and the staging area is the whole world:

Alas, on this side of the Atlantic and on that, Democracy, we apprehend, is forever impossible! So much, with certainty of loud astonished contradiction from all manner of men at present, but with sure appeal to the Law of Nature and the ever-abiding Fact, may be suggested and asserted once more. The Universe itself is a Monarchy and Hierarchy; large liberty of "voting" there, all manner of choice, utmost free-will, but with conditions inexorable and immeasurable annexed to every exercise of the same. A most free commonwealth of "voters"; but with Eternal Justice enforced by Almighty Power! (pp. 21–2).

Surely the resolution for Carlyle was not to be found in the ballot boxes which he felt would never be able to replace the natural hierarchy of God's world: the noble will always remain in high places, the ignoble in low:

To raise the Sham-Noblest and solemnly consecrate *him* by whatever method, new-devised, or slavishly adhered to from old wont, this, little as we may regard it, is, in all times and countries, a practical blasphemy, and Nature in no wise will forget it (p. 22).

His continued insistence on the futility of voting indicates the implacability of his position:

Vote it, revote it by overwhelming majorities, by jubilant unveracities or universalities; read it thrice or three hundred times, pass acts of parliament upon it till the statute book can hold no more,—it helps not a whit: The thing is not so, the thing is otherwise than so; and Adam's whole posterity, voting daily on it till the world finish, will not alter it a jot (p. 173).

The theme of the confrontation and the subsequent deadlock between Democracy and nature is reflected in Carlyle's language as well, which, although alluding to primitive animals, to Megatherions and Pythons, and mud-demons, suggests a reversal in the evolutionary process. It is as if civilization is not evolving but devolving into the primeval mud out of which it was bred. Democracy and its anarchical tendencies, its uncontrollability and unruliness, is represented by the "Irish Giant, named of Despair" who is advancing upon London, laying waste the English towns and villages:

I notice him in Piccadilly, blue-visaged, thatched in rags, a blue child on each arm; hunger-driven, wide mouthed, seeking whom he may devour: he, missioned by the just Heavens, too truly and too sadly their 'divine missionary' come at last to *this* authoritative manner, will throw us all into Doubting Castle, I perceive! (p. 94).

The scope of Carlyle's epic theme goes beyond England even to America where he sees the battle *yet* to be fought. There is still time, but Democracy with its attendant horrors will inevitably come. The theme is epical in its limitlessness, prophetic in its tone:

No! America too will have to strain its energies, in quite other fashion than this; to crack its sinews, and all-but break its heart, as the rest of us have had to do, in thousandfold wrestle with the Pythons and mud-demons, before it can become a habitation for the gods. America's battle is yet to fight; and we, sorrowful though nothing doubting, wish her strength for it. New Spiritual Pythons, plenty of them; enormous Megatherions, as ugly as were ever born of mud, loom huge and hideous out of the twilight Future on America; and she will have her own agony, and her own victory, but on other terms than she is yet quite aware of (pp. 20–1).

In terms of imagery the *Latter-Day Pamphlets* are consistently negative, and one might say that Carlyle is describing a true social hell, one which is viewed as near death, and slowly being asphyxiated. Throughout the *Pamphlets*, society is alluded to in classical terms as Stygian deeps, Phlegethon, and the mud of Lethe; yet the hell which emerges is modern. The *Pamphlets* describe a world of chaos, foul odours, vulgarity, filth, ultimate selfishness, characterized by slime, serpents, dung heaps, and finally the pig philosophy. The consciousness of the *Pamphlets* is one of pervasive contempt and disgust.[21] Yet there is some method in Carlyle's characterization of this living hell. What is suggested is a Dantesque vision, beginning with lesser or social evils and descending deeper into hell, to the source of all evil: spiritual evil, that point from which all social disorder emanates. This is symbolized by Jesuitism, the subject of the final pamphlet and the one which Carlyle felt was his best.

In "The Present Time", the first pamphlet, Carlyle circles the perimeter of hell. His descriptions are general and have an epical sweep to them. This is the *Pamphlet* which announces the theme of democracy, the advent of cosmic change. The following

Pamphlets particularize the social hell, the sickness and dehumanizing effects of institutions, and the move through the thin earth rind of "Parliaments" and "Downing Street", to the ultimate source of social corruption—egotism, selfishness—the stomach and the purse—as described in the eighth and last *Pamphlet*, "Jesuitism":

> the Human Species, as it were, unconsciously or consciously, gone all to one Sodality of Jesuitism: who will deliver us from the body of his death! It is in truth like death-in-life; a living criminal (as in the old Roman days) with a *corpse* lashed fast to him (p. 299).

The social institutions attacked throughout the *Pamphlets* are familiar—ineffective philanthropy ("Model Prisons", II); the dehumanizing effect of red tape ("Downing Street", III); mechanical rather than wise leadership ("New Downing Street", IV); hypocrisy of political rhetoric ("Stump Orator", V); uselessness of parliamentary government ("Parliaments", VI); worship of money ("Hudson's Statue", VII), and finally "Jesuitism" (VIII). The inhabitants of this social hell move centripetally from lesser to more serious sins: they range from ineffective bureaucrats such as Felicissimus Zero who gallops his thunder horse in circles and huckstering railroad kings such as George Hudson ("Copper Vishnu of the Scrip Ages") to Ignatius Loyola who inhabits the dead centre.

The centre of Carlyle's hellish vision is dominated by the pig philosophy, a form of metaphorical sensualism. All Carlyle's images of darkness, aggression, and confusion, mud-pythons, dung heaps, beaver intellect, "spiritual Vampires and obscene Nightmares" (p. 163), and the "world-wide jungle of redtape" (p. 87), are attached to this central image of the Pig Philosophy: *Schweinsche Weltansicht*, which, in effect, embraces the universe. The first principle of the Pig Philosophy states: "The Universe, so far as sane conjecture can go, is an immeasurable Swine's trough, consisting of solid and liquid, and of other contrasts and kinds; —especially consisting of attainable and unattainable, the latter in immensely greater quantities for most pigs" (p. 316). Pighood is the physical and mental condition of the world and, objectionable as it may seem, is the dominant image of the *Pamphlets* and the one toward which all others have been moving.

168

The universe, the "Swine's-trough", is a place where aggressive huckstering, the making of money, the Veritable Age of Gold reigns. In it man's duty is to consume ("to diminish the quantity of the unattainable and increase that of the attainable"); Paradise is the "unlimited attainability of Pig-wash; perfect fulfilment of one's wishes;" and justice is getting one's share of the "Swine's-trough" and "not any portion" of mine.[22] One's share is defined as whatever one can "contrive to get without being hanged or sent to the hulks". People become pigs and greedily engage in "consumerism". The system of consuming is, moreover, defended by a corrupt legal system of lawyers ("Servants of God"), and by a hypocritical church which itself is no longer able to distinguish between a heaven and a living hell. Harsh though Carlyle's satire may be, it is successful in magnifying the diseases of a capitalistic economy fostered by a growing democracy.

Seen another way, the world is poisoned, and Ignatius Loyola is the symbol of its having happened (p. 294); the dead world is seen as a "spiritual mummyhood"; the people are now devoted only to "cookery" and to "scrip", to prurient appetites, and to the acceptance of worn-out traditions as truth. The world has been infected by the "deadly virus of lying" and "prussic-acid and chloroform are poor to it" (p. 310). A fatal poison such as hydrocyanic acid or the fumes of chloroform—though actually able to destroy consciousness—are ineffective against the widespread disease of lying. In this same context Carlyle switches the image: "Jesuit chloroform stupefied us all" (p. 310). The human race is now "sunk like steeping flax under the wide-spread fetid Hell-waters,—in all spiritual respects dead, dead; voiceless towards Heaven for centuries back; merely sending up, in the form of mute prayer, such an odour as the angels never smelt before" (p. 311). It is a corrupt and foul world, rotten to the core, and a "detestable devil's poison circulates in the life-blood of mankind; taints with abominable deadly malady all that mankind do. Such a curse never fell on man before" (p. 265). Life is being destroyed:

> We of these late centuries have suffered as the sons of Adam never did before; hebetated, sunk under mountains of torpid leprosy; and studying to persuade ourselves that this is health (p. 312).

It is as if Carlyle has awakened from a dream and now faces the "consciousness of Jesuitism". It lies around him like the "valley of Jehoshaphat, . . . one nightmare wilderness, and wreck of deadmen's bones, this false modern world; and no rapt Ezekiel in prophetic vision imaged to himself things sadder, more horrible and terrible, than the eyes of men, if they *are* awake, may now deliberately see" (p. 313). Jesuitism, then, symbolizes the psychology of the new modern consciousness, now a reality.

There is, moreover, the contemptuous and bitter realization by Carlyle that Christian institutions have failed to embody a true belief for the modern world. They are blind, and their churchmen are pictured by Gathercoal (a "Yankee friend" of his) as apes " 'with their wretched blinking eyes, squatting round a fire which they cannot feed with new wood; which they say will last forever without new wood,—or, alas, which they say is going out forever: it is a sad sight!' " (p. 331). This criticism of Christian institutions is continued in what might loosely be called a modern heroic or epic metaphor. The language is oracular in tone and it is continued by Gathercoal in a passage at the end of the eighth and last pamphlet ("Jesuitism") which structurally balances the long opening set speech by the British Prime Minister at the end of the first pamphlet ("The Present Time"):

> The event at Bethlehem was of the Year One; but all years since that, eighteen hundred of them now, have been contributing new growth to it,—and see, there it stands: the Church! Touching the earth with one small point; springing out of one small seedgrain, rising out therefrom, ever higher, ever broader, high as the Heaven itself, broad till it overshadow the whole visible Heaven and Earth, and no star can be seen but through *it*. From such a seedgrain so has it grown; planted in the reverences and sacred opulences of the soul of mankind; fed continually by all the noblenesses of some forty generations of men. The world-tree of the Nations for so long!
>
> Alas, if its roots are now dead, and it have lost hold of the firm earth, or clear belief of mankind,—what, great as it is, can by possibility become of it? Shaken to and fro, in Jesuitisms, Gorham Controversies, and the storms of inevitable Fate, it must sway hither and thither; nod ever farther from the perpendicular; nod at last too far; and,—sweeping the Eternal Heavens clear of its old brown foliage and multitudinous rooks'-nests,—come to the ground with much confused crashing, and *disclose* the diurnal and nocturnal

Upper Lights again! The dead world-tree will have declared itself
dead. It will lie there an imbroglio of torn boughs and ruined fragments, of bewildered splittings and wide-spread shivers: out of
which the poor inhabitants must make what they can! (pp.
332–3).

The epic "hero" of the *Latter-Day Pamphlets* is Carlyle himself
as he takes on the role of latter-day *Vates* and epicist.[23] His heroic
mood must be seen in the familiar Carlylean context that all
history was epic, that as long as societies remained "simple and
in earnest" they knew unconsciously that their history was "Epic
and Bible, the clouded struggling Image of a God's Presence, the
action of heroes and god inspired men". Furthermore, the noble
intellect who "could disenthral such divine image, and present it
to them clear, unclouded, in visible coherency comprehensible to
human thought, was felt to be a *Vates* and the chief of intellects".
It was not necessary to ask that he write an epic or deliver a
prophecy: "Nature herself compelled him" (p. 323).

It may be said that Carlyle himself was compelled to write the
Pamphlets, and to deliver his prophecy. When he asks rhetorically, "Who are they, gifted from above, that will convert volum-
inous Dryasdust into an Epic and even a Bible?" (p. 326)—one
must feel that Carlyle himself is assuming the role of epic poet
and latter-day prophet. His contempt for the fine arts as they are
shown in the *Pamphlets* rules out his contemporaries. If these are
"Human Arts" at all, Carlyle writes, "where have they been wool-
gathering, these centuries long; wandering literally like creatures
fallen mad!" (p. 326). As Carlyle has it, the fine arts have been
converted into "after-dinner amusements; slave adjunct to the
luxurious appetites" of one "big ugly Nawaub" (p. 328)—which
all Europe has become.

His tone is strained to hoarseness, for if he has a covert "hero"
it is Sir Robert Peel who is seen as the modern Hercules who
must clean the bureaucratic Augean stables of layers of filth, corruption, of dead pedantries and accumulations of jungles of red
tape and administrative droppings. Government, in fact, is a
cesspool:

> Every one may remark what a hope animates the eyes of any
> circle, when it is reported or even confidently asserted, that Sir

171

Robert Peel has in his mind privately resolved to go, one day, into that stable of King Augias, which appals human hearts, so rich is it, high-piled with the droppings of two-hundred years; and Hercules-like to load a thousand night-wagons from it, and turn running water into it, and swash and shovel at it, and never leave it till the antique pavement, and real basis of the matter, show itself clean again! (pp. 91–2).

In another context Peel is called upon to lead England through the present morass, up the "long, steep journey" as if out of hell itself, and "snatch the standard"; and thus become a hero of his country (p. 169).

It would be easy to agree with Northrop Frye that Carlyle's style in general is "tantrum prose", the prose of denunciation, of propaganda, of rhetoric in which "we feel that the author's pen is running away with him . . ." As the prose grows more incoherent, writes Frye, the more it seems to express "emotion apart from or without intellect". It lapses into emotional jargon, consisting of "obsessive repetition of verbal formulas".[24] To a great extent this is true, but a close reading of Carlyle's *Pamphlets* shows that the writer, though angered, still has a certain control over the work. It is in essence the response of an outraged sensibility to modern madness. No reader of the *Pamphlets* can deny that Carlyle has anticipated the terrors of modernism, its nightmarish qualities, its insanity. If the *Pamphlets* are an overreaction, they nevertheless dramatize symbolically the consciousness of one man unable to cope with what he envisioned ultimately as the loneliness, the "restless gnawing ennui" (p. 335) of modern life. His responses were precipitous and spontaneous, angry and brutal, yet almost always conveying the sense of futility, of the loss of hope. Periodically Carlyle reasserted his older, hopeful visions in his direct addresses to the young men[25] of England, but these calls for redemption, for new and dedicated leaders, are lost in the overwhelming rhetorical structure of the work—a work which is unified by a myth of decadence and by a tone of impending crisis of total destruction and with virtually no hope of renovation. The inconclusiveness of Carlyle's vision—since structurally there is no myth of a future regenerated society—reveals the depth of his frustration. The *Pamphlets* are a prophetic warning, an ugly result of what has happened to one psychology when confronted with the new, the transitional, the relatively unknown:

> To the primitive man, whether he looked at moral rule, or even at physical fact, there was nothing not divine. Flame was the God Loki, etc.; this visible Universe was wholly the vesture of an Invisible Infinite; every event that occurred in it a symbol of the immediate presence of God. Which it intrinsically *is*, and forever will be, let poor stupid mortals remember or forget it! The difference is, not that God has withdrawn; but that men's minds have fallen hebetated, stupid, that their hearts are dead, awakening only to some life about meal-time and cookery-time; and their eyes are grown dim, blinkard, a kind of horn-eyes like those of owls, available chiefly for catching mice (p. 277).

It seems unlikely that if Carlyle had finished his twelve pamphlets he would have emerged from this vision of hell. He leaves himself. ironically, in the middle of things. To the many Victorians this work was deeply disappointing. It is decidedly negative: there is no tailor retailored. Rather we are left with the feeling that Carlyle's reality, his vision of England of 1850, was truly one of social and psychological chaos:

> we are not properly a society at all; we are a lost gregarious horde, with Kings of Scrip on this hand, and Famishing Connaughts and Distressed Needlewomen on that—presided over by the Anarch Old. A lost horde,—who, in bitter feeling of the intolerable injustice that presses upon all men, will not long be able to continue ever gregarious; but will have to split into street-barricades, and internecine battle with one another; and to fight, if wisdom for some new real *Peerage* be not granted us, till we all die, mutually butchered, and *so* rest,—so if not otherwise! (p. 283).

NOTES

1. The best discussion of the *Latter-Day Pamphlets* is by Albert J. LaValley, *Carlyle and the Idea of the Modern* (New Haven, 1968). Several others are valuable: Louis Cazamian, *Carlyle*, trans. E. K. Brown (New York, 1932), pp. 240–55; Julian Symons' brief comments in *TC, The Life and Ideas of a Prophet* (New York, 1952); Evan A. Reiff, "Studies in Carlyle's *Latter-Day Pamphlets*" (unpublished dissertation, Univ. of Iowa, 1937), which is helpful in showing how the Irish tour during

the summer of 1849 helped to shape the *Pamphlets*; and Judith M. C. Miller, "TC's *Latter-Day Pamphlets*: An Analysis and a Defense" (unpublished dissertation, Univ. of Arizona, 1971).

2. The comments about Jamaican blacks come from Carlyle's "Occasional Discourse on the Negro Question", *Fraser's Magazine*, 40 (1849). I have excluded this pamphlet from my discussion of the *LDP* because Carlyle decided not to include it in the *Pamphlets* in two later collections of his works, the Library and the People's editions. In the first collected edition (1858), it was presented as a "Precursor to Latter-Day Pamphlets". It will also become clear from what follows that Carlyle thought of the *Pamphlets* as the eight pamphlets issued from February to August 1850. Each one sold for one shilling, and the bound volume for nine. According to *Dyer* (pp. 129–30) there were three British editions and one American in 1850. All quotations from the *Pamphlets* are from the *Works*, XX.

3. *North British Review*, 14 (1850); Froude, *Life*, IV, 36; and W. B. Aytoun in *Blackwood's Edin. Mag.*, 67 (1850). Masson was right. The *LDP* received more notice in the press than any other single work of Carlyle's. Most of the criticism, with some exceptions—American pro-slavers and radical journals, such as the *Examiner*—was hostile. See TC, *The Critical Heritage*, ed. Jules P. Seigel (London, 1971), and *Dyer*, pp. 485–532.

4. At one point he suggests that a plan of reform could be to "Cut from one generation, whether the current one or the next, all the tongues away, prohibiting Literature too; and appoint at least one generation to pass its life in silence" (p. 209).

5. In "Jesuitism", for instance, Carlyle explicitly writes: "My friend, I have to speak in crude language, the wretched times being dumb and deaf: and if thou find no truth under this but the phantom of an extinct Hebrew one, I at present cannot help it" (p. 235).

6. What Levine has suggested for "The Negro Question" holds true to varying degrees throughout the *LDP* themselves: "The use and abuse of Carlylese", in *The Art of Victorian Prose* (New York, 1968), p. 125.

7. G. Kitson Clark, *The Making of Victorian England* (Cambridge, 1962), p. 75. The figure may even be higher. See Oliver MacDonagh, "Irish Immigration to the United States of America and the British Colonies During the Famine", in *The Great Famine*, ed. R. Dudley Edwards and T. Desmond Williams (New York, 1957), pp. 319–87, esp. p. 329.

8. Froude, *Life*, III, 423.

9. Froude, *Life*, III, 429.

10. Froude, *Life*, III, 430–1, and compare: "Since the destruction of the old Roman Empire by inroad of the Northern Barbarians, I have known nothing similar" (*LDP*, p. 6).

11. Froude, *Life*, III, 432.

12. Froude, *Life*, III, 434.

13. Froude, *Life*, III, 435.

14. The pertinent articles that he had written were: "Louis Philippe"

(*Examiner*, 4 March 1848), "The Repeal of the Union" (*Examiner*, 29 April 1848), "Legislation for Ireland" (*Examiner*, 13 May 1848), "Ireland and the British Chief Governor" (*Spectator*, 13 May 1848), "Irish Regiments of the New Era" (*Spectator*, 13 May 1848).

15. For a discussion of the interrelatedness of epic and Old Testament prophecy, see Brian Wilkie, *Romantic Poets and the Epic Tradition* (Madison, Wisc., 1965), esp. pp. 10–11. This study discusses epic as tradition rather than as genre and is valuable in showing what happened to the epic impulse during the early nineteenth century.

16. The comparison is not as strange as some might infer. The similarities between *Soul on Ice* (New York, 1968) and *Sartor* are even more striking—especially the account of Cleaver's conversion while in Folsom Prison; the chapter is called "On Becoming", a central theme in *Sartor*.

17. As will be obvious, my remarks about the epic tradition owe much to Albert J. LaValley's remarkable discussion of their use in his chapter on *The French Revolution*, esp. p. 141 ff. See also "The Epic Temper of Carlyle's Mind", in B. H. Lehman's *Carlyle's Theory of the Hero* (Durham, 1928), pp. 168–70, though the point is not developed. The opening lines of Mill's review of *The French Revolution* ("This is not so much a history as an epic poem") are echoed by Emerson and Thoreau. See *TC, The Critical Heritage*, pp. 52, 85, 290.

18. Froude, *Life*, IV, 28, and *New Letters of TC*, ed. A. Carlyle (London, 1904), II, 86. Because of the death of Peel and a general feeling of disgust, Carlyle could not go on with the twelve pamphlets as planned. The twelve became eight. Froude says how he heard Carlyle "loaded with bilious indignation flinging off the matter intended for the rest of the series which had been left unwritten, pouring out, for hours together, a torrent of sulphurous denunciation. No one could check him. If anyone tried contradiction, the cataract rose against the oracle till it rushed over it and drowned it" (Froude, *Life*, IV, 41).

19. Thomas M. Greene, *The Descent from Heaven: A Study of Epic Continuity* (New Haven, 1963), pp. 17–18, also quoted, LaValley, p. 141.

20. See LaValley (pp. 127–8) for a discussion of this image—"thin earth rind" as it appears in *The French Revolution*. The same image appears in "Ireland and the British Chief Governor": "No; and Europe has crashed together suddenly into the bottomless deeps, the thin earth rind, wholly artificial giving way beneath it; and welter now one huge Democracy." (*Rescued Essays of TC*, ed. P. Newberry [London, 1892], pp. 86–7).

21. LaValley, pp. 283–4. It resembles *Maud* and its paranoic narrator.

22. Cf. Harrold, *Sartor*, p. 232. " 'Call ye that a Society,' cries he again, 'where there is no longer any Social Idea extant. . . . Where each, isolated, regardless of his neighbour, turned against his neighbour, clutches what he can get, and cries "Mine!" and calls it Peace, because, in the cut-purse and cut-throat Scramble, no steel knives, but only a far cunninger sort, can be employed?' "

23. See John Lindberg, "The Decadence of Style: Symbolic Structure in Carlyle's Prose", *Studies in Scottish Literature*, 1 (1964), 192.

24. *Anatomy of Criticism* (Princeton, 1957), p. 328.

25. "Be not a Public Orator, thou brave young British man, thou that are now growing to be something; not a Stump-Orator, if thou canst help it. Appeal not to the vulgar, with its long ears and its seats in the Cabinet; not by spoken words to the vulgar; *hate* the profane vulgar, and bid it begone. Appeal by silent work, by silent suffering if there be no work, to the gods, who have nobler seats in the Cabinet for thee! " (p. 212). "Brave young friend, dear to me, and *known* too in a sense, though never seen nor to be seen by me,—you are, what I am not, in the happy case to learn to *be* something and to *do* something, instead of eloquently talking about what has been and was done and may be: The old are what they are, and will not alter; our hope is in you. England's hope, and the world's, is that there may once more be millions such, instead of units as now" (p. 213).

8

Frederick the Great: "That Unutterable Horror of a Prussian Book"

by ARTHUR A. and VONNA H. ADRIAN

"What my next task is to be?" Carlyle pondered in a letter (29 October 1851) to Varnhagen von Ense, the German friend whose *Memoirs* he had reviewed in the *Westminster*.[1] Confident of yet "one other Book in me", he sought a subject to demonstrate further his hero theory. Discarding Luther as of too little interest in a non-theological age, he found himself drawn increasingly to Frederick II of Prussia, "the *last real King* we have had in Europe", he told Varnhagen. Though there was as yet no full-scale life of Frederick the Great in any language, Carlyle, perhaps by way of inviting Varnhagen's reassurance, professed some doubt that this king's future fame needed any help from an Englishman. Were he "a brave Prussian", however, he would attempt such a biography "forthwith".

A few days later (14 November 1851) he declared to Lady Ashburton that "Frederick, the more I know of him, pleases me the better; a Man and King whose love of *reality* was instinctive and supreme: that is his distinction among Men,—and truly it is one of the greatest and royallest, especially in days like ours".

This predilection for Frederick was of no recent origin. Indeed, Carlyle had long felt an affinity for all things Germanic. As a twenty-four-year old student of German he had expressed admiration for Frederick; later in *Sartor Resartus* he caused Andreas Futteral to exclaim of him, "*Das nenn ich mir einen König, That*

177

is what I call a King" (II, i). Again, assembling materials for his 1840 lectures, "On Heroes and Hero-Worship—from Odin to Robert Burns", he coupled Frederick with Luther. To Emerson (27 June 1835) he elucidated a point thus: "As the great Fritz said, when the battle had gone against him, 'Another time we will do better.' " Finally in 1845 (8 October) he told his wife that he was considering a trip to Berlin "to make more acquaintance with [Frederick] and his people". So by 1851 his intentions toward "Der Grosse Fritz" had actually been taking shape for several decades.

Why did this Prussian conqueror appeal so strongly to his would-be biographer? Though Carlyle's political convictions were obviously satisfied by Frederick's forceful government and his achievement in building a powerful nation and arousing the patriotism of its citizens, the initial attraction may have stemmed no less from certain personal circumstances and qualities which Carlyle shared with his hero. Royalty notwithstanding, Frederick can at times be seen as the *alter ego* of the humble Scottish stonemason's son.

Each came from a strict Protestant background, from which he broke away to become no atheist, but a free thinker, tolerant of all religions. In this each was influenced by Voltaire, who, said Carlyle, "gave the death-stab to modern Superstition" and became, with Frederick, "the celestial element of the poor Eighteenth Century".[2] Each retained from his heritage a sober frugality and an aversion to ostentation, frivolity, and fashion. Frederick, said Carlyle, was "a King . . . without the trappings of a King". True, as an adolescent Crown Prince he had affected a foppish and Frenchified hair style and wardrobe, but he soon sobered into the mould approved by his "heavy-footed practical" father—and Carlyle. As king, except on state occasions, he affected a "Spartan simplicity of vesture: no crown but an old military cocked hat—generally old, or trampled and kneaded into absolute *softness*, if new".[3] It was headgear no less eccentric which caused smiles in railway carriages and hoots in the park when Carlyle wore his white wideawake, at whose first appearance in 1836 his wife Jane had "shrieked, nay almost *grat* [wept]". That her husband rather vaunted himself on his sartorial independence is implied by the tone of his comment to her in 1857: "Think of riding most of the summer with the aristocracy of the county, whenever I went into Hyde Park, in a duffle jacket which literally was part of an old dressing gown a year gone. Is the like on record?"[4]

Though neither Frederick nor Carlyle permitted himself more recreation than necessary to keep in trim for work, each loved horses and riding, but detested hunting. (The spiders Carlyle killed in the back garden at 5 Cheyne Row were, he boasted, the only "game" he ever pursued.) Not pleasure but work was to each a gospel—held, preached, and practised throughout his life. Carlyle's constant insistence on work as man's only excuse for being, parallels Frederick's dictum, "Man is made to work."[5] Macaulay's remark that Frederick "loved labour for its own sake"[6] applies no less to the Calvinistic Carlyle, who, even as he lamented its rigours, embraced it as the ordained curse on Adam's sons.

To Carlyle it was highly satisfying to contemplate success won by dogged labour and determination in the face of repeated obstacles. "That unquenchableness is what has drawn Carlyle to [Frederick]," said Mark Rutherford.[7] This "wonderful plodding perseverance" which he attributed to the whole German race, he was himself to emulate, however impatiently, during his thirteen-year task, spinning out his manuscript "an inch a day"—or so he declared in typically exaggerated fashion. In such travail he must have felt particularly *bruderlich* toward his hero, that "most lone soul of man, . . . continually toiling forward, as if the brightest goal and heaven were near and in view" (V, xix, 395).

That the talk and correspondence of two such men, both copious letter writers, should not be graced by social trivia or decked by bombast is no surprise. Frederick, Carlyle reiterated, was a doer rather than an idle talker, one of those great silent men who are the salt of the earth. (To Carlyle, who uttered the Word, most men were given to uttering Wind.)

It seems only fitting that two such harsh souls should be visited by continuing dyspepsia and abdominal complaints, possibly related to their melancholy and misanthropic cast of mind. As if under compulsion to identify with his hero, Carlyle adds to his report of Frederick's brief attack of "something like apoplexy" ("hemi-plegia", according to Frederick himself) the conjecture that it was "probably indigestion . . . exasperated by over-fatigue". And again quoting Frederick on his haemorrhoids, he inserts the sympathetic diagnosis "dreadful biliary affair", *biliary* being a favourite adjective to describe his own complaints (IV, xvi, 216; VI, xx, 64).

Though Carlyle's misanthropy was mingled with compassion, his inbred conviction of original sin led him to tell with obvious zest how Frederick once squelched a certain romantic who maintained that man is good by nature: "Alas, dear Sulzer, *Ach mein lieber Sulzer,* I see you don't know that damned race of creatures (*Er kennt nicht diese verdammte Race*) as I do!" (IV, xvi, 324).

Toward the female half of the *verdammte* human race Carlyle might have declared with Frederick that he was "no gallant". However different the origins and manifestations of his own lack of gallantry, Carlyle was constitutionally sympathetic with any man who shunned sentimental dalliance with women, single or *en masse.* As a husband, though, he was obviously superior to his hero, being genuinely devoted to his Jane. Yet certain parallels may be assumed. Frederick, according to his own statement, paid brief "tribute to Hymen" at the outset of his marriage.[6] It is an accepted opinion that Carlyle also paid his dues briefly—if at all. At any rate, both men remained childless. (But Jane Carlyle, perhaps unwilling to concede her husband's reputation for sexual indifference, is said to have protested to a friend, "My dear, if Mr Carlyle's digestion had been better, there is no telling what he might have done!"[9])

That the parallels between Frederick and his biographer are by no means exhausted in the foregoing paragraphs will be evident to all who have been struck by passages in *Frederick the Great* which might serve as well for autobiography, the traits stressed being those Carlyle found, or aspired to find, in himself. Even his rendering of his subject's countenance reflects not so much the Prussian king as what Carlyle saw in the mirror: "The face bears evidence of many sorrows, . . . of much hard labour done in this world, and seems to anticipate nothing but more still coming." There is the look of "pride, well tempered with cheery mockery of humour". As for the eyes, they show "a lambent outer radiance springing from some great inner sea of light and fire in the man" (I, i, 2). One is struck above all by the staunch aloneness of Carlyle and his hero, each a man of magnitude in, but not representative of, his century.

For all the initial attractions of his subject it was not without misgivings that Carlyle finally undertook what was to be his longest work, one to whose research and composition he was to give thirteen anguished years. In the first place, where could he gather information? Not in the British Museum, whose director, Anthony Panizzi, resented his charges of mismanagement—Panizzi, that social dilettante engaged in the "hollow dining and drinking Nonsense of so-called 'Literature' ".[10] To be sure, the Museum holdings included ample material on Frederick, which Carlyle might have examined in the general reading room, but he declined to expose himself to headaches from bad air, and distractions from noise and the freakish behaviour of certain readers. When he demanded instead a privileged place in the quiet of the King's Library, he was denied.[11] The refusal involved no serious deprivation, however, for he had at his behest faithful disciples to search out and copy documents in the British Museum, in the London State Paper Office, in German libraries and elsewhere.[12] Their slave labour, performed out of pure dedication to the "Master", indeed demonstrated a tenet of Carlylean doctrine: devoted obedience to the chosen *Übermensch*.

There followed a long period of vacillation and indecision, marked by lapses in hero-worship. Referring to Frederick as the "lean drill-sergeant of the World", Carlyle confessed to Lady Ashburton (16 February 1852), "I do not even grow to love him better: a really mediocre intellect, a hard withered Soul: great only in his invincible Courage, in his constant loyalty to truth and fact." Yet some four months later he could write to Varnhagen (6 June 1852), "I decidedly grow in love for my Hero, and go on; and can by no means decide to throw him up at this stage of the inquiry."

By now his scholar's conscience was urging a trip to Germany, yet he shrank from the "disgraceful wretchedness" that inevitably beset his travels. "On the whole," he wrote to Jane (13 August 1852), "there is nothing to drive me thither but a kind of shame, and a desire *not* to be a poor coward. . . . Really at heart I do not much love [Frederick]." (This some nine weeks after "I grow in love for my hero"!) On the eve of departure he announced to his brother John that he was now "*obliged* to go, there seems no honourable getting off from it" (18 August 1852).

Once abroad, his grim anticipations were realized. It was the old story: he could not sleep. German beds were impossible, their pillows shaped "like a *wedge* three feet broad". Worst of all, there were no bed curtains, and "in beds *without curtains* what Christian could give up the ghost?" The noise, too, was intolerable: loud voices in the street till midnight, the pealing of church bells, the watchman's horn with its "jackass" tone, "and a general Sanhedrin of all the dogs and cats of nature". Everywhere it was the same. "Confound . . . this abominable, sorrowful, shockingly expensive tour of Germany", he grumbled as he prepared to sail for home.[13]

For all his exertions and torments, the trip brought little reward. But "I saw where Frederick *had been*", he told his brother John, "—if that can do any good to me, I have acquired that" (3 October 1852). He might have added that after considerable search he had also acquired one graphic representation of Frederick which, he felt, revealed the inner man. (Some months later he was still fuming over the dearth of such portraits: "No mortal seemed to know of such a thing, or to be in the least want of it. . . . I said to myself a hundred times, the speaking, painting, dissertating, poetizing, most 'artistic' . . . German people, is *this* then all you can do to 'represent' a great man and hero, when the gods send you one?"[14])

But he still wavered. *"Eheu!"* he wrote in his Journal (5 December), "Shall I try Frederick, or not try him?" (Froude, *Life*, IV, 126); and to Charles Redwood, "He will walk the plank, I think, or has walked it, and I must try something else" (Wilson, *Carlyle*, IV, 453). Recalling his hero's death mask in Berlin, he pronounced it not so much "the face of a lean lion" as "alas, of a ditto *cat*! The lips are thin, and closed like pincers; a face that never yielded;—not the beautifullest kind of face. In fine why should *I* torment my domestic soul writing his foreign history?" Besides, Frederick "is not half or tenth part such a man as Cromwell, that one should swim and dive for him in that manner", he told his sister Jean (23 December 1852). The temptation to relinquish the task continued into the next year. "Very well," he told himself in March, "you have lived long without the 'Zollerns, they without you: why not continue to?"[15]

To his correspondents and his Journal he was to confide his doubts and struggles throughout the thirteen years that *Frederick* was in preparation. Actually he had wailed no less despairingly during his four-year labour on *Cromwell*; then, however, his doubts were mainly of his own powers: would the biographer be worthy of his noble subject? The question now was more disturbing: was the subject worthy of the biographer?

But in the end he resisted misgivings and began to write. The prospect looked dismal: "Only pain can now *drive* me through the subject; *led* and induced I shall never be", he told his brother John (20 May 1853). He professed no hope of proud success, only of "some day finishing" the task (Wilson, *Carlyle*, V, 34–5). As his health began to decline under the stress of work and worry his lamentations overflowed the letters and Journal for which he somehow found time. They even clogged his manuscript, delaying the progress of the narrative and adding considerably to its length.

He complained constantly of his source material—to Emerson, to his brother John, to Jane. The books he had ordered from Germany were mainly collections of dry facts, nothing but "the endless rubbish of dullards", he told Jane (23 July 1853). As he turned over tons of such matter he gave further release to his spleen by notebook jottings upon the offending volumes: "Dreadfully worthless!" "What perfectly worthless balderdash!" "Full of ignorance and mendacities." A few of his invectives attacked the unfortunate authors directly: "Oh you absurd old husky 'Psalmodist'—chanting in that dismal hypocritical manner . . . !" "You Dunce! Has cost me half an hour!" (This latter on being thrown off by a mistaken date.) One writer he dismissed as "dog gone mad . . . unfortunate barking individual"; another he addressed condescendingly, "You are rather a poor creature! thank you, however."[16]

Tribulations notwithstanding, by the summer of 1857 Carlyle was reading proof for the first two volumes. Encouragement came from Jane in Scotland, to whom the proof sheets were sent. "Oh, my dear!" she exclaimed, "What a magnificent book this is going to be! The best of all your books" (25 August 1857). (Not until later did she come to wish that Frederick had died in infancy.[17]) Though Carlyle called her "an excellent *encouraging* Goody" (25 August 1857), it was not in his nature to be sanguine, and the task was stretching ahead appallingly. Those first two volumes, by treating Frederick's forebears exhaustively, had failed to advance the hero beyond the status of Crown Prince.

And now, with Frederick's reign and military career looming ahead, Carlyle was forced, as Froude points out, "to make a special study, entirely new to him, of military science and the art of war".[18] For this he deemed it necessary to visit the various battlefields. In August of 1858, accordingly, he made his second tour of Germany. On his return he found himself so wretched and his "hand so out" that he could not take up composition again. One sleepless night he was visited by terror lest he should never finish the work. It was like the apparition of the Devil confronting Luther, or so he felt next morning. "Well, well, Herr Teufel," he resolved, "we will just go on as long as we are alive; and keep working all the same till thou do get us killed" (Wilson, *Carlyle*, V, 391).

But it was Jane whose life was soon to be endangered. Already in frail health, she had shared her husband's nervous anxiety over Frederick from the beginning and had suffered from his impatient temper—as he from hers. According to General John Sterling, who recalled a visit to Cheyne Row in 1859, she confided that her husband was then in despair over his waning respect for his hero.[19] In this same year she echoed his misgivings in a letter to his sister Jean (16 January): "He . . . ought never to have tried to make a silk purse out of a sow's ear." After her death Carlyle was to recall how "often enough it cut me to the heart to think what she was suffering by this book . . . and with what noble and perfect constancy she bore it all".[20]

As he doggedly inched his way toward the end of what he had condemned in 1859 as "that unutterable horror of a Prussian Book",[21] Jane's condition was gradually worsening. During 1864 her life was actually in jeopardy. But as the new year began she grew miraculously better, and Carlyle was fast approaching completion of his sixth and last volume. Perhaps the two circumstances were related. On a Sunday evening at the end of January he walked out with "a kind of solemn thankfulness" that he had written his last sentence: "Adieu, good readers; bad also, adieu."

In the months and even years to follow, well after he might presumably have recovered from his long toil, Carlyle was to lay his broken health and spirits at the charge of this last book, even more ruinous in its effect than his loneliness and remorse after

Jane's death in 1866. The tremors of his right hand worsened; his insomnia increased. His indigestion, by now "a fifty years story", had been "brought to a head by the unspeakable *Friedrich*", he declared in 1867, and would "evidently never much recover".[22] If, Carlylean exaggeration and the normal decline of age aside, the charge be at all admissible, one suspects continuing tension induced by a conflict peculiar to this book alone. That the hero king had proved harsh and unlovable—this might be freely admitted. But if he had also proved ignoble? Here Carlyle may have been forced into an embarrassing dilemma. Having early established his hero as worthy of reverence and emulation, and having seen this evaluation through the press in Volumes I and II, he had either to recant and destroy the unity of his work along with its intended didactic purpose, or take the saving course of suppressing or softening his growing distaste for the practical, able leader, whose duplicity, treachery, and rapacity were daily more apparent. Certain judgments of Frederick which he injected into letters and conversation, and, according to a later biographer of the Prussian king, even into the margins of books borrowed from the London Library, were omitted from his manuscript.[23] It was as if each bright coin of Frederick's virtues had its tarnished side, which Carlyle was obliged to turn up only briefly, if at all, for the reader's view. To resort to such jugglery and to justify his hero's conduct as an ignoble means to a noble goal—such manœuvring to demonstrate his own pet principle that "Right makes Might" should have strained that conscience which controls the Scots Presbyterian temper and digestive juices.

Carlyle's reputed confession in old age "that he had been mistaken about Frederick the Great", whom he now "found to be no worshipful man",[24] may be seen as the delayed acknowledgment of a revulsion he had earlier striven not to convey—perhaps not even to recognize fully. Consciously or not, he had employed a revealing phrase in a letter to Emerson (27 January 1867) when he looked back on *Frederick* as a "wrestle with . . . subterranean hydras". The torment inhering in such conflicts (and by implication, the easement of self-knowledge and confession) had already been recognized by the young Carlyle who wrote to Jane in 1835 (2 November), "It is a great misery . . . for a man to lie, even unconsciously, even to himself."

Inasmuch as this conflict, as well as the exigencies of organizing perplexing and chaotic material, had begun to torment him before the first two volumes were submitted for publication, why had Carlyle not abandoned "that unutterable horror" while there was yet time to save himself? A tangle of motives, all typically Carlylean, seems to have held him floundering, powerless to make the break toward freedom. First of all, there were practical considerations. He had settled on producing some final major work on the plea that it was for financial security in his old age, and with so much time, labour, and money already expended on Frederick, he balked at the waste involved in choosing another subject more to his liking. He was therefore urged on by the same frugal practicality he admired in his hero.

Besides, there was a moral, even religious, compulsion. To abandon a difficult task was unmanful, abhorrent to the stern religion of his childhood: Love not pleasure; love God and be wretched. The more resistant one's work, the more its inherent virtue. Then, too, there was his role of prophet to sustain, the solemn role on which his fame depended. Here was his opportunity to reaffirm those cardinal principles imparted in his previous works: the hero as a plain silent man of action, a reformer bringing order out of chaos, an ordained leader shaping the destiny of a nation. Here was his opportunity to contrast the achievements of "the *last real King* we have had in Europe" with the "do-nothingness" of Victorian England's talk-happy Parliament and its windy politicians. In short, here was his final opportunity for a prophetic blast at his own mechanistic century, so like the godless eighteenth century, except that the latter had been miraculously saved by the emergence of the true king, the Able Man ("a long way till the *next*, I fear") whose dominion was not based on "semblance" and whom the people therefore recognized and obeyed. England too must develop the mystic "eye" to recognize and exalt some saving hero of her own.

Having bestowed such heroic stature on Frederick, Carlyle must have surmised that his countrymen would hardly be persuaded to endorse his conception. Nineteenth-century England, he knew, was too insular, too complacent to look for military models beyond her own border. That "the ignorance of the English public in regards to Prussian things obstructs [Carlyle] more than anything else" had already been pointed out by his brother John, who recognized that "the book must stand or fall on English ground".[25] In any case, English readers at all interested in Frederick could turn to Macaulay's clear and compact treatment, a review essay written in 1842, and find there a viewpoint more in harmony with their own. Instead of a hero, Macaulay had delineated a malicious practical joker, a blasphemer, a tyrannical military and civic leader, a plunderer, a deceiver—in short, an utter scoundrel. He had also hinted at Frederick's homosexuality —"vices from which history averts her eyes".[26] Basically, he had illumined facets of Frederick that Carlyle kept in semi-shadow, thus forearming the public against the heroic portrait. By glorifying so unpopular a man, Carlyle, as he must have seen, weakened any receptivity toward his central plan for an autocratic government of the earnest, dedicated, highly trained and able few, a concept increasingly unacceptable in an age of extending franchise. Accustomed, however, to crying his social and political doctrines into deaf ears, Carlyle seems to have trusted to some distant future for recognition. The present "English world's stupidity upon [Frederick]", he declared in his late years, "is a small matter to me. . . . Book is not quite zero, I perceive, but will be good for something by-and-by."[27]

Whatever the public's reservations about Carlyle's Prussian subject, the work sold amazingly well and contributed substantially to his prosperity.[28] From a few confirmed devotees—notably Froude in England and Emerson in America—came extravagant praise. Equal in enthusiasm but lacking their reverence was Swinburne, whose mildest epithet for Carlyle was "virulent old Arch-Quack of Chelsea". Yet when the final two volumes were due he declared himself "ravenous with expectation", having already delighted in the earlier four, whose hero was "more comprehensible to my heathen mind than any Puritan". It was "Frederick's clear, cold purity of pluck, looking neither upward nor around for any help or comfort" that captivated Swinburne.[29] One pictures this little red squirrel casting aside the dry husk of Carlyle's preachments to get at the rich kernel of his godless hero. The *Punch* staff, however, were less avid. Discussing the first two volumes at one of their weekly dinner meetings, they rendered the terse verdict: "A waste of labour."[30]

187

From the non-literary general public came respect inspired by the awesome research behind the work, its vast scope as a history of eighteenth-century Europe—and, of course, its author's status as England's "dear old Prophet Carlyle" (so Lady Ashburton had called him) whose thunder had long been esteemed and seldom heeded. It was this automatic respect which prompted *The Gentleman's Magazine* (December 1858) to pay exaggerated homage to Carlyle's work as a "faithful history" and "exquisite work of art", verdicts which it supported by further laudatory generalizations rather than by specific analysis or example. Certain judgments (for instance, "masterly arrangement of his vast mass of facts" and "matchless skill in condensation") were in direct opposition to those of the majority of commentators. For, though the importance of the work was generally conceded, its critical reception was less than enthusiastic. Reviewed by virtually all the leading journals, it received—with the exception noted above—little or no unqualified praise.

Repeatedly censured was the choice of hero, for, commented *Fraser's Magazine* (December 1858) with true English insularity, "It is difficult to care much about Frederick and his doings." Quoting Carlyle's own deprecating statement that "Frederick's ideal, compared with some, was low . . . and only worth much memory in the absence of better", *Blackwood's Edinburgh Magazine* (July 1865) asked, "Why not have sought better, then, Mr. Carlyle?" *The Saturday Review* (25 April 1865) also cited the history's constant patronizing tone in presenting Frederick as "a heathenish old brute [who] still fought and wrought so well that anything may be forgiven". Just how well he wrought was in the main ignored, though *The Times* (18 April 1865) did recognize the notable "domestic administration" through which Frederick "consolidated the Prussian State, repaired its losses in population and wealth, and soothed the very remembrance even of its scars". Most periodicals, however, inclined to the views expressed by *The British Quarterly Review* (January 1859), which accused Carlyle of portraying "the besotted qualities" of Frederick's character as "elevated instincts", of transforming "the passions of the tyrant" into "the virtues of a legislator", of exalting "a Bill Sykes in purple" as a "legitimate hero", and of confounding "the distinction of right and wrong". Calling this Carlyle's "most mis-

188

chievous book", the October number followed with a similar condemnation: the work had trampled on "considerations of justice and truth as things too vulgar and commonplace to be taken into account when judging the actions of heroes". Similar dissent came from *The Quarterly Review* (April 1859), *The Cornhill Magazine* (July 1862), *The Athenaeum* (25 March 1865), *The Westminster Review* (July 1865), and *The North British Review* (September 1865). So, whether Carlyle exalted Frederick or apologized for him, the book was berated.

Especially offensive to Victorian complacency was Carlyle's scorn for his own nation and era. "Blessed with every comfort that liberty and enlightenment can confer, he sees in the fair, broad, honest face of England only a howling wilderness," accused *Blackwood's* (February 1859). *The Edinburgh Review* (October 1859) deplored his "elaborate ridicule of every institution and usage" of modern times. *The North British Review* (September 1865) concurred, charging him with painting the past "unduly bright" to emphasize "the inferiority of his country and time". This gave his history "a peculiar power to work mischief" on the public: "He stirs up doubt and discontent in their minds, and then abandons them to that unhallowed companionship."

But the victims of his sardonic mockery were by no means confined to his own country and time. Over the years Carlyle had cultivated a talent for derision, which he now exercised habitually and almost automatically, thereby incurring in turn the derision of reviewers who strained to outdo his own caustic tone. (To them one can only say, Thy tooth is not so keen.) One periodical, however, spoke so firmly and justly as to deserve somewhat extended treatment here. Having seen it in Scotland, Jane Carlyle wrote to her husband of "a review in the 'Cornhill' [July 1862] which would amuse you! Adoring your genius, but. . . ."[31]

This essay pronounced *Frederick* to be so "grotesquely original" as not to be subject to the usual criteria. "It must be accepted—or rejected—for what it is, and as it is: a book of strange power." The artist, so the reviewer asserted, must be allowed freedom to create as his genius dictates:

> But the teacher is allowed no such license. And as a teacher there are two points upon which we think Carlyle is open to severe

disapprobation. . . . The first of these is the painful excess of scorn, which poisons his graphic humour with cruelty and injustice. Scorn is an attitude perilous even to a mind like his, pernicious in its influence on weaker minds. Every serious man will at times be moved to indignant sarcasm at what is base. But in Carlyle, always too disposed to scorn, this attitude has become permanent, not occasional. It is no longer "shams" and charlatans that move his sardonic laughter; but much that is not base at all, good honest endeavour, is quizzed and nicknamed in contempt.

Among those inevitably made the butt of scorn, the writer mentions mathematicians and scientists: "We may allow him to estimate science as far inferior to 'spiritual insight' (somewhat misty as to what it *sees*), but we cannot forget that it is a very noble effort." Leibnitz and Maupertuis, for example, deserve better of Carlyle than repeated ridicule on the basis of the former's "long nose, bandy legs, and huge periwig (as if *those* were the most notable points in a great thinker!)" and of the latter's "big red face". These are "graphic, no doubt, but what is the sense or justice of it?" The perpetual mood of scorn is held to be as overdrawn as the "preposterous" worship of Carlyle's hero.

Attacked by a number of periodicals was the organization of material. *The North British Review* (September 1865) found the work prolix, confused, and out of proportion. *The Westminster Review* (July 1865) regretted that Carlyle had lost his "art of picturesque condensation, of loading his sentences with profound meaning and flashing out his thoughts in swift emphatic precision", a notable feature of his *French Revolution*. *The British Quarterly Review* (January 1859) accused him of merely taking his materials as they came to hand, without design or perspective. *The Quarterly Review* (April 1859) termed the book a mere "collection of sketches", which omitted "important details in some places" only to accumulate them "without mercy or evident reason . . . in others". Without its helpful index "it would be almost impossible to read the book through with profit". (Had the reviewer only known, this admirable index had been compiled as a labour of love by Carlyle's Chelsea neighbour and disciple, Henry Larkin.) The narrative was diffuse and "garbled", *The Quarterly* continued, as a result of the author's "running comments". The ratio of such interpolations to sound historical substance was

190

summed up by *Blackwood's* (February 1859) charge that never had "the pennyworth of bread borne so small a proportion to the intolerable deal of sack". Also deplored by *The Dublin University Magazine* (July 1862) was the incoherence of Carlyle's "somersault mode of narration, wherein he emulates the springing kangaroo". In short, journalistic opinion agreed that Carlyle's peculiar organization imposed a grave burden on his readers.

But in the majority of negative criticisms Carlyle's unique style appears as an even greater culprit. The pungent flavour of "Carlylese", ever an acquired taste, seems to have turned unpalatable with the years, or with the concentrated six-volume dose. Thus many a reviewer complained of such grotesqueries as invented dialogue, elliptical fragments, the eternal invectives and apostrophes, the eccentric epithets staled by the repetition: *Windbags, Mud-Demons, Dryasdusts, Phantasm-Captains, Demon Newspapers, Enchanted Wiggeries,* and the hoary spokesmen *Teufelsdröckh, Smelfungus,* and *Sauerteig.* The initiated reader of Carlyle might grasp this terminology, but for the novice, so *Blackwood's* (February 1859) maintained, a glossary was needed. (Reviewers would have been wise to acknowledge a few of Carlyle's more successful epithets as well: for example, that for Frederick's pathetic Queen, *Her Serene Insipidity of Brunswick.*)

The Edinburgh Review (October 1859) was revolted by "the nauseous depths to which [Carlyle] drags his readers for metaphors". *Fraser's Magazine* (December 1858) pronounced his work "a curious mixture of phantasmagoria and anecdote, of riotous humour, incessant quaintness, extravagance of language, and painful exactness of detail". *The Saturday Review* (2 April 1864), another addict to a bland diet of everyday language, was thankful that "the ordinary chroniclers of current events do not write like Smelfungus". For, though it was "amusing at times to guess what on earth Mr. Carlyle can mean", success brought no reward but a mere "commonplace reflection . . . twisted into an odd but striking form of expression".

The Athenaeum (3 May 1862), however, tolerated the bewildering "extravagances" and "complications" of language in view of the vitality of Carlyle's characterizations and "military descriptions", noting that "his style, when he follows the army, marches with it, echoes its guns, reflects its bayonet gleams, is in harmony with its wildest music". A later issue (12 March 1864) continues indulgent of the "intensely peculiar" expression, justly observing how "often the author's manner gives strength and picturesqueness to his matter". The consensus of journalistic opinion, however, was considerably less favourable to the vagaries of genius.

As with his earlier books Carlyle feigned to ignore critical opinion, except when "officious people" forced it upon him. Favourable or not, the reviews of *Frederick*, in so far as he noticed them, were dismissed as "no better . . . than the barking of dogs".[32] Nevertheless, the English rejection of his Prussian *alter ego* was in a sense a rejection of himself, and as such presumably held a degree of bitterness.

He must therefore, have been gratified by the response from Germany, where the work was immediately translated, widely circulated, and increasingly approved as the decade advanced. Its author was praised not only as an artist and epic historian, but also as a seer who had anticipated the rise of Germany and had prepared Europe for an expanding German Empire. Toward the end of the Franco-Prussian War, with a German victory assured, Carlyle therefore felt that a letter to *The Times* (18 November 1870) was called for to remind the English that "no nation ever had so bad a neighbour as Germany has had in France for the last 400 years; bad in all manner of ways; insolent, rapacious, insatiable, unappeasable, continually aggressive". Now he found it only just that this neighbour should have been dealt "so complete, instantaneous, and ignominious a smashing-down" by Germany, who would have been foolish "not to think of raising up some secure boundary-fence" between herself and her ancient enemy. He dwelt rapturously on the union of Prussian states that he had foreseen: "That noble, patient, deep, pious and solid Germany should at length be welded into a Nation and become Queen of the Continent instead of a vapouring, vainglorious, gesticulating, quarrelsome, restless and over-sensitive France, seems to me to be the hopefulest public fact that has occurred in my time" (*Works*, XXX, 52, 59).

Four years later Germany awarded Carlyle the Prussian Order of Merit, founded, appropriately enough, by Frederick himself. No doubt Carlyle was gratified. Yet he deprecated the honour in his usual manner, calling it a "sublime nonentity" and protesting that "had they sent me ¼lb. of good Tobacco the addition to my happiness had probably been suitabler and greater!"[33] The following year he was honoured by a note of congratulation from Bismarck on his eightieth birthday. He replied in German (10 December 1875) with keen appreciation, declaring, "What you are pleased to say of my poor history of your great King Frederich seems to me the fittest and most flattering utterance I have yet heard on this subject anywhere" (Wilson, *Carlyle*, VI, 374–5).

Actually, Bismarck's praise seems rather too general to be termed "the most pertinent . . . yet heard", consisting merely of the assurance that Carlyle's work had presented a full-length portrait, revealing Frederick to the German people like a living statue—"*wie eine lebende Bildsäule*". Carlyle's acknowledgment, however, becomes exempt from critical scrutiny when one notes that it was "with a great effort, painfully dictated" to his niece Mary, who had dutifully undertaken to answer "that wheelbarrowful" of birthday remembrances.[34]

Carlyle's letter to the *Times*, along with such subsequent evidences of his German connections and sympathies, brought on angry outbursts which reverberated into the next century, particularly during World Wars I and II. Writing to the *Nation* (14 September 1918) Stuart F. Sherman, in an article entitled "Carlyle and Kaiser Worship", recommended that the works of Carlyle be burned because of this bias. An unsigned contribution to the *National Review* (February 1923) accused him of being the "catspaw of the Hohenzollerns". And in 1927 Norwood Young held that Carlyle, by whitewashing Frederick's violence and fraud, had rendered judgments which even extreme Prussian admirers could not countenance. Such exaltation of "one of the worst men known to history", Young asserted, "came home to us in the terrible years of the Great War".[35] With World War II Carlyle was further discredited by association when the Nazis quoted him extensively in broadcasts beamed at Britain in the late thirties and early forties.

War-nurtured opinion aside, how has Carlyle's *Frederick* been regarded in this century? In 1929 Alec Wilson, unmoved by lingering post-war prejudice, but perhaps biased in favour of a fellow-Scot, said that this work surpassed other histories "as diamonds surpass coal" (V, 179). But another Scot, J. G. Robertson, well versed in German language and literature, declared it "doubt-ful if any of the acknowledged standard writings on Frederick in our day would have been essentially different had Carlyle never laboured".[36] True, the recent compact, objective, and popular treatment by Nancy Mitford does acknowledge Carlyle as a source: "a gold mine of information, both relevant and irrelevant" (p. 292), but obviously not as an influence on interpretation. With the exception of Norwood Young's notoriously anti-Carlylean *Life of Frederick the Great* (1919), other twentieth-century biographies of Frederick written or translated into English (Thaddeus, 1930; Veale, 1935; Gaxotte, 1941; Gooch, 1947; Reiners, 1960) acknowledge little or no more than the mere existence of Carlyle's work.

Other than professional historians, who are in any case armed against Carlyle's special pleading, the public today is for the most part too indifferent even to echo his 1859 damnation of the un-finished work as "that unutterable horror of a Prussian book". When years later in the gloom of his old age its author consigned it to "the belly of oblivion",[37] he was perhaps anticipating the position of Morse Peckham, who submits that this heroic book de-mands heroic readers, a species lacking today.[38] Granted, a firm grasp of eighteenth-century European history and its antecedents (even unto the tenth century) is a prerequisite to reading the work without floundering. To this must be added the diligence and patience to cope with the complexities of organization and the profusion of digressions. Those so equipped might, however, admit also to communion that small segment of readership, floundering but fascinated, which remains content with less than mastery.

Of such are those non-specialists, we who are neither historians, Carlylean scholars, nor thorough-going disciples of the prophet, but mainly devotees of a personality, one that in the beginning may call forth amusement and a measure of dissent, but finally respect, attention, and affection as well. We are those to whom the *Letters* must ever be the favourite among Carlyle's books. Thus we tend to value *Frederick* more as a revelation of its author than of its hero and his times. We consequently sieve the tough pulp to catch a pungent juice over which we linger. If we find the volume of such juice unmatched in Carlyle's previous work, it may be

194

only because no earlier work approaches the length of *Frederick*. As for flavour, it cannot have been distilled from the author's zest, for unlike *The French Revolution*, this laboured work did not come "direct and flamingly from the heart". Yet flavour is notably present, tempting one to offer samples as an enticement to a first, or further, dip into plentitude.

Any collection of memorabilia might well include that vignette of the twelfth-century Frederick Barbarossa, "greatest of all the Kaisers . . . holding the reins of the world", who chained the rebellious Governor of Milan beneath his table and forced him to lie there "like a dog, for three days", till he complied. "Those", adds Carlyle approvingly, "were serious old times" (I, v, 76–7).

Frederick's father, too, that "solid, honest, if somewhat explosive bear" (I, iii, 30), is a source of delight, in whom we meet every parent who would have his offspring walk in his own footsteps, resembling him "as a little sixpence does a big half-crown". And in the youthful Fritz, wilfully bent on "French fopperies, flutings, and cockatoo fashions of hair", who could not then or ever become an exact copy of the paternal half-crown, we recognize and sympathize with the universal teenager (I, xii, 391).

As for Frederick's paternal grandmother, Queen Sophie Charlotte, we cannot forget her attempts "to draw water from that deep well" which was Leibnitz, and her failure to hoist anything but a "wet rope with cobwebs sticking to it . . . endless rope, and the bucket never coming to view" (I, iv, 35).

For the historical validity of these and other portraits we may care no more than we do for that of Shakespeare's Hotspur and Prince Hal. It is enough that they live, and enough that events are often re-created in such seeming actuality that we experience them with all our senses. Thus with each return to that rhythmic depiction of the advancing Prussian troops we are caught up in their "intricate, many-glancing tide . . . swift, correct as clockwork . . ., tornado-storm so beautifully hidden within it" (V, ii, 27). In like manner we witness the theatrical defiance of Maria Theresa, exultant on her hilltop; or the last hours of Frederick, attended by a shivering hound and a faithful hussar; or numerous other episodes. Opposed to dull textbook exposition, this method of Carlyle's is the essence of his virtue. Yet it is only an intermittent virtue, for such passages, composed *con amore*, mingle unevenly with series of disjointed paragraphs transcribed directly, though with disarming apology, from "rough Notebooks". This unevenness, along with ponderous jocularity, crusty rebuke ("pooh, you—!"), and footnotes combining documentation with damnation, are none the less savoured by the reader attuned to the quirks of Carlylean personality. Thus lured, he may grapple eventually with the titanic history entire.

But what of the book's future, that "by-and-by" which Carlyle foresaw in one of his rare moods of optimism?

That the reading public increasingly demands ease and brevity amounts to a prediction of further dwindling readership for such epics as *Frederick*. Along with ease and brevity the public also demands what it is pleased to term relevance, a quality which today's democratic society finds lacking in this history. But universal and eternal relevance is exactly what Carlyle himself regarded as the chief merit of his last work. And who can predict tomorrow's concept of relevance? As chaos and the decline of moral responsibility continue to blight our lives, who can say that the pendulum will not swing, however lamentably, toward the autocrat hero? Then, with the accompanying emergence of *Frederick* from "the belly of oblivion", we should doubtless find both governor and governed pursuing that unheroic method of mining the text for usable nuggets—such only as would sustain the authoritarian regime. Thus the prophecy in the final paragraph of Carlyle's history would be fulfilled: that "the Nations universally . . . bethink themselves of such a Man and his Function and Performance, with feelings far other than possible at present".

NOTES

1. Since letters cited will eventually be in *CL*, references are generally given only by date and name of addressee.
2. See Carlyle's "Voltaire" (1829) and letter to Emerson (25 June 1852).
3. *History of Friedrich the Second, Called Frederick the Great*, 6 vols (New York, 1859–66), I, i, 1. Subsequent references are to this edition and given in the text.
4. See Carlyle's letter (June 1836) to his brother John and another to Jane Carlyle (2 July 1857).
5. Nancy Mitford, *Frederick the Great* (New York, 1970), p. 247.

6. See his review essay on Thomas Campbell's *Frederick the Great and His Times* in *The Works of Lord Macaulay* (London, 1904), VI, 667.
7. W. Hale White (Mark Rutherford), *Letters to Three Friends* (London, 1924), p. 67.
8. Mitford, *Frederick*, p. 76.
9. See Margaret Oliphant's comments on Carlyle in *Macmillan's Magazine* for April 1881, pp. 487–95.
10. See Carlyle's letter to Varnhagen von Ense (6 June 1852).
11. Wilson, *Carlyle*, IV, 478–9.
12. *Ibid.*, V, 125.
13. See his letter to Jane Carlyle (9 Sep. 1852) and Wilson, *Carlyle*, IV, 442.
14. Letter to J. Marshall (13 March 1853), British Museum, Egerton MSS. 3032.1–33.
15. *Ibid.*
16. *"Carlyliana"; being the Opinions of TC on some books relating to the "History of Frederick the Great"* (London, privately printed, 1883).
17. Moncure D. Conway, *Autobiography* (Boston, 1904), pp. 394–5.
18. Froude, *Life*, IV, 86–7.
19. See Sterling's letter in the *Times*, 11 Jan. 1917.
20. See Carlyle's note in *Letters and Memorials of Jane Welsh Carlyle*, ed. J. A. Froude (London, 1883), p. 243.
21. Letter to Marshall (28 Nov. 1859), Egerton MS.
22. Letter to John Carlyle (31 Aug. 1867).
23. Norwood Young, *Carlyle, His Rise and Fall* (London, 1927), p. 294.
24. M. D. Conway, *TC* (New York, 1881), p. 105.
25. Letter to Marshall (13 Feb. 1857), Egerton MS.
26. *The Works of Lord Macaulay*, VI, 649.
27. Froude, *Life*, IV, 354.
28. Wilson, *Carlyle*, V, 328.
29. See his letters to Burne-Jones (15 May 1883) and Pauline, Lady Trevelyan (15 March 1865) in *The Swinburne Letters*, ed. Cecil Y. Lang (New Haven, 1959–62).
30. Diary of Henry Silver, entry for 10 Feb. 1859, in the *Punch* Library.
31. *Letters and Memorials of Jane Welsh Carlyle*, p. 102.
32. Froude, *Life*, IV, 228, quoting TC's Journal.
33. Letter to John Carlyle (14 Feb. 1874).
34. *Ibid.* (15 Dec. 1875).
35. *Carlyle, His Rise and Fall*, p. 366.
36. *Cambridge History of English Literature*, XIII, 20.
37. *Reminiscences* (Norton), I, 201.
38. *Victorian Revolutionaries* (New York, 1970), p. 45.

9

Frederick the Great

by MORSE PECKHAM

It is difficult to write about Carlyle's *History of Friedrich II of Prussia Called Frederick the Great,* for it seems a pointless and useless undertaking. Almost no one has read it, and it seems unlikely that anyone will read it because of a mere essay. Those who find this essay valuable will probably conclude that they are saved the trouble of reading the work; while those who dislike the essay will decide that it has not offered convincing reasons for undertaking the book itself. During the fifteen years since I first read it, constant inquiry among other Victorian scholars has not uncovered anyone else who has done so. In fact, one scholar who has written in some detail about it and with an air of considerable authority turned out only to have skimmed through it. Another, one who likewise found the work to be a failure, does not give me the impression that he has done more than a rapid skimming. When I recommend reading *Frederick* to other Victorian scholars, my enthusiasm is received with scepticism and more often than not a politely but barely concealed implication that my judgement is grotesque. To be sure, one friend to whom I recommended it did read it and, though he detested Carlyle, thought it to be a marvellous book. But then, he was not a Victorian scholar but a music critic, and besides he died not long thereafter.

I shall make no attempt, therefore, to argue that *Frederick* is a success or a failure, a great book or a poor one. When I first read it I felt that I was having one of the greatest and most thoroughly satisfying reading experiences of my life. My second reading was less agreeable, but it was done not at leisure but under deadline pressure. I look forward to reading it again, but at my ease and after I have retired. I think it is a fascinating and wonderful work. If one wants to understand Carlyle and the culture of the nineteenth century one should read it; if one wishes professional success and status, to read *Frederick* is clearly unnecessary, since so many Victorian scholars who enjoy both have not troubled to do so. Rather, I shall be concerned with certain rhetorical peculiarities in *Frederick* and in proposing explanations for them, since they raise interesting questions not only about Carlyle but also about the very nature of writing history.[1]

1

Approaching *Frederick* initially as a piece of historical discourse, one first notes the oddness of its proportions. Almost a third of the work is over before Friedrich succeeds to the throne. The last half of his reign takes up a little less than a tenth of the whole. Thus almost 60% of the work is concerned with the years from 1740 to 1763. This is the period of the Silesian Wars; Friedrich invaded Silesia in December, 1740, less than seven months after his accession. Moreover, Books I to III, almost 10%, are principally taken up with the history of Brandenburg and of the Hohenzollerns before the accession of Friedrich's father, Friedrich Wilhelm. Books IV to X, about 23%, ostensibly taken up with Friedrich's youth, are as much concerned with Friedrich Wilhelm as with his son. Thus anyone who wishes to read a balanced account of the career of Friedrich will be both disappointed and puzzled.

A clue to this way of laying out the work is to be found in the great space and immense detail devoted to Friedrich's campaigns and above all to his battles. Carlyle himself visited most of the battle-sites, and it is obvious that no one who had not done so could have written about the battles as he did. If he could not go to the field itself, he procured the most accurate and informative maps and descriptions he could lay his hands on. Two themes of the book emerge here, that of struggle and that of reality.

The theme of struggle emerges in the long accounts of the history of Brandenburg and of the Hohenzollerns, though it is not explicitly set forth until Book XXI. Carlyle is discussing the rapid recovery of Prussia from the devastations of the Third Silesian War:

> Prussia has been a meritorious Nation; and, however cut and ruined, is and was in a healthy state, capable of recovering soon. Prussia has defended itself against overwhelming odds,—brave Prussia; but the real soul of its merit was that of having merited such a King to command it. Without this King, all its valours, disciplines, resources of war, would have availed Prussia little. No wonder Prussia has still a loyalty to its great Friedrich, to its Hohenzollern Sovereigns generally. Without these Hohenzollerns, Prussia had been, what we long ago saw it, the unluckiest of German Provinces; and could never have had the pretension to exist as a Nation at all. Without this particular Hohenzollern, it had been trampled out again, after apparently succeeding. To have achieved a Friedrich the Second for King over it, was Prussia's grand merit (XXI, i, 8).

The interactions of Hohenzollerns and Brandenburg, the long history that lay behind the achievement of "Prussia's grand merit", is the theme of the first three books.[2] It is on the one hand the struggle of the Hohenzollerns to establish themselves, and on the other of the people of Brandenburg to establish themselves as an independent nation. The central theme is the struggle of Brandenburg and the Hohenzollerns to adapt themselves to each other, a struggle almost completed by Friedrich Wilhelm, who left to Friedrich an army and a disciplined population. In the Silesian wars Friedrich consummated the century-old struggle and created a modern nation.

Carlyle conceived of his task as the creation of an epic, the first true historical epic, although he was convinced that his cultural situation did not allow him to create that epic.

> Alas, the Ideal of History, as my friend Sauerteig knows, is very high; and it is not one serious man, but many successions of such, and whole serious generations of such, that can ever again build up History towards its old dignity. . . . "All History is an imprisoned Epic, nay an imprisoned Psalm and Prophecy," says Sauerteig there. . . . But I think all real *Poets*, to this hour, are Psalmists and Illiadists after their sort; and have in them a divine impatience of lies, a divine incapacity of living among lies. Likewise, which is a corollary, that the highest Shakspeare producible is properly the fittest Historian producible (I, i, 17–18).

Arms-and-the-man is the theme of epic, and to Friedrich the Electorate of Brandenburg and the Kingdom of Prussia were his arms, forged by his Hohenzollern ancestors.

But the joint struggle of electorate and family to realize themselves and each other was not enough to account for Friedrich. Not only must the arms be forged but also the man. Hence the long and lovingly detailed discourse on the reign of Friedrich Wilhelm, and on what, for Carlyle's purposes, was the real point of that reign, the fearful conflict between father and son, the result of which was the creation of a man and a king out of a sensitive, dilettantish, Francophile prince. It is therefore of great significance to the design of the work that Carlyle makes much of the reconciliation of father and son, of Friedrich's grief at his father's death, of his love for his father, and particularly of his continuation of his father's internal policies and administrative personnel. Thus by the end of the original first two volumes (Books I–VIII) both country and man are forged and ready for each other.

The next twelve months (IX–XX) are taken up almost entirely with the three Silesian wars, except for seven months of peace after the accession and two intervals of two and ten years (Books XI, XIV, and XVI). From these wars Friedrich and Prussia emerge, the one as finally a true King, the other as finally a true Nation. Book XXI, which Carlyle calls a "loose Appendix of Papers", is not a "finished Narrative" simply because to his theme such a finished narrative would be inappropriate. All that was needed was a demonstration that in the last twenty-three years of his reign, Friedrich truly ruled a consummated nation. The whole metaphysical point is to be found here.

In the chaos of the eighteenth century—that it was a chaos the French Revolution, to Carlyle, sufficiently proved—Friedrich had created an island of social order. Not that he was alone. Carlyle saw in that chaotic century of lies two other focal points of truth. One was Voltaire; the other was Pitt. Carlyle judged Voltaire to be no more perfect than Friedrich, yet he saw him as a counterpart. Voltaire had an intellectual grasp of his cultural situation; Friedrich, whom Carlyle saw as intellectually superficial, nevertheless had a practical, non-intellectual grasp of a similar sort. Pitt stands on the sidelines; he helps Friedrich, but his help is validated by his intelligence in grasping that America must be

English not French, France, of course, being at once the most brilliant and the most corrupt of eighteenth-century nations. America is presented as the hope of the future; Pitt was great because he saw that hope as something that would be destroyed if France controlled America.

Further, Carlyle saw the nineteenth century as the inheritor and the continuator of the collapse of eighteenth century culture in the French Revolution. The first chapter of Book I begins with that theme and the first chapter of the final book reiterates it, "New Act,—or, we may call it New *Part*; Drama of World History, Part Third" (XXI, i, 2). This is not a casual remark here, but a proper introduction to that Book. The work cannot be allowed to end triumphantly, heroically, in a blaze of Friedrich's glory. Friedrich, it is true, created an island of order, but it was bound to be temporary, since it came toward the close of Part II of World-History. The world in which Carlyle was living was the opening chaos of Part III. That is why the true Historical Epic lay far in the future, why Carlyle could not write it. To do so it would be necessary to understand the meaning of Part III, and though Carlyle guesses at it—("unappeasable Revolt against Sham-Governors and Sham-Teachers,—which I do charitably define to be a Search, most unconscious, yet in deadly earnest, for true Governors and Teachers")—the result of that search cannot be envisioned. Friedrich, he implies in the next sentence, is not particularly significant for what he did, but that he existed may be of the highest relevance. At the beginning of Book I Carlyle writes, "To many it appears certain there are to be no Kings of any sort, no Government more; less and less need of them henceforth, New Era having come" (I, i, 16). At the beginning of Book XXI he defines Part III of World-History as "the breaking-out of universal mankind into Anarchy, into the faith and practice of No-Government" (p. 2). That is why he says in Book I, "My hopes of presenting, in this Last of the Kings, an exemplar to my contemporaries, I confess, are not high" (I, i, 17). In short, if Carlyle has understood World-History, true Governors and true Teachers—political and moral agents of social control and management—will arise; if he has not, mankind will find a way of living satisfactorily without social control and management. Since Carlyle cannot be sure of how the problem is to be resolved, if at all, he cannot write a true Historical Epic, since such an epic would require an understanding of the meaning of World-History. He can only show the struggle, he can only demonstrate how one man became a true King, but he cannot be sure that such struggle and becoming can really be useful. (I cannot forbear interpolating that, disagreeable as the notion may be, I cannot imagine mankind without techniques of social control and management. My reason is that notions of society without social control and management are founded upon love, but love, in all its forms, appears to me to be the most stringent and oppressive of the various modes of social control and management. Possibly Carlyle was hinting at this when he proposed that Part II of World History began with Christ and ended with the French Revolution.) The future, then, may not need such exemplars as Friedrich, or, on the contrary, it may need them but be unable to use them. From this point of view the real hero of *Frederick* is Carlyle himself, for he engaged in and persisted in the immense struggle to complete the work without any confidence that it was worth completing. This is the difference between the redemptionist Carlyle (and Marx) of the 1830's and 1840's and the Carlyle of *Frederick*.

The theme of *Frederick*, then, is the theme of all Carlyle's work from before 1830: the struggle to create order out of chaos, and the struggle to penetrate through shams and lies to reality. However, the notion that that penetration is redemptive is now gone or at best has suffered a severe attrition. What had sustained Carlyle so long, up to *Latter-Day Pamphlets*, was the conviction that the penetration through lies and shams revealed the reality of the world as a symbol of the divine, or that the hero was a symbol and instrument of the divine. All this has disappeared from Frederick. We hear often enough about the Laws of Nature and the Laws of God, but we are not informed precisely what those laws are, except that they tend on the whole to be disagreeable, and except that the heroic man can face their disagreeableness and act in spite of it. Indeed, Carlyle's conception of God becomes remarkably like that of Kierkegaard's at much the same time: from the belief in God no moral or metaphysical propositions can be deduced. The only reality the not very intelligent or perceptive Friedrich was capable of was the reality of creating an island of order, in the chaos of the eighteenth century, the reality of knowing what he wanted; yet his island was to be washed away by the French Revolution. The best Carlyle can suggest is that Friedrich's achievement enabled Prussia to survive several inferior Kings, the French Revolution, and Napoleon. Thus the marked difference between *Frederick* and the works of the 1830's and 1840's is not sufficiently explained (and to my mind not at all explained) by postulating failing powers or loss of "creativity" (whatever that is). One must recognize a radical difference of vision. Recent writers on *Frederick* have been young (and platitudinously liberal). Their rejection of the work may, possibly, be a function of their youth (and their ideology), not of their critical insight nor of their social comprehension.

2

A second oddity of Frederick is typographical. A very large portion is in small print. It was the result of a very idiosyncratic decision, and I have never seen it discussed, though it seems impossible that it has never been commented on. Why did Carlyle set up this additional barrier to the reader?[3]

Many of these small-print passages are, to be sure, quotations from letters and other documents, but most of them are not. Some of them are summaries of documents; others are elaborations of minor points; for only a few of them is there any suggestion that they can be profitably skipped by all but persevering and determined readers. A sampling of how they are introduced will be of some interest. "Says one whose Note-books I have got" (I, i, 58); "says one of my old Papers" (I, i, 75); "the following Excerpt" (I, i, 77); "perhaps I had better subjoin a List (V, i, 15); "the following stray Note" (V, iii, 31); "accept this Note, or Summary" (V, iii, 39); "a most small Anecdote, but then an indisputably certain one" (V, v, 48); "One glance I may perhaps commend to the reader, out of these multifarious Notebooks in my possession" (IX, vi, 78); "excerpted from multifarious old Notebooks" (IX, viii, 91); "the following chronological phenomena of the Polish Election" (IX, viii, 95); "As to the History of Schlesien . . . I notice . . . Three Epochs" (XII, i, 4); "Read this Note" (XII, ii, 17); "says an Excerpt I have made" (XII, ii, 20); "and this of Smelfungus" (XVI, iii, 233); "I have something to quote, as abridged and distilled from various sources" [it is not a quotation] (XVI, vi, 273); "says a certain Author" [unidentified] (XVI, viii, 306); "take this brief Note" (XVIII, vii, 228); two paragraphs without introduction, but placed in quotes (XVIII, viii, 264); "Smelfungus takes him up, with a twitch" (XVIII, ix, 304); "For our poor objects, here is a Summary, which may suffice" (XX, v, 299); "some glances into the Turk War, I grieve to say, are become inevitable to us!" (XXI, iv, 100); "a rough brief Note" (XXI, v, 132); "Here, saved from my poor friend Smelfungus (nobody knows how much of him I suppress), is a brief jotting, in the form of rough *memoranda*, if it be permissible" (XXI, v, 181).

A thorough study of all the small-print passages, the categories into which they fall, and their various introductions, when present, as they usually are, might be of considerable interest, but probably would not change drastically the impression one gets from a thorough reading of the entire work. One group, as suggested, consists of direct quotations from letters and other documents. Here the small print is clearly a typographical convention. The effect of the other group, however, is quite different. For these passages Carlyle has innovated not merely a typographical convention but one that may properly be called a rhetorical one. The effect is by no means one that indicates that the material is skippable or unessential in any way. Often enough the effect is quite the contrary; it is an effect of emphasis. There seem to be two quite different functions, subordination, and superordination.

In the first category are materials which only remotely impinge upon Friedrich, events which affect his activities and his purposes, but only indirectly, though some other agency. Although it is not in small print, the following passage gives some clue to this function. It is about the Italian War from 1742 to 1748. "War of which we propose to say almost nothing; but must request the reader to imagine it, all along, as influential on our specific affairs" (XIV, ii, 381). And every now and then there is a reminder that it is indeed going on, and occasionally more than a reminder, sometimes in small-print passages. Excellent examples of this kind of subordination are to be found in the accounts of Wolfe in Canada (Books XVIII and XIX). What Carlyle was attempting to do is clear enough. To carry out his theme of Friedrich creating an island of order in the European chaos of the eighteenth century, he had to present that chaos both vividly and in considerable detail. To feel Friedrich's struggle, the reader has to feel as intimately what he was struggling against. The effect is certainly precisely that. As the reader continues to burrow his way through the book, gradually he gains, as several readers at the time noticed, an extraordinarily comprehensive and detailed imaginative grasp of the political life of Europe during the twenty-three years of Friedrich's role as Friedrich Agonistes, not Carlyle's own epithet but justified by the identification of Friedrich with Samson Agonistes in Book I (p. 5). From this tremendous detail emerges a pattern of forces marshalled against him, at various times and in various combinations, England, France, Austria (above all), Russia and Sweden. I know of no sustained historical discourse, even of much lesser length, in which the general contours of political and military events emerge with such grandeur and clarity. The convention of subordination by small print certainly, I think, contributes greatly to this. Such a passage is to the large print as a subordinate clause is to an independent clause. The equivalent of a logical articulation is achieved in large-scale historical articulation.

The second category, superordination, is equally important. The effect is cinematic, a close-up, together with a slowing down of the tempo of narration. A more appropriate nineteenth-century term would be "vignette". One of Carlyle's constant minor themes is the difficulty of getting a clear picture of Friedrich, or of his contemporaries, such as Voltaire or Czar Peter III. Just as Friedrich's effort was to penetrate through the shams and lies and illusions of the eighteenth century, so Carlyle presents himself as engaged in an equivalent struggle to penetrate through the mass of documents and formal histories—subsumed under the imaginary Prussian historian Dryasdust—to get at the living reality of a human being. The large-print discourse, then, carries forward the events in a more or less normal historical rhetoric, but it is apparent that Carlyle recognizes such narrative rhetoric as an abstraction, a simplification, a reduction to a spurious order of the infinitely complex interactions of human beings. The small-print superordination not only serves, then, to penetrate through that abstraction and to offer relief from it, but also—and this is the most important effect—to reveal its abstract character.

Moreover, the conventions of rhetorical articulation of sub-ordination and superordination effected by small print are them-selves part of a larger and even more interesting rhetorical strategy, the dissolution of the narrator into a group of narrators. First, of course, is "I". This is the modest struggling historian, attempting to set forth clearly the history of Friedrich, to disen-tangle immense complications, such as the Schleswig-Holstein question, or the case of the Miller Arnold, to present clearly what cannot be presented clearly, a battle, to explain the movements in Friedrich's campaigns. Above all—and this is of the highest importance—the "I" is struggling with an immense accumulation of documents. This "I" often calls himself "Editor". This not only emphasizes the physical presence of the documents but also links Frederick with Carlyle's truly editorial role in *Cromwell* and with the fictitious editor of *Sartor Resartus*, also struggling with a confused mass of miscellaneous documents from which he has to construct some kind of meaning. Closely related to this primary "I", and almost identifiable with him, is the "I" of some previous stage in the construction of the book. This former "I" has left behind him note-books, scraps of paper, annotated maps, and so forth, which the current "I" uses. Part of the humour of the current "I" is the pleasure he takes in burning up materials he no longer needs. More remote is an unnamed "predecessor", transparently Carlyle himself. Dramatized in this figure is the experience every researcher has of feeling that his earlier notes must have been made by someone else, a justified feeling, since as one studies and writes one does become a different figure. Still more remote is the unnamed tourist, transparently again Carlyle himself. Here also is dramatized the feeling that the historian in his study, consulting his notes and his documents, is not the same man as the historian in the field, actively engaged in exam-ining the battleground, or the palace, or the gardens, or the portrait. All these figures are anonymous, and each indicates a different and psychologically accurate relation of the historian to his materials.

Over against these are two named figures, each with quite a different function. "Sauerteig" is the author of the discussion of Ideal History, of the identification of history with imprisoned epic, quoted above. "Sauerteig" means yeast, or leaven. He is the ultimate interpreter not of history itself but of the historian's activity. He is the meta-historian. At the opposite pole is "Smelfungus", presumably meaning "smelling of the mould of ancient documents". He is the polar opposite of Sauerteig. He is the researcher; he occasionally seems to be Joseph Neuberg, Carlyle's immensely valuable assistant. He is spoken of with contempt and affection, and with sorrow for his endless and often profitless efforts, for he often produces the useless or the barely usable. He is, therefore, a useful means of subordination, a way of bringing in material of very peripheral interest, which is, however, at least above the level of the negligible, though often enough he turns up with that as well. These two figures likewise indicate psychologically accurate relations of the historian to his materials.

Against these named and nameless figures is the enemy of all of them, Dryasdust. He is not only the unimaginative, noninterpretative historian, usually Prussian; he is not even competent and reliable in presenting his materials. He is particularly incompetent—and he often gets cursed for this—in providing indices; either they are non-existent or they are bad. Thus he is as unimaginative in comprehending the relation of the historian to his documents as he is uncomprehending of the extreme pole of the competent construction of historical discourse—meta-history, the role of Sauerteig. Dryasdust cannot give a rational account of a sequence of events of any complexity; he cannot even construct a simple chronological table of such a sequence. He is entirely overwhelmed by the maelstrom of historical documentation; he himself is only caught up in the perpetual whirlwind in the dustbin of historical documents. He is therefore a constant threat to the other narrators; without knowing it, he continuously undermines and subverts the activity of constructing a historical discourse. And he too is an aspect of Carlyle, of the narrator of the narrators, as he is of any historian.

This dissolution of the narrator into a variety of roles is of the highest interest. It is a device which, without compromising *Frederick* as historical discourse, nevertheless pulls it into the general field of art. The narrator, as increasingly in the novels of the time, *Vanity Fair* for example, the "I" is not a category with a fixed and stable set of attributes.[4] He becomes something like the central figure of a major work of fiction, a proper-name category with a constantly changing set of attributes for which there is no attribute which subsumes the remaining attributes into a coherence. Thus the narrator resembles not only the narrator of sophisticated fiction but also the narrator of many lyric poems and of the informal essay. This dissolved narrator, in fact, tends to become more interesting, because of attributional discontinuity, than Friedrich himself, who shows greater attributional stability and coherence than Friedrich Wilhelm, his father, a character recognized by some of Carlyle's contemporaries as one of the great creations of English literature.

This attributional dissolution of the narrator into various named roles is on the central line of Romanticism, the separation between self and role, as George Herbert Mead pointed out many years ago. The usual procedure in Romantic fictions of one sort or another, including poetry, is the creation of an anti-role, the Bohemian, the Artist, the Dandy, the Virtuoso, and the Historian.[5] The anti-role establishes and defines the self, which, of course, is a pure concept and has no empirical existence, or at best is a feeling-state, a sense of continuity as one shifts from one social role to another. In dissolving and subdividing the anti-Role of the Historian, Carlyle has gone one step further in this, anticipating Nietzsche, who insisted that the effort to create a coherent interpretation of his thousands of aphorisms and paragraphs would be a profound miscomprehension of what he was trying to do. Carlyle has shown the similarity of the construction of anti-Roles to the construction of socially validated roles. The self, as it were, can manifest itself only in roles, and from this point of view, even the creation of an anti-Role itself belongs to the socialization process. The personality is thus revealed not as a manifestation or embodiment of the self but as part of the social world from which the self is alienated. This is again an instance of the radical difference between the redemptionist Carlyle of the years before *Latter-Day Pamphlets* and the Carlyle of *Frederick*.

Nevertheless, the continuity of the self behind the roles is symbolized. The prose style is that symbolization; for whatever role is being played, even a minor role not yet mentioned, the Translator, there is a stylistic continuity. However, that continuity is by no means identical with the style of Carlyle's previous writings. It is different from the style of *Latter-Day Pamphlets*, in which appears an unusually high percentage of complex sentences. On the other hand, *Frederick* shares with the *French Revolution* and *Latter-Day Pamphlets* a most unusually high percentage of sentence-fragments. Again, only *Past and Present* and *Latter-Day Pamphlets* show a higher average of expressive punctuation marks than *Frederick*, to which the average in *Heroes and Hero-Worship* is equal. The latter, of course, was designed for public presentation in lectures, and *Past and Present* was written after several years of public lecturing. *Latter-Day Pamphlets*, on the other hand, was specifically polemic, designed to bring about changes in attitudes and action. Sentence-fragments and expressive punctuation are the marks of a style aimed at oral delivery. The self underlying the various roles in *Frederick* can be usefully categorized as a man speaking to other men, but a man separated from other men by an alienation more thorough-going than at any previous stage in Carlyle's life. Thus the style of *Frederick* is often more like Carlyle's journal style than is the style of any of his other published works. This is perfectly consonant with the implications drawn above from the passages on No-Government, and with the conviction that the true Historical Epic cannot be written at the present time by anyone.[6]

But this is not all, for that alienation is further dramatized by the narrator's alienation from the task he is engaged on, the construction of a history of Friedrich. That this alienation was perfectly sincere is indicated by Carlyle's journal entries at the time. That sincerity, however, is of no importance; the evidence for it serves little more than to support a rhetorical analysis developed from other evidence. It is more interesting that the alienation from the task itself is consonant with Carlyle's lack of conviction that the whole enormous effort was worth the trouble it was taking to do it. All of the devices so far discussed are employed to dramatize that alienation from the effort. *Frederick* is unique in the way it forces on the reader an awareness of the narrator's struggle with documents and with previous histories on this and related subjects. Everyone who attempts to construct a discourse from primary and secondary materials and from his own notes experiences that struggle; but the normal and socially

validated attributes of the scholarly narrator's role are the suppression of that awareness, the presentation of an air of quiet
confidence, and a dramatization of perfect competence, even
though in fact the author is constantly trembling with professional
anxiety. The competence of the scholar and the historian is one
of those shams and illusions and lies, one of those "unveracities",
which Carlyle is attacking. This is often dramatized amusingly, as
when the narrator admits he has lost a note, or has inadvertently
destroyed it, or can no longer locate the source of a quotation or
a reference. The highly unsatisfactory and fundamentally incompetent behavioural processes of the scholar and historian are thus
brought out into the open. Perhaps this is why younger scholar-
critics have rejected *Frederick*. Their professional ambitions and
longings for validated professional status do not permit them to
become aware of and examine the illusory and unveracious
attributes of the social role they are playing. That incompetence
and wasted effort are fundamental attributes of humanity is
neither an attractive nor a sustaining notion. Nevertheless, it
sustained Carlyle through the immense struggle of writing
Frederick. It is worth speculating on how this could have been
the case.

3

In the first place Carlyle saw the ultimate task of the historian
as the interpretation of historical events:

> That the man of rhythmic nature will feel more and more his
> vocation towards the Interpretation of Fact; since only in the vital
> centre of that, could we once get thither, lies all real melody; and
> that he will become, he, once again, the Historian of events,—
> bewildered Dryasdust having at last the happiness to be his servant,
> and to have some guidance from him. Which will be blessed indeed.
> For the present, Dryasdust strikes me like a hapless Nigger gone
> masterless: Nigger totally unfit for self-guidance; yet without master
> good or bad; and whose feats in that capacity no god or man can
> rejoice in.
> History, with faithful Genius at the top and faithful Industry at
> the bottom, will then be capable of being written. History will then
> actually *be* written,—the inspired gift of God employing itself to
> illuminate the dark ways of God (I, i, 19).

211

This is spoken by Sauerteig, the yeast of historical discourse, the metaphysical historian. In this passage two things are to be noted: interpretation as the ultimate task of history, and the insistence that though history may be the gift of God which illuminates the dark ways of God, the time for the exercise of that gift has not yet come. This is Sauerteig's hope. The fact that it resides in the realm of hope, however, suggests something about how Carlyle was able to sustain himself. The central epistemological thesis of Romanticism, not often uttered but constantly exemplified, is the irresolvable tension between subject and object. In this passage the hope for the future historian appears to be, for history at least, that the interpretation of fact, the illumination of the dark ways of God, will ultimately involve a resolution of subject and object. But it is to be remembered that this is Sauerteig speaking, and that Sauerteig is a role. Thus what he says is displaced from Carlyle's own position. A hope is offered, to be sure, but the ultimate Romantic position of non-resolution of subject and object is not ultimately compromised. It is as if Carlyle were stating that Sauerteig's hope has its primary attractiveness in its emotional satisfaction, that such satisfaction cannot be rejected simply because it is satisfying, but also that it cannot be accepted on the same grounds either. This is one of the more subtle Romantic epistemological strategies, one at which Browning was particularly adept. "The tension between subject and object is irresolvable, but insofar as that proposition is itself object, it is necessary to maintain an irresolvable tension between the subject and that proposition as object." It was a very Hegelian way of considering the problem.

Frederick, then, rests upon an historian's alienation from his task of constructing an historical discourse, but the task could be, in spite of that, continued since it was sustained by the Romantic epistemology of subject-object tension. That alienation, moreover, particularly as it is manifest through the reader's intense awareness of the historian's unsatisfactory struggle with the documents and already existing instances of historical discourse, raises a further question about historical discourse which cannot be answered in terms of the Romantic epistemology, at least as it had developed for Carlyle and his contemporaries. That question is, What is historical discourse, really? Now there is a fallacy in Sauerteig's remarks, a fallacy revealed by the actual discourse of *Frederick*. The historian does not in fact interpret fact, that is, historical events. He interprets documents and historical discourses. Carlyle seems to have some self-conscious inkling of this. He urged the student of history to seek for portraits, just as he himself collected all the portraits of Friedrich he could acquire. The portrait, he said, was "a small lighted *candle*, by which the Biographies could for the first time be read with some human interpretation".[7] Though I do not know of any passage in which he spelled it out or even hinted at it, other than this one, here, at any rate, Carlyle seems to have had some notion that there is a profound difference between interpreting fact and interpreting documents. The latter, the historian's task, is the interpretation of language before him, not of events in the past. The past is inaccessible; only language is accessible. The historian constructs a linguistic discourse which is related, somehow or other, to a selected assemblage of discourses, a package of discourses held together by the wrappings of the package, not by internal affiliation. Their affinities are elected, but the historian does the electing.

History, then, is language about language, language that refers to language. A notion of history thus is properly subsumed by a notion of language, and the question, "What is history?" resolves itself into the question, "What is language?" One can find a way into this maze by focusing upon the term "refer". Now it seems to be reasonably clear that language does not refer. "Refer" when applied to language is a metaphor. Human beings refer; *language* does not do anything. It consists of signs to which human beings respond. Furthermore, responses to particular signs are not stable over time nor at any given moment, since to any single sign an indefinably wide range of responses is always possible. Further, human beings *learn* how to respond to signs and learn, with considerable imprecision, what responses to a given sign or set of signs are appropriate in a given situation or set of situations. Like Fritz Mauthner, and others before him, I think the most adequate resolution of this problem is to define language as instructions or directions for performance, effective only for those who have been previously instructed how to respond to those directions, even when the proper response is to produce further linguistic utter-

213

ances. Such a position avoids completely any notion of immanent meaning and accepts fully both conventionality of meaning and the imprecision (that is, the constant flow of innovation) which is characteristic of responses to language. Much else remains to be said about historical discourse, but a conclusion about history from this notion of language can serve to explain the extraordinary and unique character of *Frederick*. A historical discourse is a set of instructions for reading primary and secondary documents originating in the past. The drama of *Frederick* is the drama of an historian struggling to learn how to read his documents.

The charm of historical discourse is its capacity to elude our human demands for the probable, a demand to which fiction is disgracefully obedient. If one likes to read history, merely for the sake of reading history, Carlyle's *History of Friedrich II of Prussia* offers a hugely enjoyable experience. Beyond that it derives a further interest because it raises questions of great interest both about historical writing in Carlyle's own cultural situation and about the philosophy of history, or more precisely, the philosophy of historical discourse.

NOTES

1. A few bibliographical details may be of some interest, particularly since the first edition is less frequently encountered, in my experience, than the Centenary Edition.
   First edition: Vol. I, Books I–V, pp. 634, 1858; Vol. II, Books VI–X, pp. 694 (with index to p. 712), 1858; Vol. III, Books XI–XIV, pp. 759 (index to p. 770), 1862; Vol. IV, Books XV–XVII, pp. 615 (index to p. 632), 1864; Vol. V, Books XVIII–XIX, pp. 639, 1865; Vol. VI, Books XX–XXI, pp. 698 (index to p. 781), 1865. The total pages (excluding indices) amount to 4,039. The first instalment (Books I–X, 1858) ends with the death of Friedrich's father, Friedrich Wilhelm; the second instalment (Books XI–XIV, 1862) recounts the events through the First Silesian War and Friedrich's subsequent two years of peace; the third instalment (Books XV–XVII, 1864) carries the account through the Second Silesian War, Friedrich's ten years of peace, and the first year (to March, 1757) of the Third Silesian or Seven Years' War; the fourth instalment (Books XVIII–XXI) concludes that war (1762) and in Book XXI gives a summary of Friedrich's last years (1763–1786).
   Centenary Edition: Vol. I, Books I–IV, pp. 435, 1897; Vol. II, Books

V–VIII, pp, 406, 1897; Vol III, Books IX–XI, pp. 413, 1897; Vol. IV, Books XII–XIV, pp. 501, 1898; Vol. V, Books XV–XVI, pp. 410, 1898; Vol. VI, Books XVII–XVIII, pp. 435, 1898; Vol. VII, Books XIX–XX, pp. 494, 1898; Vol. VIII, Book XXI, pp. 321 (index to p. 390), 1898. Total pages (excluding index): 3,415.

The work is about the same length as Gibbon's masterpiece. Comparison is difficult because so many passages in *Frederick* are in smaller type. References in the text are (by Book, chapter and page) to the *Works*, XII–XIX.

2. Here "Prussia" means what it meant when Carlyle was writing, all the territory of the former Electorate of Brandenburg. As King of Prussia Friedrich was in fact *King* only of E. Prussia, separated from Brandenburg by W. Prussia, acquired in 1772 by the first Polish partition (except for Danzig).

3. The large print yields about 2,160 characters to the page; the small print about 2,910. If 900 pages in the Centenary edition are in small print, and if those pages were printed in the larger type, there would be about 300 pages more than the present 3,415, an additional bulk of less than 9 per cent. Since 900 is probably too high a figure, though not extremely far off, a reasonable guess would be that if the entire book were presented in the large-type font, not including the index, it would grow by about 7 per cent or perhaps 240 pages. In the original edition there might have been about 300 additional pages, or 50 pages per volume. The cost of paper might have been responsible for the decision to print much of the book in small type, but the book was so splendid and even luxurious a piece of publishing that this explanation is most unlikely. The immediate model was probably Macaulay's *History of England*. The decision to use smaller type may have been the publisher's, but, in view of Carlyle's fame and prestige, it seems most likely to have been Carlyle's.

4. See my "Discontinuity in Fiction", *The Triumph of Romanticism, Collected Essays* (Columbia, S.C., 1970), pp. 318–40.

5. See my "The Dilemma of a Century", *id.*, pp. 36–57.

6. I owe the above information to the kindness of Professor Robert Lee Oakman III of the University of South Carolina, who has allowed me to use his unpublished dissertation, *Syntax in the Prose Style of TC, A Quantitative, Linguistic Analysis*, Indiana Univ. 1971. Professor Oakman is not responsible for my statement about Carlyle's journal style.

7. "Project of a National Exhibition of Scottish Portraits", *Works*, XXIX, 405.

10

Carlyle's Pen Portraits of Queen Victoria and Prince Albert

by C. R. SANDERS

Despite his many expressions of scorn for aesthetics and what he called "dilettantism", some of Carlyle's deepest instincts were those of an artist, and it is a great mistake not to assume that usually he quite consciously wrote as an artist. *Sartor Resartus* is a combination of several literary genres deliberately brought into harmony with one another; *The French Revolution* unites history treated philosophically with what Carlyle thought of as an epic poem in prose, with echoes of Homer recently read in Greek ringing in his ears as he wrote; the "Death of Edward Irving" he himself spoke of as a kind of classical funeral oration, like that in Shakespeare which Antony delivers over Caesar's dead body; and he never grew weary of reading, writing, and theorizing about biography as an art form, the complex function of symbols, and the mysterious powers and problems of language.

He was least an artist when he wrote about his health, denounced the people or institutions which he disliked, moralized, prophesied, or preached. He was most an artist when his eyes came into play and when his intellect interpreted and his imagination shaped what he had actually seen. There can be little doubt that he was one of the greatest picture writers of all time or that, deliberately setting out early in his life to make for posterity as full, vivid, vital, and trustworthy a record of his time as possible, he deserved the title which his contemporaries gave him and which has continued to be accepted, that of the "Victorian Rembrandt".[1] His purpose here was linked in his mind with the important part that he played in bringing about the establishment of National Portrait Galleries in England and Scotland.

Perhaps none of his pen portraits is more interesting to examine with artistic technique in mind than those which he made of Queen Victoria and Prince Albert. Like the thirty or forty other major pen portraits produced by Carlyle, they create their effect and gradually build up the precise conceptions and images he wished to suggest through an accumulative process, as over a long period of years he saw the subjects of his portraits from time to time, corresponding to the way in which a painter requires a series of sittings by his subject before he finishes his portrait. In Carlyle's work, as in a painter's, as his subjects presented themselves from various points of view he modified the general conception, with such changes of line, colour, tone, and emphasis as seemed needful. Yet each new view of his subjects was remarkably fresh, and each new stroke of the pen in recording his impressions seems uncontrived and spontaneous.

One of the most striking powers which Carlyle exercises in drawing his pen portraits, even those of his Queen and Prince, is that of intellectual and artistic dominance. This he achieves in considerable part through the extensive use of diminutives. The young Victoria is a "poor little thing" or "poor little lassie" or "poor little Queen" or "unhappy little child" or "her little Majesty taking her bit departure for Windsor". Carlyle refers to "this little wedding of hers" and describes her as "small, sonsy and modest,—and has the ugliest task, I should say, of all girls in these Isles". Similarly, Prince Albert is "a sensible lad". Nicknames have the same function, as in Carlyle's well-known longer works. The Queen is "poor little Victory" or "little Queen Victory".

Dominance in Carlyle carries with it the right to evaluate and judge. All of his portraits, like most of those by Chaucer, Browning, and Yeats, are appraisal portraits. His subjects are not merely described but are weighed on the scales of his philosophy of life. More than once Carlyle expresses very serious misgivings about the young Victoria's ability to play her role of Queen well. On one occasion when some of her subjects cheer for the Queen as she passes along the street but one refuses to do so and says, "I vont holler!" Carlyle adds, "Neither did I holler at all." When he read

217

a newspaper story indicating that the Queen had been unjust and even stupid in dealing with one of her maids of honour, he commented, "The little Queen behaved like a hapless little fool." Sometimes these judgments take the rather unpleasant form of direful predictions concerning the future of England under such rulers, whether the ruler be Queen Victoria or her son the Prince of Wales.

The dislike of Dandyism and worldly glitter which is often expressed in his longer works also appears in his pen portraits. He is somewhat scornful about the pageantry of Victoria's marriage as "Victory's gilt coach and other gilt coaches drive out". He cares little for the spectacle of the Coronation Procession: "Crowds and mummery are not agreeable to me"; and he describes what he sees as "all gilding, velvet and grandeur". He is just as scornful in commenting on the Glass Palace during the summer of 1851 and speaks of it as a mass of insignificant ostentation under the sponsorship of "King Cole, Prince Albert and Company". In their indictment of Vanity Fair Carlyle and Thackeray have much in common.

If at times Carlyle's evaluations seem too narrow and Puritanical and if he appears to carry the principle of dominance too far, he makes amends by a wealth of convincingly real pictorial detail, by the life with which all his portraits are endowed, by the skill with which they are clearly related to the life of their time and its significant events, by the extent to which his subjects are made to reveal their own inner nature in dramatic action, and by the deep strain of compassion in Carlyle's own nature which usually leads him to identify his subjects with himself as fellow creatures sharing in the common lot of humanity with all its suffering and all its joys. As one reads through his portraits of Victoria and Albert arranged chronologically, one senses a progression through a series of chance glimpses, explosive comments, quick, valid perceptions mixed with prejudice, flashes of light illuminating not only the subjects themselves but to a considerable extent the whole Victorian Age in the background—all moving in a kind of crescendo toward two scenes fully acted out and fully painted in which the real Carlyle meets the real Prince Albert and the real Queen in clear light where there is no distortion and where Carlyle's sense of proportion, perspective, emphasis, and balance has now made its last needful adjustment. Something very much like this takes place in the development of the pen portrait of Coleridge, which reaches its final stage in *The Life of John Sterling*, and in nearly all of his other major pen portraits.

Nothing could be more vivid or memorable than the pictorial details, almost Chaucer-like in their quality, which Carlyle gives us. Albert has a "well-built figure of near my own height, florid *blond* face (with fair hair); but the eyes were much better than I had fancied; a pair of strong steady eyes, with a good healthy briskness in them"; and he wears "loose greyish clothes". At the time of her meeting with Carlyle, Victoria comes "gliding into the room in a sort of swimming way, no feet visible"; and after the meeting she "sailed out as if moving on skates". In 1867 she "still looks plump and almost young (in spite of one broad wrinkle that shows in each cheek *occasionally*)". She is "all gentle, all sincere-looking, unembarrassing, rather attractive even;— *makes* you feel too (if you have sense in you) that she is Queen". Details in the setting are not overlooked: the tea-cups are of "sublime patterns", but the coffee is "very black and muddy". In earlier glimpses of the Queen, Carlyle's use of picturesque Scottish words do much to spice his descriptions and make them fresh and vivid. Touches of humour often enliven his portraits. At least one appears in those of Victoria and Albert when Victoria is misled by Sir James Clark into "mistaking the wind and protuberance of a certain maid of honour's *digestive* apparatus for something in the *generative* (Gott in Himmel!)".

As in all his other writings, Carlyle here places a very high value on good manners. Prince Albert when he meets Carlyle is a model of courtesy and as he leaves mentions Carlyle's works and backs out as a token of recognition of Carlyle's eminence as a writer; and Carlyle writes of Queen Victoria, "It is impossible to imagine a *politer* little woman."

The use of metaphor also counts for much in these pen portraits. The young Queen's throne is a "frail cockle on the black bottomless deluges".[2] At the time when frenzied young men were shooting at the Queen, Carlyle, though fully aware of the need for social and economic reform in that day, declares that the would-be assassins were like "a man that wanted the steeple pulled down" but who had to be content with flinging "a stone at the gilt weathercock". The Crystal Palace, though sponsored by Prince Albert, is the emblem of the "profoundest Orcus, or belly of Chaos itself". He describes the "deep bow of us male monsters" when the Queen appears; and Mrs George Grote is spoken of as "a tall old Gearpole" ["Irish-weaver implement"—T.C.].

Carlyle's subjects are never placed in a vacuum, and the social and economic background against which they are presented and which often involves them in dramatic interplay with the incidents and forces of their times is never artificial or contrived in such a manner as to suggest a mere stage setting. As we observe the young Queen, trembling with fear and sometimes even weeping, we learn that she has many enemies among the Tories. We sympathize with her when she cannot even take a ride in her carriage without being shot at by young fanatics. We also sympathize with Prince Albert when false rumours damage his reputation and during his unpopularity about 1854. We admire him when he joins forces with Carlyle in establishing National Portrait Galleries and when he shows a lively, informed, and intelligent interest in German studies and German culture. We assay the quality of the Queen's taste in terms of the part she had in determining the architecture of the Albert Memorial; and we admire her as she listens patiently to Carlyle's discourse on Scottish history and lore. Questions concerning England's relation to France, Germany, Russia, and India are also an integral part of the background.

Extremely important in Carlyle's delineations of his subjects is the skilful use of other persons bearing somewhat the same relation to them that the supporting characters in drama bear to the principal members of the cast. His technique here strongly suggests that of Boswell, whose *Johnson* was a lifetime favourite with him. In Carlyle's portraits, Victoria, "poor little fool", quarrels with her mother, puts the aggressive and formidable Mrs George Grote in her place, cuts short Professor Grote when he threatens to lose himself and others in labyrinths of erudition, pretends politely to listen for a time to Sir Charles Lyell's discourse on geology, asks Robert Browning, who was at work on *The Ring and the Book*, "Writing anything?" and then like Pontius Pilate turns quickly away without waiting for an answer, finds her own excellent manners greatly enhanced by the personal charm and corresponding excellent manners of Lady Augusta Stanley, and her own attractiveness enhanced by the loveliness of her daughter Princess Louise. Yet the threatening incompetence of the Prince of Wales and what Carlyle considers the questionable activities of Alfred Ernest Albert, Queen Victoria's second son, rise like clouds upon the horizon. Prince Albert, at times idealistic and visionary, appears at a great disadvantage when contrasted with Arkwright, whose head was full of practicality and common sense. On the other hand, a Prince Albert ready to sponsor such an admirable project as a National Portrait Gallery is greatly to be preferred to a Sir Anthony Panizzi, Keeper of Printed Books in the British Museum, who, Carlyle believed, was concerned altogether with the kind of librarianship that stressed ostentatious exhibitionism and impressive statistics relating to the annual budget and other administrative matters.

But the quality that gives the greatest value to Carlyle's pen portraits is their humanity and the sense of human kinship which he feels with his subjects, often accompanied by a feeling of deep compassion for them. The young Queen during the trying early years of her reign is "a sister situated as mortal seldom was". In 1838 he writes: "Poor Queen. She is much to be pitied." Prince Albert is far from being a mere figurehead but is "truly a handsome flourishing man and Prince" who after his meeting with Carlyle at Windsor was spoken of as "the young Brother Mortal I had just been speaking to". It is significant that the banker-poet Samuel Rogers, not usually associated with sentimentalism, rises greatly in Carlyle's esteem when, in the period of the Queen's early unpopularity, he defends young people in general and the young Queen in particular. The bond between Carlyle and the Queen is greatly strengthened by deep sorrow. Her gracious message sent to him after the death of his wife in 1866, is expressed in terms of her own sense of loss when her husband died about five years before. And his chief thought as he describes for his sister his meeting with the Queen is what the meeting would have meant to Jane, if she could have been alive to know about it.

So much then for comment and analysis. Let us now read the pen portraits themselves in chronological sequence and see how they move toward a kind of climax when Carlyle meets first Prince Albert and then the Queen. What follows these meetings is brief, mere epilogue, as the years and distant memories close in on an old man who had seen much and served his Queen and country well.

TC to Margaret A. Carlyle, 9 November 1837:
We heard nothing of Queen Victoria and her dinner yesterday except the jowling of the bells.[3]

TC to Alexander Carlyle, 26 November 1837:
I enclose a Portrait of Queen Victoria poor little thing, whom I have never seen yet; they say it is as like her as another. It will need pasting together at the edges (the edging will); it was too big to go into the letter,—or, lo, Jane has done it with no need of pasting![4]

TC to John A. Carlyle, 12 April 1838:
Going thro' the Green Park, I saw her little Majesty, taking her bit of departure for Windsor. I had seen her another day at Hyde Park Corner coming in from the daily ride. She is decidedly a pretty-looking little creature; health, clearness, graceful timidity looking out from her young face; "frail cockle on the black bottomless deluges," one could not help some interest in her, as in a sister situated as mortal seldom was. The crowd yesterday, some two thousand strong, of loungers and children, uttered no sound whatever, except a kind of thin-spread interjection *"Aihh!"* from the infantile part of it, one old Flunkey in tarnished laced hat was the only creature I saw salute, he got a bow in return all to himself Poor little Victory![5]

TC to Margaret A. Carlyle, 12 April 1838:
Yesterday, going thro' one of the Parks, I saw the poor little Queen. She was in an open carriage, preceded by three or four swift red-coated troopers; all off for Windsor just as I happened to pass. Another carriage, or carriages, followed; with maids of honour &c: the whole drove very fast. It seemed to me the poor little Queen was a bit modest nice sonsy little lassie; blue eyes, light hair fine white skin; of extremely small stature: she looked timid anxious, almost frightened; for the people looked at her in perfect silence; one old liveryman alone touched his hat to her: I was heartily sorry for the poor bairn,—tho' perhaps she might have said as Parson Swan did, "*Greet* not for me brethren; for verily yea verily I greet not for myself." It is a strange thing to look at the fashion of this world![6]

TC to Jean Carlyle Aitken, 6 July 1838:

A Miss Fergus[7] from Kirkcaldy was here staying: I had to accompany her to see the Coronation Procession; we had been invited to the Montagues' window, but sh*d* not otherwise have gone. I had even a "ticket to the Abbey" (a thing infinitely precious), but gave that decidedly away. Crowds and mummery are not agreeable to me. The Procession was all gilding, velvet and grandeur; the poor little Queen seemed to have been *greeting* [weeping]: we could not but wish the poor little lassie well; she is small, sonsy and modest, —and has the ugliest task, I should say, of all girls in these Isles.[8]

TC at a dinner given by Richard Monckton Milnes in 1838:

Poor Queen! She is much to be pitied. She is at an age when she would hardly be trusted with the choosing of a bonnet, and she is called to a task from which an archangel might have shrunk?[9]

TC to John A. Carlyle, 16 April 1839:

Sir James [Clark] has got into a scrape lately and led the Queenkin into one; mistaking the wind and protuberance of a certain maid of honour's *digestive* apparatus for something in the *generative* (Gott in Himmel!), and quite roughly requesting said maid of honour to *confess*! The little Queen behaved like a hapless little fool,—and indeed looks like one now (very strikingly since last year, to my sense), and seems very generally to be thought one. Unhappy little child.[10]

TC to Margaret A. Carlyle, 11 February 1840:

Yesterday the idle portion of the Town was in a sort of flurry owing to the marriage of little Queen Victory. I had to go out to breakfast with an ancient Notable of this place, one named Rogers the Poet and Banker; my way lay past little Victory's Palace, and a perceptible crowd was gathering there even then, which went on increasing all the time till I returned (about one o'clock); streams of idle *gomerils* [block-heads] flowing in from all quarters, to see one knows not what,—perhaps Victory's gilt coach and other gilt coaches drive out, for that would be all! It was a wet day too, of bitter heavy showers, and abundant mud: I steered, by a small circuit, out of their road altogether, and except the clanking of some bells in the after part of the day heard no more of it. Poor little thing, I wish her marriage all prosperity too;—but it is her business, not mine. She has many enemies among the Tories, who repeat all kinds of spiteful things about her; she seems also to have abundance of obstinate temper, and no great overplus of sense:

I see too clearly great misery lying in store for her, if she live some years; and Prince Albert, I can tell him, has got no sinecure by the end! As for him, they say he is a sensible lad; which circumstance may be of much service here: he burst into tears, in leaving his little native Coburg, a small quiet town, like Annan for example; poor fellow, he thought I suppose how he was bidding adieu to *quiet* there, and would probably never know *it* any more, whatever else he might know![11]

TC to John A. Carlyle, 15 February 1840:

I did attend Rogers's Dinner, as appointed. . . . I decidedly liked Rogers a little better. His love of young people is itself a good sign. He defended the poor little Queen, and her fooleries and piques and pettings in this little wedding of hers.[12]

TC to Alexander Carlyle, 17 February 1840:

Queen Victory has got her bit wedding over; the people are all accusing her, poor little dear, how she has quarrelled with her mother, openly insulted her; how she has done this and that! I am heartily sorry for her, poor little fool; but for the poor little fool's *Twenty Millions of people* I am infinitely sorrier. Bad days are coming, as I often *spae* [foretell].[13]

TC to Margaret A. Carlyle, 4 June 1842:

It was precisely on that Wednesday [2 June] that the Queen had been shot at. These are bad times for Kings and Queens. This young blackguard, it seems, is *not* mad at all; was in great want, and so forth; it is said they will hang him. Such facts indicate that even among the lowest classes of people, Queenship and Kingship are fast growing out of date.[14]

TC to Margaret A. Carlyle, 4 July 1842:

On Saturday night it was publicly made known that [John] Francis, the man who last shot at the Queen, was not to be hanged, but to be sent to Botany Bay, or some such punishment. Well, yesterday about noon, as the Queen went to St. James' Chapel, a third individual [John William Bean] presented his pistol at the Majesty of England, but was struck down and seized before he could fire it; he and another who seemed to be in concert with him are both laid up. There is no doubt of the fact. The two are both "young" men; we have yet heard nothing more of them than that. The person who struck down the pistol (and with it the man, so vehement was he) is said to be a gentleman's flunkey; but I do not know that for certain and have seen no newspaper yet. . . . Are not these strange times? The people are sick of their misgovernment, and the blackguards among them shoot at the poor Queen: as a man that wanted the steeple pulled down might at least fling a stone at the gilt weathercock. The poor little Queen has a horrid business of it,—cannot take a drive in HER *clatch* without risk of being shot![15]

TC to Jane Welsh Carlyle, [13 August 1842]:

Yesterday I did not see Charles Buller; on arriving at Charing Cross I found the Parliament just *then* in its agonies, and that there was no chance of him at the Temple. I stept down rather, to look at the Queen for an instant. She did pass, she and Albert, looking very much frightened, red in the face; but none shot at the poor little thing, some even gave a kind of encouraging cheer. "No, me? *I vont holler!*" said some of the populace near me; neither did I *holler* at all.[16]

TC to Joseph Neuberg, 25 July 1851:

To look once at this Glass Palace was (if you forgot all else) perceptibly pleasant; but to have gone to study, to think, or to learn anything in it, would almost have driven a serious man mad. Who can bear to look on *Chaos*, however gilded the specimens shown? Very empty persons only! "Improvement in Manufactures?" I have often said: "The grandest specific set of improvements ever made in manufactures were effected not in a big Glass Soapbubble, presided over by Prince Albert and the General Assembly of Prurient Windbags out of all countries, but under the torn hat, once, of a Lancashire Pedlar [Richard Arkwright] selling washballs and cheap razors thro' the Hill-country,—Pedlar and Barber who chanced to have a head that he could employ in *thinking* under said Hat!"[17]

TC to Jane Welsh Carlyle, 10 September 1851:

I had no idea till late times what a *bottomless* fund of darkness there is in the human animal, especially when congregated in masses, and set to build "Crystal Palaces" &c under King Cole, Prince Albert and Company! The profoundest Orcus, or belly of Chaos itself, this *is* the emblem of them.[18]

TC to Lord Ashburton, 8 September 1853:

Edward Hyde, the great Chancellor, first Earl of Clarendon, is the only Englishman I have ever heard of attempting seriously to form a Gallery of English Portraits. . . . I have no hesitation in asserting that of all Galleries whatsoever the one that has in Nature the *best* right to exist on English Funds were a Gallery of Portraits of Historical English. If the Prince Consort would be pleased to take up this important and neglected Enterprise, I love to persuade myself he has the means both inward and outward of doing much to accomplish it. . . . That the Prince himself should be Sovereign of the thing,—the Prince, or somebody possessing the qualities of mind which I privately ascribe to the Prince;—who should do the operation in much more silence than is common: this seems to me to be an essential condition. From Committees and After-Dinner Oratory,—alas, what can we expect? We know these sad entities, some of us; and all of us are beginning to know,—to our cost! And if the Parliament would give no money on these terms, I believe, even in that worst case, the Prince might make more real progress with money he could spare of his own, than with the Parliamentary money granted on the common terms. And just as George the Third's modest, solid and excellent Library is *worth* far more than Panizzi's huge expensive unsound and ostentatious one, and calls forth a blessing yet on the faithful and really human soul of that simple King (instead of a *non-blessing* on certain other *in*human, pedant, and merely showman souls),—so might the Prince's Gallery of English Portraits, conducted even on his own resources if he could get no other on fair terms, be a blessing and a credit to this country.[19]

TC to Lady Ashburton, 11 January 1854:

Come, then; and comfort poor Prince Albert, who is really getting into turbid water at present. Poor soul: Louis XVI said once, "What have I done to be so loved?" Thou (probably) "what to be so hated?" The answer in both, "Nothing! "[20]

TC to John A. Carlyle, 27 January 1854:

Abundance of rumour still abt Prince Albert (poor soul), but no sensible person that I meet takes the least share(?) in it.[21]

TC to Lady Ashburton, 9 November 1854:

Yesterday I went to Windsor, as arranged; was met on [all?] hands by the due facilities; had in fact good success, and much reason to thank the beneficent individualities who made all roads so smooth for me there. The Collection of Engraved Portraits, Miniatures &c &c far exceeds, in quantity and quality any I had ever had access to; . . . a larger proportion were of interest to me, in my present affair [the writing of *Frederick the Great*], than I could at all have expected. . . . Glover is an intelligent handy cheerful man, of London-Offical nature; not wanting in what learning is needful to him; . . . he was civility itself to me. . . . I had four very good hours there, and saw much that I shall remember: the only thing was, I *talked* a great deal too much (having acquired no art of keeping silence, even when I wanted to do so, fool that I am!),—and flurried all my nerves, even had there been no other mischief in it!

Towards 4 o'clock there came a light footstep to the door; I still busy among 100 Frederick Portraits did not look up, till Glover said, "Prince Albert!"—and there in fact was his Royal Highness, come for a sight of the monster before he went;—bowing very graciously, and not advancing till I bowed. Truly a handsome flourishing man and Prince; extremely polite (in the English way too);—and with a far better pair of *eyes* than I had given him credit for in the distance. We had a very pretty little dialogue: about Frederick's Portraits first (and your despised Picture now turned to the wall at Bath House, the original of which is well known to H.R.H., came in among other things); after which, by a step or two, we got into the Saxon genealogies, Elector Frederick the Wise, Martin Luther, Wartburg, Coburg, and had the whole world free before us! Very fair indeed: but a noiseless, almost voiceless *waiter* glided in just at this time, out of whom I caught the words, "gone out to the Terrace";—whereupon, after a minute or so, his R.H., our Dialogue winding itself up in some tolerable way, gracefully vanished (back foremost, as I noticed, the courteous man!), and I saw him no more. That was about the finale of my day; and I need not deny, was a pleasant, not a painful one,—and left me with a multiplicity of thoughts, inarticulate and other, about the young Brother Mortal I had just been speaking to; thoughts surely not of an ungrateful unrecognizing nature, whatever else they might be in the confused and confusing epochs of the world!—— That is the history of my day; which I thought good to lay at your Ladyship's feet, that you may see how "the pleasure of the Lord prospers in your hand," when you do kindnesses to your friends.[22]

TC to Jean Carlyle Aitken, 10 November 1854:

The day before yesterday I went to Windsor; for the sake of innumerable Portraits, Engravings, Miniatures &c which I had got access to there. It is some 20 and odd miles off: one of the beautifullest Palaces,—for situation &c much the beautifullest I ever saw.

Built on a sheer steep Hill (high for those parts, and beautifully *clothed*); commanding an immense plain, the richest in the Island; with Oak forests, with the River, with &c &c to all lengths. I regarded little or nothing of that; but proceeded straight to my Print rooms, where a Mr. Glover, the "Librarian" of the place, was extremely kind to me, and I saw really a great many things that may be useful in my operations; and had four diligent and goodish hours out of a day. I mean to go back when the weather is brighter (for Pictures and old eyes), and when "the Court" is not there. Towards 4 o'clock, while I was busy with a hundred Prints of *Frederick*, there came a soft step to the door; I did not look up till Glover said, "Prince Albert!"—and there in truth was the handsome young gentleman, very jolly and handsome in his loose greyish clothes, standing in the door; not advancing till I bowed. His figure and general face were well known to me, well-built figure of near my own height, florid *blond* face (with fair hair); but the *eyes* were much better than I had fancied; a pair of strong steady eyes, with a good healthy briskness in them. He was civility itself, and in a fine simple fashion: a sensible man withal. We talked first of Fred*k*'s Portraits; then went, by a step or two, into the *Saxon genealogy* line, into the Wartburg, Coburg, Luther, Frederick the Wise (that is the Prince who caught up Luther, put him safe into the Wartburg; he is *Ancestor* of Albert); we had there abundant scope of talk, and went on very well, the Prince shewing me a Portrait he had copied of "Fred*k* the Wise" (not ill done), telling of a Luther Autograph he had (from Coburg, and a joke appended to the getting of it there),—when a *domestic* glided in upon us, murmured something, of which I heard, "gone out to the Terrace!" (Queen out, wants you,—he had been in Town all morning)—whereupon, in a minute or two, our Dialogue winding itself up in some tolerable way, P*ce* Albert (prince of Courtesy) bowed himself out, back foremost and with some indistinct mention of "your *Works*," which did not much affect me; and so ended our interview. I had had an indistinct questionable anticipation of some such thing all day; but tho*t* too I was safe, having *met* his carriage on the railway as I came. However, it was managed as you hear; and I was not ill pleased with it, nor had any reason,—*well* pleased to have it over as you may fancy.[23]

TC to John A. Carlyle, 10 November 1854:

The day before yesterday I was at Windsor, looking into Portraits, Prints, Miniatures &c (by private favour),—saw many a thing; and at length "the Prince" himself, with whom there was a pleasant enough little Dialogue; of which you shall know all the particulars one day, if you like. *Hat nichts zu bedeuten.* I returned home, much flurried by my day's travel and activity; and have had a worse dose of cold ever since.[24]

TC to Lady Ashburton, 18 November 1854:
   There should really be a place found for that picture of the Boy Frederick Drumming: yes indeed! there are 3 or 4 prints of it at Windsor, all rather coarse and bad; the Prince Consort suggested the original at Charlottenburg (as yet ignorant that there was a first-rate Copy in these parts).[25]

TC to John Forster, 5 July 1855:
   By the bye, thinking about Lemoin[n]e yes[terday?] I reflected, before getting home, that he seemed to have no *evidence* whatever, beyond his own surmise and suspicion, of Prince Albert's having interfered at all in the matter of the *Débats* Paragraph or Article? Knowing to what length suspicion can go in the mind of an angry Frenchman, I incline to think Lemoin[n]e most probably altogether mistaken, and Louis Napoleon (in whom I have traced much of the *Housebreaker* talent, touches of the Truculent-Flunkey, and nothing of the Heroic hitherto) probably himself the *sole* author of that Lemoin[n]e operation. "To put down the Press in France": what good or evil can the Press of France do to that poor Gentleman? The Press of England, not put down or *puttable*, is what he hangs on!— Give him the benefit of this doubt I charge you; think not *worse* of your Prince than you were wont, except upon new *evidence.*[26]

TC to Lord Ashburton, 18 January 1856: after Prince Albert through Lord Ashburton had offered to lend Carlyle his copy of Clausewitz, *On War*, 3 vols (1833):
   I suppose it is not seemly for the like of me to thank H.R.H. the Prince Consort in word or message of any kind; but I hope you will, on some good occasion, indicate for me how sensible I am to this mark of humanity in high places.[27]

TC in conversation with William Knighton, 28 November 1855: in reply to the question "Is there yet any hope for England?":
   None; *for a hundred years we have been going downhill fast,* losing faith and hope. *What kind of a boy is this that is to be our King of England next? The German race we have imported from*

the Continent has been a heavy, stupid race. Prince Albert is an exception. He looks forward, I think, and is preparing for what he foresees—that those boys of his will live in troublesome times; but he cannot say so, of course.[28]

Conversations of Sir Charles Gavan Duffy with Carlyle, ca. 1865:
I [Duffy] asked who was responsible for the disappointing effect of the Albert Memorial. The person to be contented, he said, was the Queen. She lived in such an atmosphere of courtly exaggeration that she ceased to comprehend the true relation and proportion of things. Hence the tremendous outcry over Prince Albert, who was in no respect a very remarkable man. He had a certain practical German sense in him too, which prevented him from running counter to the feelings of the English people, but that was all. He was very ill-liked among the aristocracy who came into personal relations with him. Queen Victoria had a preternaturally good time of it with the English people, owing a good deal to reaction from the hatred which George IV had excited. Her son, one might fear, would pay the penalty in a stormy and perilous reign. He gave no promise of being a man fit to perform the tremendous task appointed him to do, and indeed one looked in vain anywhere just now for the man who would lead England back to better ways than she had fallen into in our time.[29]

Lady Augusta Stanley to Dr John A. Carlyle: soon after the Queen had received news of Jane Welsh Carlyle's death:
Osborne: April 30, 1866.
Dear Dr. Carlyle,—I was here when the news of the terrible calamity with which your brother has been visited reached Her Majesty, and was received by her with feelings of sympathy and regret, all the more keen from the lively interest with which the Queen had so recently followed proceedings in Edinburgh. Her Majesty expressed a wish that, as soon as I could do so, I should convey to Mr. Carlyle the expression of these feelings, and the assurance of her sorrowful understanding of a grief which she herself, alas! knows too well.
It was with heartfelt interest that the Queen heard yesterday that Mr. Carlyle had been able to make the effort to return to his desolate home, and that you are with him.[30]

TC's reply to Lady Augusta Stanley:
Chelsea: May 1, 1866.
Dear Lady Augusta,—The gracious mark of Her Majesty's sym-

pathy touches me with many feelings, sad and yet beautiful and high. Will you in the proper manner, with my humblest respects, express to Her Majesty my profound sense of her great goodness to me, in this the day of my calamity. I can write to nobody. It is best for me at present when I do not even speak to anybody.[31]

TC to Sir Henry Parkes, 27 April 1868:
   One set of Newspapers seemed to be filled with the Duke of Edinburgh [Alfred Ernest Albert (1844–1900), 2nd son of Queen Victoria] and his to me thrice-unimportant speakings and doings. These I took no interest in at all, and indeed fled from, as from an afflictive object. I am sorry you have spent £100,000 on that young gentleman, and am much afraid it won't pay! Our "Statesmen" (if we have still any such animal among us) had, most probably, nothing to do with that mission of him to the Antipodes [as commander of the *Galatea* on a world cruise, 1867–71]; it must have been Mamma, merely, and the wish to be rid of him for a while.—Yesterday there came a "telegram" to the effect that some of you had shot him at Sydney (poor soul), not quite killed him but tried it; which I found agitating several people,—tho' not much me, in its present state of mere telegram and uncertain rumour. Poor England will have to prepare herself for quite other disasters, atrocities and brute anarchisms at home and abroad, even if it be true![32]

TC to John A. Carlyle, 6 March 1869:
   Hoho! Here is Froude;—and there was one great thing of all to tell you: interview with Sacred Majty, Thursday last, at "The Deanery" by an appointt a week before. I one of four,—and I may partly think the main one perhaps. Sacred My was very good; thing altogr decidedly insignift, do *tiresome*; and *worsened* a kind of cold I had (and am still dropping with on this very sheet). Abt all whh I will not say a word more, unless specifically *desired* by some of you![33]

TC to Jean Carlyle Aitken, 11 March 1869:
   "Interview" took place this day gone a week; nearly a week before that, the Dean and Dean*ess* (who is called Lady Augusta Stanley, once *Bruce*, an active hard and busy little woman) drove up here, and, in a solemnly mysterious, though half quizzical manner, invited me for Thursday, 4th, 5 P.M.:—Must come, a very "high or indeed highest person has long been desirous," etc., etc. I

saw well enough it was the Queen incognita; and briefly agreed to come. "Half past 4 COME *you!*" and then went their ways.

Walking up at the set time, I was there ushered into a long Drawingroom in their monastic edifice. I found no Stanley there; only at the farther end, a tall old *Gearpole* of a Mrs. Grote,—the most wooden woman I know in London or the world, who thinks herself very clever, etc.—the sight of whom taught me to expect others; as accordingly, in a few minutes, fell out. Grote and Wife, Sir Charles Lyell and ditto, Browning and myself, these I saw were to be our party. "Better than bargain!" "These will take the edge off the thing, if edge it have!"—which it hadn't, nor threatened to have.

The Stanleys and we were all in a flow of talk, and some flunkies had done setting coffee-pots, tea-cups of sublime patterns, when Her Majesty, punctual to the minute, glided softly in, escorted by her Dame in waiting (a Dowager Duchess of Athol), and by the Princess Louise, decidedly a very pretty young lady, and *clever* too, as I found in speaking to her afterwards.

The Queen came softly forward, a kindly little smile on her face; gently shook hands with all three women, gently acknowledged with a nod the silent deep bow of us male monsters; and directly in her presence everybody was if at ease again. She is a comely little lady, with a pair of kind clear and intelligent grey eyes; still looks plump and almost young (in spite of one broad wrinkle that shows in each cheek *occasionally*); has a fine soft low voice; soft indeed her whole manner is and melodiously perfect; it is impossible to imagine a *politer* little woman. Nothing the least imperious; all gentle, all *sincere*-looking, unembarrassing, rather attractive even;—*makes* you feel too (if you have sense in you) that she is Queen.

After a little word to each of us in succession as we stood,—to me it was, "Sorry you did not see my Daughter," Princess of Prussia (or "she sorry," perhaps?), which led us into Potsdam, Berlin, etc., for an instant or two; to Sir Charles Lyell[34] I heard her say, "Gold in Sutherland," but quickly and delicately cut him *short* in responding; to Browning, "Are you writing anything?" (he had just been publishing the absurdest of things! [nothing less than *The Ring and the Book*]); to Grote [35] I did not hear what she said: but it was touch-and-go with everybody; Majesty visibly *without* interest or nearly so of her *own*. This done, Coffee (very black and muddy) was handed round; Queen and Three women taking seats (Queen in the corner of a sofa, Lady Deaness in opposite corner, Mrs. Grote in a chair *intrusively close* to Majesty, Lady Lyell modestly at the *diagonal* corner); we others obliged to stand, and hover within call. Coffee fairly done, Lady Augusta called me gently to "come and speak with Her Majesty." I obeyed, first asking, as an old infirmish man, Majesty's permission to *sit*, which was graciously conceded. Nothing of the least significance was said, nor *needed*; however my bit of dialogue went very well. "What part of Scotland I came from?" "Dumfriesshire (where Majesty might as well go some time); Carlisle, *i.e.*, *Caer-Lewel*, a place about the antiquity of King Solomon (according to Milton, whereat Majesty smiled); Border-Ballads (and even old Jamie Pool slightly alluded to,—not by name!); Glasgow, and even Grandfather's ride thither,—ending in mere *psalms* and streets *vacant* at half-past nine P.M.;—hard sound and genuine Presbyterian *root* of what has now shot up to be such a monstrously ugly Cabbage-tree and Hemlock-tree!" All which Her Majesty seemed to take rather well.

Whereupon Mrs Grote rose, and good-naturedly brought forward her Husband to her own chair, *cheek by jowl* with her Majesty, who evidently did not care a straw for him; but kindly asked, "Writing anything?" and one heard "Aristotle, now that I have done with Plato," etc., etc.—but only for a minimum of time. Majesty herself (I think àpropos of some question of my *shaking hand*) said something about her own difficulty in writing by dictation, which brought forward Lady Lyell and Husband, mutually used to the operation. After which, talk becoming trivial, Majesty gracefully retired,—Lady Augusta with her,—and in ten minutes more, returned to receive our farewell bows; which, too, she did very prettily; and sailed out as if moving on skates, and bending her head towards us with a smile. By the Underground Railway I was home before seven, and out of the adventure, with only a headache of little moment.

Froude tells me there are foolish *myths* about the poor business; especially about my share of it; but this is the real truth;—*worth* to me, in strict speech all but nothing; the *myths* even less than nothing.[36]

TC's entry in his "Journal," 15 March 1869:

It was Thursday, 4th March, 5–6.30 P.M., when this pretty "Interview" took place. Queen was really very gracious and pretty in her demeanour throughout: *rose* gently in my esteem, by everything that happened, did not fall in any point. Sister Jean has got a brief sketch of the thing,—on her earnest request. The "Interview" was quietly very mournful to me; the one point of real interest a sombre thought, "Alas, how it would have cheered *Her* bright soul (for my sake), had she been here!" To me, with such prospects close ahead, it could not be much, and did indeed approximate to melancholy well-meant *zero*.[37]

Disraeli to TC, 27 December 1874:

I have advised the Queen to offer to confer a baronetcy on Mr. Tennyson, and the same distinction should be at your command, if you liked it. But I have remembered that, like myself, you are childless, and may not care for hereditary honors. I have therefore made up my mind, if agreeable to yourself, to recommend Her Majesty to confer on you the highest distinction for merit at her command, and which, I believe, has never yet been conferred by her except for direct services to the State. And that is the Grand Cross of the Bath.

I will speak with frankness on another point. It is not well that, in the sunset of life, you should be disturbed by common cares. I see no reason why a great author should not receive from the nation a pension as well as a lawyer and a statesman. Unfortunately the personal power of Her Majesty in this respect is limited; but still it is in the Queen's capacity to settle on an individual an amount equal to a good fellowship, and which was cheerfully accepted and enjoyed by the great spirit of Johnson, and the pure integrity of Southey.[38]

TC to Disraeli, 29 December 1874:

Yesterday, to my great surprise, I had the honour to receive your letter containing a magnificent proposal for my benefit, which will be memorable to me for the rest of my life. Allow me to say that the letter, both in purport and expression, is worthy to be called magnanimous and noble, that it is without example in my own poor history; and I think it is unexampled, too, in the history of governing persons towards men of letters at the present, as at any time; and that I will carefully preserve it as one of the things precious to memory and heart. A real treasure or benefit *it*, independent of all results from it.

This said to yourself and reposited with many feelings in my own grateful mind, I have only to add that your splendid and generous proposals for my practical behoof must not any of them take effect; that titles of honour are, in all degrees of them, out of keeping with the tenour of my own poor existence hitherto in this epoch of the world, and would be an encumberance, not a furtherance to me; that as to money, it has, after long years of rigorous and frugal, but also (thank God, and those that are gone before me) not degrading poverty, become in this latter time amply abundant, even superabundant; more of it, too, now a hindrance, not a help to me; so that royal or other bounty would be more than thrown away in my case; and in brief, that except the feeling of your fine and noble conduct on this occasion, which is a real and permanent possession, there cannot be anything to be done that would not now be a sorrow rather than a pleasure.[39]

TC to John A. Carlyle, 1 January 1875:
You would have been surprised, all of you, to have found unexpectedly your poor old Brother Tom converted into Sir Tom, Bart., but, alas, there was no danger at any moment of such a catastrophe. I do however truly admire the magnanimity of Dizzy in regard to me: he is the only man I almost never spoke of except with contempt, and if there is anything of scurrility anywhere chargeable against me, I am sorry to own he is the subject of it; and yet see, here he comes with a pan of hot coals for my guilty head![40]

TC in conversation with Mrs Anstruther, summer 1878:
He [Disraeli] has done great harm to the Queen, persuading her to believe anything. Then by giving her this title of Empress of India he secured her good will. "Peace with honour" indeed! There is no peace at all. He has provoked the enmity of Russia, instead of conciliating her and gaining a friend and a powerful ally.[41]

*   *   *

Thus it was that the independent spirit and the critical mind, indispensable to a true artist, remained with Carlyle to the very last. That he was able to maintain them consistently testifies not merely to his great talent as an artist and integrity as a person but to the high quality of British democracy in his day, which granted privileges touching the Monarchy itself to a gifted writer of very humble Scottish origin. Ben Jonson, the Elizabethan writer most like him in temper, tone, courage, and vigorous, rough-grained individualism, would never have spoken of his Queen with the freedom or with the tenderness with which Carlyle spoke of his.

NOTES

1. See my "The Victorian Rembrandt: Carlyle's Portraits of His Contemporaries", *Bulletin of the John Rylands Library*, 39 (March 1957)

521–57. Since I wrote this article I have discovered that John Sterling and Friedrich Althaus, were also among Carlyle's contemporaries who compared him with Rembrandt. Interestingly enough, the common element in the two which both stress is humour. Possibly the earliest comparison of Carlyle with Rembrandt is to be found in a passage in John Sterling's "Carlyle's Works", *London and Westminster Review*, 33 (1839), 20: "It becomes evident why the humorous lies so near as has often been remarked to the pathetic and sublime: how they pass into each other by perpetual undulations and successions, with a play and interfusion of vital energy from one to the other: so that the homely farce of a Rembrandt and a Bunyan, of a Hogarth and a Fielding, lies under and supports conceptions of which the tenderness and lofty passion will never fade from human hearts." For Althaus, see "Thomas Carlyle. Eine Biographische-Literarische Charakteristik", *Unsere Zeit*, II (July 1866), 23.

2. Quoted by Carlyle: untraced but possibly from an old ballad.
3. NLS, MS 520.62. William IV was succeeded by Victoria on 20 June 1837.
4. Edwin W. Marrs, Jr., *The Letters of TC to His Brother Alexander* (Cambridge, Mass., 1968), p. 432.
5. NLS, MS 523.57.
6. NLS, MS 520.70.
7. Elizabeth Fergus, who later married Comte Carlo de Pepoli.
8. NLS, MS 511.52.
9. From the *Autobiography* of Sir Archibald Alison, I, 413, quoted in Wilson, *Carlyle*, III, 47.
10. NLS, MS 523.63.
11. NLS, MS 520.89.
12. NLS, MS 523.74.
13. Marrs, p. 478. According to Lytton Strachey, Victoria broke away from the influence of her mother, the Duchess of Kent, soon after she became Queen. See *Queen Victoria* (London, 1921), pp. 73–4. Friction with the Tories rose in part from the Queen's insistence that the nation settle £50,000 a year on Prince Albert at a time when there was much poverty in the country.
14. C. T. Copeland, *Letters of TC to His Youngest Sister* (Boston and New York, 1899), p. 125.
15. Copeland, pp. 127–8. Queen Victoria was first shot at on 10 June 1840 by a youth of eighteen named Edward Oxford, son of a mulatto jeweller of Birmingham. Oxford was later declared insane. In 1882 the Queen was shot at by a youth named Roderick Maclean. Strachey writes: "This was the last of a series of seven attempts upon the Queen, attempts which, taking place at sporadic intervals over a period of forty years, resembled one another in a curious manner. All, with a single exception, were perpetrated by adolescents, whose motives were apparently not murderous, since, save in the case of Maclean, none of their pistols was loaded" (pp. 375–6).

16. NLS, MS 611.108. From 1842 to 1851 Carlyle seems to have had few glimpses of the Queen and Prince. We know, however, that he and the Queen attended the same performance of Bulwer-Lytton's *Richelieu*, produced by Macready in 1848. Carlyle declared at the time that he felt quite sorry for the Queen, condemned to sit and see a king as wicked, weak, and contemptible as Louis XIII in this play. On 15 May of the same year he and Queen Victoria saw the same performance of another play, Dickens and his friends playing in *The Merry Wives of Windsor*. See Francis Espinasse, *Literary Recollections and Sketches* (New York, 1893), p. 267; and Edgar Johnson, *Charles Dickens* (New York, 1952), II, 646.

17. NLS, MS 551.18.

18. NLS, MS 613.348.

19. Wilson, *Carlyle*, V, 42–3. This passage is part of a much longer prospectus on the subject sent in an envelope addressed to Lady Ashburton and labelled "For Lord Ashburton (on a rainy day)".

20. Supporters of Palmerston helped to spread wild rumours concerning what many believed was Prince Albert's Prussian-like high-handedness in his desire to dominate the government and, near the outbreak of the Crimean War, his leaning toward Russia. See the broadside entitled "Lovely Albert" in Strachey, pp. 242–3.

21. NLS, MS 524.95.

22. MS., the Marquess of Northampton.

23. NLS, MS 515.89.

24. NLS, MS 515.88. See also Carlyle's note in J. A. Froude, *Letters and Memorials of Jane Welsh Carlyle* (London, 1883), II, 249.

25. MS, The Marquess of Northampton. For a copy of "The Little Drummer", see Carlyle's *Frederick the Great*, in *Works*, XII, opp. p. 370, with Carlyle's comment on the merits of the picture and of the Ashburton's copy on p. 372.

26. MS, Victoria and Albert Museum. John Marguerite Émile Lemoinne, (1815–92), French journalist, was on the staff of the *Journal des Débats* from 1840 to 1892. John Forster (1812–76), best known for his biography of Dickens, edited the *Examiner* from 1847 to 1855.

27. MS, the Marquess of Northampton. According to Wilson, Sir James Stephen told Carlyle that when Prince Albert proposed a pension for Carlyle during the years when George Hamilton Gordon, fourth Earl of Aberdeen (1784–1860) was Prime Minister (1852–55), Aberdeen shuddered, shook his head, and said that such a thing was impossible because of Carlyle's "heterodoxy" (*Carlyle*, III, 265).

28. Wilson, *Carlyle*, V, 255.

29. *Conversations with Carlyle* (London, 1896), p. 229.

30. Froude, *Life*, IV, 320–1.

31. *Ibid.*, p. 321.

32. MS., Mitchell Library, Sydney, Australia.

33. NLS, MS 526.88.

34. Distinguished British geologist (1797–1875), often regarded as the father of modern geology.
35. George Grote (1794–1871), English banker, historian, and educator, best known for his *History of Greece* (1846–56).
36. A. Carlyle, ed., *New Letters of TC* (London and New York, 1904), II, 252–5. "The Court Circular", 13 March 1869, carried the following item: "Her Majesty on Thursday last had the pleasure of becoming personally acquainted with two of the most distinguished writers of the age—Mr. Carlyle and Mr. Browning. These eminent men—who, so far as intellect is concerned, stand head and shoulders above their contemporaries—were invited to meet the Queen at the residence of the Dean of Westminster." Quoted by Betty Miller, *Robert Browning: A Portrait* (London, 1952), pp. 246–7. Wilson says that after the Queen and Carlyle had talked the Queen told Browning, "What a very singular person Mr. Carlyle is!" *Carlyle*, VI, 186; quoted from C. E. Norton's *Journal*, 23 March 1869. Later in telling Ruskin and Joan Severn about his meeting with the Queen, Carlyle said that after describing to her the beauties of Galloway he got his chair on her dress and had to move it. *Praeterita, Works*, ed. Cook and Wedderburn (London and New York, 1909), XXXV, 539–40. According to Wilson, Mrs Anna Maria Pickering wrote that the Queen was much affronted with Carlyle for asking permission to be seated and declared that she would see no more literary men but that she later not only had an interview with Dickens but was charming to him. Wilson comments that she had probably not read the beautiful story of how Frederick the Great insisted that old Ziethen take a chair "while he himself remained standing before him". *Carlyle*, VI, 187–8. For Carlyle's statement that "the Queen came gliding into the room in a sort of swimming way, no feet visible", see *ibid.*, p. 184.
37. A. Carlyle, ed., *New Letters of TC* (London and New York, 1904), II, 255–6n.
38. Wilson, *Carlyle*, VI, 343–4.
39. *Ibid.*, pp. 344–5. Carlyle believed that the Countess of Derby had been chiefly influential in having the honour offered to him. For an incomplete text of his letter to her, 30 Dec. 1874, see Froude, *Life*, IV, 431–2.
40. Wilson, *Carlyle*, VI, 345.
41. *Ibid.*, p. 429. Several related details may be added. After Carlyle's interview with the Queen in 1869, Princess Louise came to see him at Cheyne Row and presented him with a portrait she had made of the historian J. L. Motley. Gerald Blunt once asked Carlyle, "Do you think the Queen has read your books?" Carlyle replied, "She may have read many books, but I do not think she has read mine." In Carlyle's extreme old age Sir Bartle Frere wrote him to request an interview for the Prince of Wales, Albert Edward. Carlyle denied the request, saying, "I am too old. He might as well come and see my poor old dead body." *Ibid.*, pp. 187, 458.

11

Froude and Carlyle: Some New Considerations

by K. J. FIELDING

Of all writers on Carlyle the most quoted and the least liked is James Anthony Froude. Able, bitter, contentious and tactless, he has left his mark on the study of Carlyle, not simply in the way he used the papers that came into his hands but in the manner in which his own opinions and personality appear in his selection and in what he says himself. The impression he leaves is not entirely an unlikeable one. Yet his chief fault is not simply that he is rather an inaccurate editor, but that he so strongly leaves the impression of being untrustworthy.

There are several excuses to be made for him. He was hasty because he persuaded himself that his duty to write a biography was onerous but unsought. He is clear and decisive even when he is wrong, many of his editorial mistakes are forgivable, and it is now really much less important that he omits, misreads, changes punctuation and capitalization, or even that he garbles texts, than that he relies too heavily on what Carlyle had to say about himself in his journals and his letters. Yet there should be no question of thinking that this treatment of texts, facts and evidence was acceptable according to the usual standards of his time, though there might have been a better case for this if he had not insisted that he meant to set a new standard of truth telling, and that he was not a conventional romantic biographer. He claimed to give "a complete account" of Carlyle's "character", in which "there should be no reserve, and therefore I have practised none".[1] But

239

for this kind of work Froude had neither the sympathy, the knowledge, the nerve, the judgment, nor the time.

Even so, Froude has his champions, especially his most recent biographer, Waldo Hilary Dunn. It was even Dunn's belief that Froude "far surpassed Carlyle", and that "in the final analysis" he "emerges as an outstandingly more able and representative man".[2] Yet his biography is more than partisan. Whether in his study of *Froude and Carlyle* (1930) or in his biography (2 vols, 1961, 1963) Froude can do no wrong. "I have found", wrote Dunn, "no reason to question any of Froude's statements"[3]; and no less complacently, between his own first and second book, "no reason to necessitate any revision".[4]

Now the accuracy and character of Froude and the disputes that arose almost immediately after the publication of his edition of Carlyle's *Reminiscences* and his *Life* are almost nothing in themselves. They matter only because, if we are to understand Carlyle, it may be helpful to be clear about the authority of those who wrote about him. For myself, I find that, although Froude is sometimes right in matters of dispute, almost everything he says is open to question; he contradicts himself; and he even sometimes seems to be unaware of what he is saying. However unpleasant and petty the disputes that arose between Froude and others after he had written on Carlyle, they raise certain questions about his reliability as a biographer. For Froude still stands in our way. His is still the standard *Life*; he is the authority for the text of the passages he provides from Carlyle's journal; and he has given us a decisive portrait of Carlyle which has firsthand authority. As biographer, he had the use of all Carlyle's private papers, some of which are now inaccessible. Many of his own papers were destroyed. However open to criticism, therefore, his biography will always be indispensable.

A recent discovery of legal papers associated with Carlyle's Will, his manuscripts and copyrights, allows questions to be raised which not only bear upon Froude but which affect his interpretation of Carlyle. The documents are musty and confused, they carry us into the middle of one of the most undignified squabbles in literature, but they also allow us a chance to re-assess the more important issues involved. Waldo Dunn, secure in unrestricted access to the Froude family papers, professed to regret that the question of who owned the literary manuscripts Carlyle left behind him at death had never come into court. The one person whom it would have been disastrous to put into the witness-box was Froude, and possibly the man to see this most clearly was his own friend and co-executor Sir James Fitzjames Stephen, the eminent lawyer, critic and judge.

My own interest in this began with my discovery of these legal papers. After joining the editorship of the new Carlyle *Collected Letters* in 1967, I looked at his Will to trace the history of some of his papers. (It is convenient that, though there are various manuscripts and printed copies, the text of the Will is correctly given in Froude's *My Relations with Carlyle* [1903]). From the names of the witnesses I saw who the solicitors were who had drawn it up; and, as they happened to be the same as Charles Dickens's, I did then what I had done with Dickens fifteen years earlier: wrote to the firm and then went up to London to see them.

I was not quite so fortunate as I had been before, but I was allowed to examine a large deed-box and to remove it to the temporary keeping of the National Library of Scotland. Examination showed that what it chiefly contained was correspondence with Carlyle's executors, Froude and Sir James Fitzjames Stephen. Much of it was the old unseemly story, familiar from Froude's *Relations* and the rejoinder to it, *The Nemesis of Froude* (1903) by Alexander Carlyle and Sir James Crichton-Browne, and I do not mean to go over every detail of the affair again. Nor, in what is retold, when there are corrections to previous accounts, shall I explicitly point them all out. Earlier biographers are unreliable, and the notes should be enough to show how this account derives from the new papers. It is certainly different from the one given by Froude.[5]

It is necessary to begin by turning to Carlyle's Will (dated 6 February 1873) which was no doubt drawn up with some contempt for lawyers and according to his own ideas about wording. What mainly concerns us is the disposal of his literary papers; but, especially with the original documents before us, it is impossible for a biographer to disregard this as the last expression of Carlyle's *will*, so emphatically is it stamped with his character yet so incompetent as a testament of his wishes. It bears his mark strongly, from its opening insistence that he is to be buried at Ecclefechan with his parents "since I cannot be laid in the Grave at Haddington" with Jane, to the signatures of the witnesses at the end: John Hare, Butler at Palace Gate House (residence of John Forster) and Frederic Ouvry, Solicitor, from whose offices I had collected the papers.

The question of who were to be the executors and trustees was important: one was John Forster, Carlyle's old friend and trusted adviser in business matters, and the other his brother, Dr John Aitken Carlyle. The Will then states that if John dies first his place is to be taken by the youngest brother, James Carlyle; and, if Forster is unable to act, his place is to be taken by "my friend", James Anthony Froude.

Certain dispositions are made next: some small sums of money, books for Harvard, and Carlyle's watch to his Canadian nephew, Thomas Carlyle. Then it disposes of the rest of the property, at the same time characterizing (in a typically Carlylean way) all those who were to be most closely connected with his uncertain intentions. For the Will shows itself to be, in all its associations and expressions, not at all like the formal drafting of a lawyer but as the personal utterance of Carlyle; so that, even when he comes to deal with the most important question of the disposal of his books, copyrights, manuscripts and papers, it continues in the same discursive personal tone.

Dr John Carlyle, "my ever dear and helpful Brother", is said to have no need of help or money. As a result he is left the lease of the Chelsea house and all its contents except those "hereinafter bequeathed specifically"; and, simply as a "memento", he is to have the remainder of "my small and indeed almost pathetic collection of books". Yet later, as we see below, with two special exceptions, he was to have "My other manuscripts". There is thus already some uncertainty about what is meant by a *manuscript*, which may be anything from an unpublished holograph (written with publication in mind), or family letters and papers. Meanwhile, Carlyle goes on to write of one or two of them in particular:

> My manuscript entitled "Letters and Memorials of Jane Welsh Carlyle" is to me naturally, in my now bereaved state, of endless value, though of what value to others I cannot in the least clearly judge; and indeed for the last four years am imperatively forbidden

242

to write farther on it, or even to look further into it. Of that manuscript my kind considerate and ever faithful friend James Anthony Froude (as he has lovingly promised me) takes precious charge in my stead. To him therefore I give it with whatever other fartherances and elucidations may be possible, and I solemnly request of him to do his best and wisest in the matter, as I feel assured he will. There is incidentally a quantity of Autobiographic Record in my notes to this Manuscript; but except as subsidiary and elucidative of the text I really put no value on such. Express biography of me I had really rather that there should be none. James Anthony Froude, John Forster and my Brother John will make earnest survey of the Manuscript and its subsidiaries there or elsewhere, in respect to this as well as to its other bearings; their united candour and partiality, taking always James Anthony Froude's practicality along with it, will evidently furnish a better judgment than mine can be. The Manuscript is by no means ready for publication; nay the questions How, When (after what delay, seven, ten years) it, or any portion of it, should be published, are still dark to me; but on all such points James Froude's practical summing up and decision is to be taken as mine. The imperfect Copy of the said Manuscript which is among my papers with the original letters I give to my niece Mary Carlyle Aitken, to whom also dear little soul, I bequeath Five hundred pounds for the loving care and unwearied patience and helpfulness she has shown me in these my last solitary and infirm years. To her also I give at her choice, whatever Memorials of the Dear Departed One she has seen me silently preserving here, especially the table in the Drawing-Room at which I now write and the little Child's Chair (in the China Closet) which latter to my eyes has always a brightness as of Time's Morning and a sadness as of Death and Eternity when I look on it; and which, with the other dear Article, I have the weak wish to preserve in loving hands yet awhile when I am gone. My other manuscripts I leave to my Brother John. They are with one exception of no moment to me. I have never seen any of them since they were written. One of them is a set of fragments about James the First . . . But neither this latter nor perhaps any of the others is worth printing. On this point however my Brother can take counsel with John Forster and James Anthony Froude and do what is then judged fittest. . . . In regard to all business matters about my Books . . . Copy rights, Editions and dealings with Booksellers . . . John Forster's advice is to be taken as supreme and complete, better than my own could ever have been. His faithful wise and ever punctual care about all that has been a miracle of generous helpfulness, literally invaluable to me in that field of things. Thanks, poor thanks, are all that I can return, alas! I give the residue of my personal estate to my Trustees before named. . . .

The remainder of the estate is then divided between Carlyle's five remaining brothers and sisters, or, if they were to die before him, their children at the age of 21. These were the two other brothers, Alexander and James, and the three sisters, Mrs Austin, Jean Aitken, and Janet Hanning. This specifically and most importantly includes Carlyle's copyrights which were thus part of the astate under the direction of his trustees:

Finally:

> To my dear friends John Forster and James Anthony Froude (Masson too I should remember in this moment and perhaps some others) I have nothing to leave that could be in the least worthy of them but if they, or any of them, could find among my reliques a Memorial they would like, who of Men could deserve it better. No man at this time. . . .

So there is Carlyle in 1873, at the age of seventy-seven, setting down his wishes in mainly clear and obviously personal terms. Had he died then, with John Forster as his executor, there would have been no difficulties. For Forster was a remarkable man, a powerful and efficient literary agent, who had been acting for many years as Carlyle's adviser in dealings with publishers; he had been a good friend of Jane's, and he was both discreet and dominant enough to have ensured that no disputes would have persisted between any of the parties. But Forster died in 1876, and Dr John Carlyle in 1878. Conditions changed, new executors were needed, and I think we may accept what Froude says in the *Life*, that Carlyle—realizing that there were sure to be biographies whether authorized or not—asked Froude to tell the story of his life. In fact, it seems that as early as 1873 he began to deposit some of his papers with him.

Yet then (in November 1878) at the age of eighty-three and without Forster to advise him, Carlyle added a codicil to his Will, dictating the terms to a clerk who no doubt submitted it to Frederic Ouvry for advice. But Ouvry was an old man himself who was to die a year after Carlyle, and so Carlyle's intentions, never entirely clear, were left more confused than ever. His first idea, in fact, had been to keep the matter mainly to himself, and it was only because of the prudence of his niece, Mary Aitken, that the solicitors were informed. She wrote:

30 Oct. 1878

. . . Mr. Carlyle, my Uncle, being anxious to add a Codicil to his Will directing that what he has bequeathed to his Brother, Dr. Carlyle, should on the death of Dr. Carlyle revert to me or to my heirs, I should be much obliged if you would send a Clerk able to take down his directions, either tomorrow or on Friday the 1st. Nov. . . .

Mr. Carlyle's own wish is that I myself write out this Codicil; but I think it a better and more satisfactory plan to make this application to you.

New executors and trustees were to be appointed: first Froude, once more, and then Sir James Fitzjames Stephen. Stephen was a most forceful man, in his younger days he had been a brilliantly unfair critic contributing mainly to the *Saturday Review*, an advocate of devastating one-sidedness and really superior power. He was an historian of criminal law, and author of *Liberty, Equality and Fraternity* (1873) written in answer to Mill. He is mentioned only once in Froude's *Life of Carlyle*, in reference to a speech at Edinburgh which Carlyle found "a very curious piece of work indeed", though he thought Stephen "very honest . . . with a huge, heavy streak of work in him".[6] At the same time, Stephen was an illiberal man who seems to have meant to be just but who was often blinded by his own powers of advocacy. Between the signing of the codicil and Carlyle's death he was made a High Court judge, and in all the disputes that follow he was naturally respected because of his position and the clarity and tenacity of his arguments. He was also a personal friend of Froude.

So, in the codicil, the gift of the drawing-room table was withdrawn from Mary Aitken and transferred to Stephen: "I know he will accept it as a distinguished mark of my esteem. He knows it belonged to my honoured Father in Law and his daughter, And that I have written all my Books on it except only Schiller." In its place Mary was given a Screen: "She knows by whom it was made and I wish her to accept it as a testimony of the trust I repose in her and as a mark of my esteem for her honourable veracious and

245

faithful character and a memorial of all the kind and ever faithful service she has done me."

The Times (9 April) made much of its amusement at the airs with which Carlyle bequeathed "his old watch or his writing table as if it were a big estate with a title attached". It noticed a touch of self-idolatry, and saw the "curious will" as a sign of "the ultimate judgement to be pronounced on his character. . . . A reaction is now in operation. . . . Counterblasts, loud and decided, are about to be blown"; Froude's editing of the *Reminiscences* may have set it off but, whatever the cause, "Let the counterblast blow." The *Times* leader on the "curious will" is itself a curious reaction.

A more practical and immediate difficulty for the new executors was that the new codicil was extremely vague about Carlyle's papers and copyrights. It will be remembered that, with the exception of Carlyle's annotated "Letters and Memorials of Jane Welsh Carlyle" (bequeathed to Froude), the "imperfect Copy" (i.e. original MSS) of the same work and some of Jane's other original letters (bequeathed to Mary), all Carlyle's other papers had originally been left to Brother John. This was specifically stated: he was to have "My other Manuscripts" *and* the contents of Cheyne Row. This time neither manuscripts nor papers were specifically mentioned, although everything previously left to John (except the lease of the house itself) was left "to my Niece Mary Carlyle Aitken", who was to receive "all such of my Furniture plate linen china books prints pictures and other effects [therein] . . .".

Had all of Carlyle's papers been left undisturbed at Cheyne Row, it would presumably have been clear that they were to go to Mary with the rest of its contents. If one supposes that she were not to have had the contents, or if the papers were arguably not among the "contents" since some were placed elsewhere, then they would have belonged to the estate, and thus to the residuary legatees who were Carlyle's brothers and sisters, or their children. In both cases the copyright (controlled by the executors) would have been theirs and not Mary's. But there are a number of problems we ought to be clear about if we are to understand the behaviour of Froude and Mary Aitken Carlyle.[7]

The first of these is that (by 1878) Carlyle had entrusted—at different times—a large number of papers to Froude, and that neither he nor Froude had made a written note of the terms on which they were passed over. Meanwhile, the ageing Carlyle had told Mary that they were *hers*, and that the papers in Froude's hands were ultimately to be returned to her. Although this was repeated before witnesses, it was apparently not until 1879 that this was made clear to Froude who then willingly accepted it. But once again there was no written record, and neither Froude nor Mary was sure what Carlyle had said to the other. Secondly, arising from the uncertainty of ownership, there were problems of copyright which are almost equally confused. Finally the position was further complicated by the variety of manuscripts involved. Among these were: (i) the composite manuscript of the *Reminiscences*, which was among the papers belonging to Mary but entrusted to Froude,[8] which with Carlyle's assent was already in proof as he was dying and published within a month of his death; (ii) the mass of journals, letters and papers, so carefully preserved by Carlyle, which were also apparently Mary's though temporarily with Froude; and (iii), there were "The Letters and Memorials of Jane Welsh Carlyle", the fair copy of which with some of Jane's letters was certainly bequeathed to Froude with the consequent presumption that the copyright was his although even here there were complications. How far, for instance, Froude might stretch the bequest of manuscripts "farthering and elucidating" the *Memorials* was quite undefined, and it must remain uncertain whether his copyright in the "fair copy" (in Mary's hand) might be affected by the bequest to Mary of what was the original autograph manuscript, even though it was known to Carlyle as "the imperfect copy of the same Memorials . . . with the original letters".

Involved as all this may appear, there can be no full understanding of the relations of Froude to Carlyle without them, and certainly they are essential to understanding the tussle for control of the Carlyle archive between Froude and Carlyle's niece Mary.

Mary Aitken was the daughter of Carlyle's younger sister Jean who lived in Dumfries; and, after he paid a visit to her in the summer of 1868, she returned to London with her uncle as his secretary and companion for the rest of his life. She and her mother are barely mentioned in Froude's last two volumes, neither is indexed, and her presence in Cheyne Row is ignored: her name is given twice, in quotations from Carlyle, and she is mentioned once merely as an anonymous "someone to write for him" (II, 416). Yet the part she played in Cheyne Row can be seen more clearly in such a record as William Allingham's *Diary* (London, 1907), or the reports of other visitors. For Mary remained with her uncle even after her marriage with her cousin Alexander Carlyle in 1879, they cheerfully accepted his company even when they went away on their honeymoon, and her first child was born at Cheyne Row, where "our baby" was a source of pride and wonder to his great-uncle. Obviously, at the time of her uncle's death, no one knew him more intimately.

Yet during Carlyle's lifetime Froude (and perhaps her uncle too) usually regarded Mary with masculine condescension. In his eighties Carlyle still writes of his niece as "dear little soul", and Froude's term for her (even within his own family) was "the little girl".[9] Yet when Carlyle died she was a married woman of about thirty-five, whose correspondence shows that she was both intelligent and sensible. Twelve years with Carlyle had taught her a great deal. She expresses herself well, and she was clearly at ease with the distinguished friends of his old age.[10] Letters about her uncle's business affairs are not only in her hand, but were frequently left for her to word, even for example in dealing with Frederic Chapman on copyright. Yet Mary and Alexander Carlyle were obviously aware of Froude's air of patronizing aloofness; and of their uncle's friends we find that it was only Froude who disagreed with them. The situation between Mary, Froude and Alexander was probably already a sensitive one to be exacerbated by the terms of the Will. It is true that they were apparently on friendly enough terms just after Carlyle's death when (after an initial misunderstanding) Mary was ready to write, "Mr. Froude has been uniformly kind and generous to me" (22 Feb. 1881). But, once their disagreements had grown, Froude was to write resentfully to Ouvry's partner, Farrer:

> I blame myself for all this mass of confusion, but it rose from this single cause: that I told Carlyle (when he told me that Mary C. had been very violent with him about the small provision that was made for her) that he might feel easy about her future, for I

would treat her as if she were a daughter of my own. One does not look for this slippery treatment from a woman to whom one has undertaken to be a quasi guardian (20 Oct. 1881).

The difficulty was that Mary did not want or need a guardian, and as soon as she was allowed to read a copy of the *Reminiscences* she was clear that if a guardian was needed for anyone it was Froude. For though Froude was editor of the *Reminescences*, the manuscript and copyright (as he eventually conceded) were hers.

Yet no prior consideration before Carlyle's death had been given to the copyright question, nor to the division of profits to come from publishing the *Memorials*, the *Reminiscences* or the biography; at least, none on which there was any written memorandum. In the disagreements that followed it was accepted, without much dispute, that Carlyle had meant the gift of the papers to make up to Mary for the rather slight provision he had otherwise made for her.[11] Legally, if Mary could establish that the manuscripts of the *Reminiscences* had been given her with the other papers, then the *prima facie* assumption would be that the copyright was hers also; and the same was true of anything written by Carlyle in the main group of papers. But this had all been left uncertain. It rested on her word, on comments by Carlyle in front of others, and on Froude's intermittent admissions—followed by his retractions. There was nothing written.

Carlyle himself had been too old and tired to bother with it, and he had simply exerted himself to leave it in the hands of someone he thought well-disposed. Rather similarly, he allowed Froude to cast himself in the role of reluctant biographer, while stating in the Will "express biography of me I had really rather that there should be none". Froude even asserts that he had not known he was to be an executor.[12] He thus had every reason to complain, as he did vehemently, that he had been put in a false position. At the same time he was at fault for letting it happen. He bemoans the fact, for example, that when entrusted with the papers he was given no inventory; yet he took none himself. He was ex-editor of *Fraser's* and an established writer who cannot have been innocent about copyright. No doubt he fully intended to be generous, but he was the kind of man who expected to be trusted even when he made mistakes. Even his friend Sir James Stephen was soon reduced to writing to their solicitor in exasperation, "Froude seems to me to have no idea of the legal effect of anything" (24 Oct. 1881).

Carlyle died on 4 February 1881, and in less than ten days Froude wrote to *The Times* to say that the *Reminiscences* would be out within a few weeks. All of them, he stressed, except the essay on Mrs Carlyle, would be printed "exactly as Mr. Carlyle left them". Mary Carlyle then made a friendly objection to Froude's remark in the same letter that Carlyle's papers had been "made over" to him; and as a result he wrote again on 25 February to say that they "belong to his niece . . . to whom he directed me to return them". Even so, when the book was published, there was no reference to Mary in the Preface either as owner of the manuscript or copyright and, until they were reminded, the publishers did not send her a copy of the book. Yet, when Mary consulted the executors' solicitor about the copyright, he confirmed, "Mr. Froude does not question your right to it" (28 April). Mary was deeply concerned: not so much about the payment as about how the work had been edited, and it was soon made clear to her that she was generally held to be involved. For some of the *Reminiscences* refer to old friends of Carlyle whom he had written about with the same scathing intimacy he used in his private letters and journals. It was obviously raspingly painful to their surviving relatives, and Froude admits that Carlyle had warned him to take care. The result was that the daughters of both Lord Jeffrey and Mrs Basil Montagu wrote promptly to complain—not to Froude, but to Mary.

It is not new that the *Reminiscences* caused offence, since it has always been known that Froude not only gave pain but so offended the families of some of Carlyle's correspondents that letters were destroyed. It is now clearer why they objected so strongly; and what we can now see, for the first time, is how Mary was involved and that it was the beginning of their differences.

Mrs Montagu's daughter was Anne Benson Procter. Mary had sent her protest on to Ouvry with a copy of her reply (8 March 1881), and presumably he sent it to Froude. Mrs Procter evidently met the comments on her mother and step-father by saying that she would publish a selection of Carlyle's letters to her parents which would make an entirely different impression. Mary tried to dissuade her, but whatever reply Mrs Procter received from Froude she went on to issue a pamphlet of *Letters Addressed to Mrs. Basil Montagu and B. W. Procter by Mr. Thomas Carlyle*, prefaced by her justification. Carlyle's comments in his essay on Edward Irving are dismissed as "shameful", "malicious" and "malignant lies". He had come to London as a "raw young Scotchman", her parents had befriended him, and yet while accepting their hospitality he had written falsely about them and left his comments to be published after his death. His satiric comments were, in fact, made not only on her parents but on step-brothers and sisters, and apparently kept for publication while Mrs Procter remained on friendly calling terms with Carlyle. His remarks *are*, in the circumstances, quite unforgivable and Mrs Procter's reply is entirely justified.

At the time Mary sent on Mrs Procter's first letter she still had not read the *Reminiscences* but, once she had received a copy, she mildly complained to Ouvry that she "understood it well enough. It is a grievous pity that such things should have been printed a month after my Uncle's death. It was Mr Froude's *'reticence'* which he most of all trusted; this hurrying-off to the market-place with everybody's dirty linen shews with what results. But I suppose it is no use to speak of it" (9 March 1881).

Mrs Procter delayed a month in publishing her reply, and then sent it to other interested parties. Among them may have been Mrs Empson, daughter of Lord Jeffrey, who had been honoured by an essay to himself. Some of it a daughter might have been proud of, but there is another side to it: the work is tinged with contempt, and it is not only frank about Jeffrey's "habit of flirting . . . like a lap-dog", but calls Mrs Empson's children "of strange Edinburgh type", her husband "long-winded" and "jargoning", and herself "abstruse, timid, enthusiastic", "perhaps . . . jealous", and "a morbidly shy kind of creature" with "the air of a . . . spoiled child". Carlyle also remarks of Jeffrey's letters to himself and Jane, that he has lost sight of them, at which point Froude cheerfully breaks in, "All preserved and in my possession.—Editor." It was to recover these letters that Mrs Empson first wrote to Froude, then Mary:

You cannot fail to understand that the tone of Mr. Carlyle's "Reminiscences" . . . must have greatly shocked and amazed me. It will not surprise you that . . . I cannot bear the idea of any letter of my father's . . . appearing in any publication referred to by Mr. Carlyle—& that I feel it absolutely needful to have them in my possession. On writing to Mr. Froude to reclaim them, he tells me that it is from you, I must ask them, & that if you are willing he will return them without delay. I now write to ask this & under the circumstances I think it impossible you should refuse it.[13]

There was no legal obligation for their return, but Mary wrote to Ouvry:

It is natural enough that she should ask to have her Father's letters sent to her, not knowing to what uses they may be put & I am most willing she should receive them, but it is not less natural that I or any member of my Uncle's family should find it most painful to have another similar work to Mrs. Procter's published from these materials (9 April 1881).

Froude was evidently forbidden to print any of Jeffrey's letters in the biography, and presumably he sent back those that he had sorted out; the result of his frankness, apparently, was that it not only lost the letters for himself and Mary, but the Carlyle-Jeffrey correspondence was destroyed.

Certainly Mrs Empson was not appeased, since in 1887 Mary was unwise enough to write to her again to present her with a copy of the corrected edition, edited for her by Charles Eliot Norton. By then she was even optimistic enough to hope that Mrs Empson might let her have copies of any Carlyle letters she might still possess. But although some important omissions had been made, Mrs Empson sent the book back, since "for obvious reasons I should not wish to have it in the house". She went on:

I was greatly shocked when Froude published those Reminiscences as I consider my Father deeply wronged. . . . The account given of his London life is also quite untrue—how untrue probably no one but myself, now alive, knows. . . . I wrote to Froude to express my sense of injury—his only explanation was that he had not thought I was alive. I leave you to judge how this could satisfy me or my daughters. . . . As to the relations between my father & your uncle which you tell me you wish to verify I do not think that there is anything more to be said than that my father had a very considerable friendship for Carlyle & his wife (a friendship which I even at that day regretted—a regret which these Rem. certainly abundantly justify.)[14]

Obviously this response to her uncle and his work dismayed Mary. Her own papers are now mainly unavailable or not preserved, but there is something to show that several friends were amazed at Froude's lack of judgment. One of them remarks that it seemed as though "private persons have *no* feelings to be hurt";[15] and David Masson ends his review of the *Reminiscences* in the *Scotsman* (9 March) by saying that "as a whole, it must honestly be said that its publication . . . is a mistake"—one for which he blames the editor. Froude confesses that the book was received "with a violence of censure for which I was quite unprepared"; yet in writing *My Relations With Carlyle* he omits the reasons and seems quite unable to see how acutely it concerned Mary.

Her answer was to ask Ouvry whether, since the copyright was hers, she could not either suppress Froude's edition or publicly correct his "blunders, as he has in many cases made my uncle say exactly the contrary of what he has written to me. I shall also be obliged by Mr. Froude's returning to me 'the imperfect copy' of the Ms. called Jane Welsh Carlyle, which is bequeathed to me by Uncle's Will. My haste to claim this will be excused by Mr. Froude's own in printing it" (27 April). Since Froude had acknowledged that the copyright *was* hers, she discovered that though nothing could be done about the first edition she could certainly see to it that there were no more, and that it might even be possible to bring out a corrected version, as she did subsequently. Froude, who had also "forgotten" to return her copy of part of the chapter on Jane Welsh Carlyle, was extremely disturbed, and the dispute grew hotter.

Once Mary was able to read her "imperfect copy" she was even more upset than Froude, and there was a new bout of letters in *The Times*. Her first (5 May) points out that Carlyle had left written instructions on the manuscript that it was not to be printed without "fit editing", and that when he was dead "fit editing" would probably be impossible. Froude replied (6 May) to say that these instructions had been countermanded by what Carlyle had said to him personally and in the Will. Mary's response (7

May) was to point out that the Will had also implied that, though he was to have the final decision, he would be wise to take advice—and that he should be willing to take it now. Clearly Froude was offended at public exposure by "the little girl"; and so, merely reserving the manuscripts explicitly bequeathed him, he publicly stated that:

> The remaining papers, which I was directed to return to Mrs. Alexander Carlyle as soon as I had done with them, I will restore at once to any responsible person whom she will empower to receive them from me. . . . [She] can have them all when she pleases (*Times*, 9 May).

This was crucial but, as he confessed to Stephen, he had simply replied in a fit of irritation without any intention of giving up the biography "the greater part" of which he said he had already written.

Much of the rest of the story has already been published in the accounts by Froude, by Alexander Carlyle and by Waldo Dunn: it is their *interpretation* which needs re-examination rather than a questioning of the facts. In Waldo Dunn's life of Froude, for example, he speaks of Mary's behaviour as "virtual blackmail", and he is blindly unable to account for her concern about the manuscripts except by supposing that she coveted their "probably large monetary value".[16] He seems entirely ignorant of the fact that they were actually her own manuscripts, that they had been given to her, that Froude admitted it, she was able to produce witnesses, and that it would have been strange if she had not seen their value. He says nothing about the way in which she was willing to return the Jeffrey letters to Mrs Empson, and he ignores the fact that she offered to give up £1,500 due to her for the first edition of the book if Froude would relinquish the biography and return her papers immediately. Dunn made a mean charge, and is particularly foolish in saying that as Carlyle "had disposed of the matter in his Will, he doubtless thought it unnecessary to do anything further".[17]

For the position was clear: Froude had publicly stated that the papers were Mary's and that she could have them when she pleased. Her solicitors sent for them immediately—and Froude withdrew his undertaking. Obviously he had had second thoughts and was restrained from his folly by Sir James Stephen. The day on which Mary sent for her papers, Froude wrote a distraught letter to his solicitors:

> . . . So far as I am individually concerned she can have them at once—but a question occurs to me which as an Executor I have to consider. Whose are those papers at the moment?—They were sent to me six years ago without a word as to their future destination, and I was told to burn freely. Two years ago Mr. C. told me that when I was done with them I was to give them to Mary C. But he has not left them to Mary C. in his Will. Marys right seems to devolve through use—am *I* in law the present owner? or are the Papers part of the general Estate.
>
> Kindly give me what guidance you can. Mary C. must have them somehow but I have to mind what I am about—if they belong to the general Estate I require (do I not?) Sir James Stephens assent (11 May).

The message had got through from Stephen. If he and Froude refused to admit that the papers had been given to Mary, then they must be regarded as belonging to the general Estate, whatever the verbal understanding with Carlyle, whatever promises had been given, and whether the other members of the Carlyle family wished to deprive Mary of them or not. The "blackmail" is in the other hand.

The next day Froude drew up what seems to be a more formal letter based on instructions from Stephen—it is formal because it is to the executors' solicitors and meant to provide them with a better basis for negotiation:

> . . . You have only to assure me that the papers which I was to return to Mrs. Carlyle are in law hers and I shall give them up with pleasure.
>
> But I must make one further provision. The papers were given to me to make use of for Carlyle's Biography. I have been for 8 years at work on them and a certain use I mean to make of them. It will not be much but it will be something.
>
> I cannot hereafter have a claim raised that I have no right to make this or that extract from Carlyle's or Mrs. Carlyle's journals or from letters. The journals and letters were put in my hands that I might make such extracts. Carlyle's memory is as dear to me as it can possibly be to Mrs. A. Carlyle.
>
> I honoured and loved him above all other men that I ever knew

or shall know. It is my duty to show him as he was & no life known to me will bear a Sterner Scrutiny. But he wished—especially wished—his faults to be known. They were nothing, amount to nothing, in the great balance of his qualities. But such as they are they must be described.—Surely by no unfriendly hand (12 May).[18]

His claim to have been working on the letters for six years has been advanced to eight: it may well have been less. His private admission that Carlyle had told him to give the papers to Mary (because they were hers) is replaced by a challenge to her to establish that her uncle had given them to her formally The rhetoric is heightened, "Mary C." is even called "Mrs. A. Carlyle", and he seeks to change the grounds for disagreement. Up to this point the objections had mainly been to his reckless manner of "editing" which hurt Carlyle only because it made him seem so treacherous a friend. It was Carlyle's acquaintances (dead or alive) who were to suffer from Froude's devotion to the "truth". Now he takes his stand on its being his positive duty to show Carlyle's faults as well. We must not be unfair to Froude; but this is the point at which the breach between Froude and Mary Carlyle was complete and at which a new round of negotiations was to begin.

The "practicality" of Froude could not stand being challenged, and his place as a negotiator had to be taken by Sir James Stephen. As might be expected Stephen's tactics, if doubtfully fair, were sound in law. He knew that there could be no written record of the gift of papers, if for no other reason than that with a partially paralysed hand Carlyle had long found it impossible to write, for this was why Mary had been needed as a secretary. So that even though, in due course, Mary's solicitors were able to show that it was well understood that the papers were hers, Stephen protected Froude by resolutely refusing to admit it. His instructions to counsel were far from impartial or complete, and he chose to argue that it was uncertain whether the papers had been given to Froude or Mary. His own duty as executor, he maintained, was to protect the rights of the residuary legatees; and he continued to maintain this even when it was clear that those whose interests he claimed to represent did not want him to. Then, even though he had no intention of letting the case go to court, both he and Froude were ready to use this as a threat, which means in fact that it was they who were putting pressure on Mary though they knew that whatever the law might be they could hardly set aside Carlyle's express wishes. It was perfectly clear to Froude's party that there was no real problem about his being allowed to complete the *Life*; but, as the *Reminiscences* had already shown, the crunch might well come when the original documents could be checked against the way he had used them. So that, although private, public, spoken and written promises had all been made that the papers were Mary's and a first instalment had been given up, Stephen refused to concede that this was so in law until Froude was guaranteed all the time he needed and until he could exact some concession to secure Froude literary control over the *Reminiscences*. It is this which the bulk of the new papers, the old ones used by Dunn, and all the small print in the appendix to *The Nemesis of Froude* are really about. Their monetary value had nothing to do with it; it was a struggle for the control of the Carlyle archive arising from lack of faith in Froude.

Unfortunately, as the dispute dragged on years later, it even brought up questions about Carlyle's sexual competence, his marriage, and the way he and Jane treated each other. According to Froude much of this had been in his mind from the moment he undertook to write the *Life*. He had been told various stories on the doubtful authority of Geraldine Jewsbury which he could hardly have meant to repeat about the old man when he accepted his task.[19] But it seems that the more he was rattled by criticism from Carlyle's family and friends, the more determined he grew to make the most of his story. His final two volumes are written in a different tone from the first two; and Froude at last resorted to the old trick of leaving his own account to be published after his death. As a result many of the details of this story, pathetic in themselves, have been discussed to the pitch of absurdity: especially, *did* Carlyle, in a fit of temper, once bruise Jane's wrists or arms? We don't know; and if he did it is not clear how it was to excuse Froude. The whole subject eventually drifted into gossip. The only new point about this in the Farrer-Stephen papers is that, as early as 1884 Froude evidently believed that he was bothered by it:

. . . I dread a controversy which may force me to tell an incident that has been my greatest difficulty from the beginning.—*Once* only once that I know of, the quarrelling led to actual physical violence, and there is an allusion to it in the part of Mrs. C's journal which I have suppressed. The effect would be miserable if this were known —It has been a weight on my own neck for the last 13 years (28 Oct. 1884).

Froude did not in fact "know" anything except from Geraldine Jewsbury, and he was to keep the dreaded secret by leaving it for his children to publish. It is typical of Froude that, in spite of his declared ambitions as a biographer, he did not know when to tell the "truth" and when to be silent. Apart from this he was innocent enough but overcome by the responsibility.*

I do not want to go over the old ground. The essential weakness both of Froude's case and character can be seen in the fact that he and Stephen were reluctantly forced to yield to Mary. When not flustered by opposition they always recognized that Carlyle meant her to have his papers, and that he had even given them to her in effect in his own lifetime. They could hardly do otherwise in the face of two written statements of Froude made when Carlyle was living: —"I perfectly understood that all the papers were to be returned to you when I had done with them" (10 Feb. 1880), and, "It has, however, long been settled that you were to have the entire collection when I had done with it" (12 Feb. 1880).[20] Yet it was with the utmost unwillingness that they ultimately lost control over them. Throughout the remainder of 1881 Froude threatened to compel Mary to resort to the law to establish her claim, and Stephen and the solicitors had to restrain him. There were many good reasons, the main one being that the question was a moral as well as a legal one in which Froude would show up badly, and there was the other consideration that (though ready to support Froude) Stephen was not prepared to accept liability for any legal expenses that might result from actions to satisfy his friend's hurt pride. Nor can he have been confident about how Froude's contradictions would have stood cross-examination. Legal brinkmanship continued, therefore, until a frail compromise was reached.

---

* In fairness to Froude, he *was* accused of having torn a page out of one of Jane's journals, which he had not done. This meant that his children could save their father's posthumous reputation at the expense of his "loved and honoured friend" by publishing the manuscript (*My Relations With Carlyle*) which he had left them for the purpose.

In brief its terms were: (*i*) that Mary should have the copyright of the *Reminiscences* but that, somehow, Froude was to be thought of as having reserved "literary control"; (*ii*) Mary was to be given an inventory of the papers, "with a Memorandum, that subject to Mr. Froude's right to make use of them for the purpose of his biography they belong to Mrs. Carlyle,"—accepted, although the inventory was to be a sketchy one and she may never have received the memorandum; (*iii*) Froude was to keep what had been specifically bequeathed to him; (*iv*) the papers were to be returned to Mrs Carlyle as soon as Froude had done with them for writing the biography;—all accepted, with the stipulation that Froude should have time to correct the second edition, and with some uncertainty about what letters and notebooks of Jane's he might keep. The terms were arrived at by correspondence and were never drawn up in a single document. One can sense that everyone but Froude was relieved to be reaching a workable compromise. There was a temporary lull, therefore, as some of the papers were sent back and the biography completed.

Yet once the papers were in her hands, Mary's position was stronger. She went on to arrange for Norton's edition of the *Reminiscences* in America, and even to persuade Froude to agree to an English edition as well.[21] In time, Alexander Carlyle also brought out the *New Letters and Memorials of Jane Welsh Carlyle* (1903). Alexander Carlyle and Norton were to devote much of their lives to the Carlyle papers and to demonstrating the editorial sins of Froude. Though not blameless for pursuing him in this way, it must be understood that Froude was oddly careless in the way he treated texts. It is true that he lamely offered to correct later editions if he could be allowed to consult the papers again; but the fact is that if the letters and journals quoted in his biography were to have been edited to exact standards the whole edition would have to have been reset, which would have been impossible. His disdain for Mary and Alexander Carlyle had left its mark and their response is understandable. His defeat left him exasperated and unhappy.

There are letters to William Allingham, among other unused papers in the National Library of Scotland, which suggest that he also suffered from Froude, and that he and his wife shared Mary's opinion.[22] They imply that little would have been lost if Froude had carried out his threat to give up writing the biography, since an exchange for Allingham could well have been for the better. They also thought that (at Mary's request) he might have edited some of Carlyle's miscellaneous unpublished papers.[23] No reader of the *Diary* can have closed it without an affection for its writer and Mary may well have had him in mind as a biographer. In 1870 he had noted, "Mary tells me she said to her Uncle—'People say Mr. Allingham is to be your Boswell', and he replied, 'Well let him try it. He's very accurate' " (p. 202). We have only Mary's side of a limited series of letters, but we find her writing to him quite cheerfully about "the Froude affair". By 22 October 1881, for example, she reports on the second phase, after Stephen has taken over, that she has come to believe him "worse than Froude. . . . He plants his portly figure between Froude and me", determined to wrest a concession. What she says is perfectly clear and consistent; and yet Allingham pacifically advised her how to avoid an open conflict (as she had intended) and she did as he said. But both Froude's accounts and the paper he persuaded Sir James Stephen to write for him are biased and incomplete; and although Sir James never lost his air of judicial impartiality in his letters, Froude reveals both his weakness and his better nature.

In 1882 we find him at last ready to give up more of the papers after publishing his first two volumes: they included letters up to 1835, "Edward Irving's letters, Mrs. Basil Montagu's letters, and a few others" (Froude to Farrer, 20 May). Evidently there were still some delays, but he was anxious now to have everything settled:

> . . . As soon as I have finished my own work and published what I mean to publish Mrs. Carlyle shall have *everything*—such of "Jane Welsh Carlyle's" letters diaries &c as I do *not* mean to publish as well as all the rest,—because hereafter a complete edition of the whole of the MSS.—I mean the whole remains of both Carlyle & his wife—will certainly be demanded—and the papers ought to be kept together (18 July 1882).

For Froude's sake it would be better to stop here, where he shows that he appreciates the papers' importance and even means to be magnanimous, but perhaps the strain of finishing was too much for him. When he had completed the last two volumes he wrote to Farrer again:

My work is done.—It is time for the long talked of dinner, when you & I and Stephen can celebrate the close of our adventures in this matter. . . .

The Letters &c. will now be given up to Mary Carlyle. I must however go over my extracts & quotations in a last examination to make certain that no errors have crept in. It occurs to me that perhaps it might be well if *some one of your people* was to go over them with me. I have to do with a dangerous & very vindictive person, very reckless of statement and unscrupulous in the accusations which she may bring. It will be easy for her when the Papers are in her hands to insist that this & that is wrongly quoted and I shall have no means of setting myself right. She is at this moment bringing out in America a rival edition of the *Reminiscences* although I have always refused to allow her any literary control of it.

Think over my suggestion—& when you come here we can talk about it (26 Oct. 1884).

He seems to have forgotten that (if he wanted to) he could have kept the papers for a second, corrected edition; yet Froude may have already realized that, in a sense, his work was beyond correction. No law clerk could help him, and it remains astonishing that he was so careless about detail even when he was afraid to be caught out. At the same time his friends seem to have persuaded him to take a little longer, and perhaps the text we now have is one that (by his standards) *had* been guardedly corrected. For, by November, he still had the papers and was distressed to discover that Mary was demanding them:

. . . I have answered that the Biography has first to be completely revised but that I told you that they would be in your hands before Xmas. At the same time by bringing out this Edition of the Reminiscences in America she has broken the promise which she made me in her uncle's life time to make no use of these Papers without consulting me. I was satisfied with that promise & therefore said nothing to him on the subject—as I otherwise might have done. I have therefore been thinking seriously whether we might apply for power to deposit the whole Collection in the British Museum where they would be open to every one. You and Stephen can judge whether this would be possible. To me it would be a quite infinite relief (Froude to Farrer, 8 Nov. 1884).

Froude begins to seem almost unbalanced. It can hardly pass that here is a further admission that the manuscript of the *Reminiscences* was meant to be Mary's, and presumably the whole collection—always subject to his paternal supervision—and that he is not to be bound by his promises though she ought to have kept hers. Even with the celebration dinner in view, Farrer's heart must have sunk to find that his client still somehow believed that, to teach Mary a lesson, an uncertain "power" might be applied for to withhold her papers. Ultimately, of course, Mary and Alexander Carlyle needed no prompting to see that most of them went to the National Library of Scotland.

In this account I have tried to give the story with a respect for the facts, but without pretence that its conclusions are impartial though I hope they are fair. Froude has already been described as careless, inaccurate, patronizing, and so lacking in judgment as sometimes to be unbalanced. He was not dishonest, but he lacked self-understanding so badly that he easily gives that impression. His abilities were remarkable, but it is not too much to say that in some ways he was a fool. Mary Carlyle appears to have been determined, intelligent and truthful. Sir James Stephen was always an advocate, acting strictly within the law but ready to suppress the truth to support his cause. There is no point in whipping up controversy: these conclusions are re-stated because we have no clear or accurate biography of Froude. Mary Aitken Carlyle was not mercenary, as Dunn decided; she did not marry hastily in order to get her dying uncle's papers into her hands, as Froude's daughter suggested to Dunn; she wanted what was hers, but she did not "nag", "badger", "blackmail", tell lies, or act like a "she-demon", as Dunn tells his readers or as Froude told his friends.

Apart from this, what difference does it make to our knowledge of Carlyle and Froude? Perhaps a considerable one, although some of the implications remain to be thought about. At the simplest biographical level we know rather more about them both, and in a most general way we are able to make a better estimate of Froude's biography. Its chief value remains, like many Victorian biographies, as a repository of documents; and certainly a re-examination of the *Life* makes one see why control of the papers was so essential to Froude. It is mainly the work of the Carlyles, and most of Froude's task lay in arrangement and copying, though it was accepted that he should have the entire receipts of payment from the publishers even though they were Mary's papers. He confessed himself, "it may be said that I . . . have thus produced no 'Life', but only the materials for a 'Life' ". The same, of course, is true of the *Reminiscences*, which were edited by Froude only in the sense that he had them copied for the printer. Yet *both* Froude *and* Mary deserve our gratitude for respecting the papers that were entrusted to them. Carlyle had occasionally thrown out the injunction to select and burn, but whether in Froude's indiscretion or his wisdom he faithfully preserved them. It is fortunate for us that John Forster died before his friend, since had he lived to act as an executor he would have thinned them remorselessly.[25]

The disputes may also remind us how opinionated Froude could be, and how this may have distorted our view of Carlyle. We also notice how curiously he divided his volumes. When he began, the first two volumes were designed as *Thomas Carlyle, A History of the First Forty Years of His Life 1795–1835*, which is logical provided one thinks of a man's maturity and old age as needing about the same space as his youth and childhood. The final two volumes had to be *A History of His Life in London, 1834–1881*. But of *Life in London* the first volume covers the period from 1835-1848, leaving for the last one the years 1849 to 1881, the period when material is still abundant, when Froude knew him personally, but when he inevitably ran out of space. For Froude was decidedly a disciple of Carlyle's later period, and so what we have is a biography placing a disproportionate emphasis on Carlyle's early life written from the point of view of someone whose sympathies and special knowledge belong to the later period. Froude, for example, is far more interested in the ageing Carlyle's self-styled "remorse" about Jane than his early radicalism. The circumstances of the quarrel about the papers may also have affected the second half of the biography not only by reinforcing the commitment to finish in two volumes, but by tempting him to rely even more on direct quotation (at which he was weakest) and to make less of personal knowledge than he might.

Yet his two letters about the importance of keeping the collection together suggest that by the time he had finished he had begun to see their enormous value. No doubt he was well able to arrive at this conclusion himself; but it is also abundantly clear that although Carlyle was sometimes worried about their publication his remarks about burning them were largely affectation. Discussing the subject with a friend of Mazzini shortly after the latter's death, he approved of Mazzini's habit of burning all intimate letters as soon as possible, but to her surprise disagreed with it as a general rule.[26] It is self-evident not only from his enormous accumulation of correspondence, but the care with which they were kept and annotated. He was a prose-poet of memory who had come to be doubtful of immortality and overwhelmed by the need to reassure himself of the existence of those he had known and loved. No less, in his letters and journals and in everything he wrote, he had the pleasure and discomfort of feeling that he did so for posterity. His self-concern is enormous, and at times hateful to him, hence the instructions to "burn", "express biography of me I had really rather that there should be none", and the outburst to Allingham (*Diary*, p. 196), "Write my autobiography? I would as soon think of cutting my throat with my pen-knife!" But he may well have realized, at other times, that he was a short-range thinker with a supreme power of expression, often capable of his best in speech, diary and correspondence, but too self-questioning to write anything which was fully self-consistent and self-developing in design.

Certainly this is suggested by one path his reputation has taken. For though volumes of the *Collected Letters* have only recently begun to appear, other collections of the Carlyles' letters have long attracted more interest than his major works, and new collections such as those of the letters to Emerson and to his brother Alexander have been given an editorial treatment that fresh editions of the works now lack.[27] The Carlyles' observations in letters, journals and contemporary comment of all kinds are what possibly give them at present their largest claim on our attention.

Yet Carlyle is more than a Victorian Pepys or Boswell; he deserved his reputation as a great writer in his own time, and he saw more deeply into men and society than either. But even his major works have some of the same qualities we find in his papers: they are a collection of sure and rapid insights, not easily connected unless he found the right subject or related them to himself. The swift and compact accumulation of observations is the principle of Carlyle's composition, as well as the process of his thought. He may make a fantasy in this way as with *Sartor*, or he may devise a quasi-epic structure for the *Pamphlets*, but he is so concerned with the actual that any theory he takes up disintegrates as he worries at it. When troubles of his own time press directly on himself he can turn to and deal with them. But essentially he is a critic: able to write with wonderful expressiveness and insight even in the wilds of Craigenputtoch if he is provided with the twenty-six volumes of Diderot or the complete works of Voltaire, reliant on translation to begin writing, pleased to find a master in Goethe, but as an original artist never completely satisfying. It is this which gnaws at him. History is his refuge, and it is in his historical studies that he is most original, working painfully over the French Revolution, Cromwell and Frederick until he masters them by finding a pattern in their events or imposing one on them of his own.

"All books", he says, "are in the long run historical documents." He chooses to write histories because, hard as he finds it, he believes that only in writing could he feel himself fully come *alive*. Yet he finds that his insight comes partly in proportion to the difficulties surmounted and so, whatever the task (as with *The French Revolution*), he feels he must grapple with it, "seize it, crush the secret out of it, and make or mar".[28] He speaks of his plight as a writer facing the life of Cromwell:

> For many months there has been no writing here. Alas! what was there to write? About myself, nothing: or less if that was possible. I have not got one word to stand upon paper in regard to Oliver. . . . I seem to myself at present, and for a long while past, to be sunk deep, fifty miles deep, below the region of articulation, and, if I ever rise to speak again, must raise whole continents with me. . . . I am, as it were, without a language. . . . I wish often I could write rhyme. . . .[29]

Poetry he could never write because he could not bring himself to speak of contemporary poetry as anything *but* rhyme. His general philosophy was to declare that no general philosophy was possible, and his outlook when faced with creating anything not centred on himself was almost blank. The only difference between the Everlasting No and the Everlasting Yea is self-will. Listing various

schemes for books, he notes: "Life consists, as it were, in the sift-
ing of huge rubbish-mounds, and the choosing from them, with
ever more or less error, what is golden and vital to us."[30] About
the same time, he declares: "Neither does Art &c., in the smallest
hold out with me. In fact, that concern has all gone down with me
like ice too thin on a muddy pond. I do not believe in 'Art.' "[31]
After writing *Heroes*: "I sometimes feel as if I had lost the art of
writing altogether; as if I were a dumb man. . . . I do lead a most
self-secluded, entirely lonesome existence. 'How is each so lonely in
the wide grave of the All?' says Richter."[32] It is not *all* Carlylean
"exaggeration". He sees the desperate nature of being a writer,
and that he is dependent on rousing himself into a state destructive to his "nerves"; yet, finally, because so few will listen to him
after 1850, he turns to *Friedrich II of Prussia*, making supreme
demands on himself and his readers.

The French Revolution is a great exception for which reasons
might be given, but, apart from this, it is arguable that Carlyle's tremendous powers produced works which were fragmentary—though
no doubt his fragments are greater achievements than most men's
life-work. Yet it is in his private papers that he often expressed
himself best because (to use his own terms) they are about *himself*, and this is what he believed in—*himself*. This is not always
enough, even for Carlyle; but a justification can be found near the
start of his published *Cromwell*: they "hang there in the dark abysses
of the Past; if like a star almost extinct, yet like a real star. . . .
These Letters will convince any man that the Past did exist!"[34]

Illustration from *Punch's Almanac* (31 Dec. 1881), showing that
March 1881 had been memorable for Froude's besmirching Carlyle on
publishing the *Reminiscences*.

NOTES

1. Froude, *Life*, III, 4 and 7.
2. Dunn, *James Anthony Froude, A Biography, 1818–1856* (Oxford, 1961), I, 9.
3. Dunn, *Froude, A Biography, 1857–1894* (1963), II, 472. There are pointed comments on Dunn and Froude by Gertrude Himmelfarb, *Victorian Minds* (London, 1968), "James Anthony Froude: A Forgotten Worthy", pp. 236–48.
4. Dunn, *Froude, A Biography*, II, 477–8.
5. NLS, MS. Acc. 5074, referred to hereafter as the Farrer-Stephen papers. I am greatly indebted to the kindness of Messrs Farrer & Co. The papers include many letters, some autograph, others legal copies, and several in both forms; but there is no point in distinguishing for the present purpose between originals and accurate legal copies, so that citation only by date means that the text is taken from these papers.
6. Froude, *Life*, IV, 423, where Carlyle's rather odd comments on Stephen's speech mean that he was contemptuous of his relative moderation in willingness to tolerate parliamentary government.
7. In judgment on legal points I have been guided by the present extensive papers, such previously published documents as those in the appendix to *The Nemesis of Froude*, and W. A. Copinger, *The Law of Copyright in Works of Literature and Art* (London, 1870, 2nd edn 1881).
8. The manuscript of the *Reminiscences* is a composite one, including the chapter on TC's father, "James Carlyle", written in January 1832; chapters on Edward Irving, Lord Jeffrey and others, written in 1866–7; and pieces combined to make the chapter on Jane Welsh Carlyle, mainly written in 1866. The latter is much more in the form of a journal than either Froude or Norton allow us to suppose. All but "James Carlyle" are in NLS. There is nothing to be gained by distinguishing between the different parts of the MS at every reference.
9. Dunn, *Froude, A Biography*, II, 483.
10. See especially NLS, MS 1777, but there are many other miscellaneous letters of Mary Carlyle in NLS.
11. The bequest to Mary by the codicil of the lease of the house in Cheyne Row, previously left to Dr John Carlyle, was convenient but almost worthless; its probate value was nil, since with only $2\frac{1}{4}$ years of the lease to run its rentable value was balanced by the cost of putting it into good condition again at the end of the lease.—Farrer-Stephen papers.
12. *My Relations with Carlyle*, p. 29. Froude falls into the dilemma of bemoaning that Carlyle did not tell him about his intentions, and denouncing "the absurdity" of the supposition "that I, being in constant and confidential communication with Carlyle, did not know his wishes".—Quoted, Dunn, *Life of Froude*, II, 491. A similar contradiction is noted by *Dyer*, p. 215, in Froude's claim to have consulted Carlyle

on various questions while also saying that (at this time) Carlyle was incapable of understanding what they meant.

13. NLS, MS 1777.113. Froude again admits Mary's right to possession.

14. NLS, MS 1777.163, 29 June.

15. NLS, MS 1777.121, unidentified correspondent from Forres (15 May 1881) who also asks, "Was Froude his *secret* enemy or what? or is it the overweaning conceit which gets naturally into the blood of all writers."

16. Dunn, *Life of Froude*, "blackmail", II, 486; "monetary value", II, 476, and Dunn, *Froude and Carlyle*, p. 30.

17. Dunn, *Life of Froude*, II, 477.

18. Froude was rather taken with the wording of the last paragraph; Stephen obligingly quoted it back to him, when he wrote his "privately printed" letter for Froude to distribute in self-justification (*The Late Mr. Carlyle's Papers*, 1886, reprinted in *My Relations*), and Froude used some of it again, as if a fresh thought, in writing to Lady Derby, as quoted by Herbert Paul, *Life of Froude* (London, 1905), p. 329.

19. Not necessarily because Geraldine Jewsbury was a bad witness, but her evidence was unwritten, came orally from Mrs Carlyle, was repeated (presumably as a broken confidence) to Froude, and is unverifiable. Yet she *may* be right.

20. These letters are quoted and referred to in *Nemesis*, pp. 87 and 140–1, were never denied by Froude, and were accepted by Dunn in *Froude and Carlyle*. (It needs to be appreciated that whereas I have worked mainly from the Farrer-Stephen papers, Dunn worked exclusively from the Froude family set of documents, and that there is still probably a Mary Carlyle set in existence (part given in *Nemesis*) among which the originals to these may still be found.)

21. Dunn, *Froude and Carlyle*, pp. 91–5.

22. NLS. MS 3823.

23. The proposal to edit some of the unpublished papers for *Fraser's* had occurred to Allingham and Mary previously, in 1876, but Mary (to whom Allingham recognized they belonged) changed her mind.— *Nemesis*, p. 144.

24. *Life*, I, xv.

25. By analogy with his treatment of both the Dickens papers and his own: see K. J. Fielding, "New Letters from Charles Dickens to John Forster, How They Were Found", *Boston University Studies* in English, II (1956), 140–9.

26. *Nemesis*, p. 145.

27. *The Correspondence of Emerson and Carlyle*, ed. J. Slater (New York, 1968), and *The Letters of TC to His Brother Alexander*, ed. E. W. Marrs, Jr. (Cambridge, Mass., 1968).

28. *Life*, II, 466.

29. *Life*, III, 279.

30. *Life*, III, 422–3.

31. *Life*, III, 421. Compare, for example, two entries in the Forster manu-

script: "What is 'Art'? I confess myself entirely unable to say. For my own share, I have as good as no Art: —more pity" (f. 95 v.); "Why look on revolutions? Are men never great but in revolution? Why, truly, yes occasionally; and yet oftenest enough also, far oftenest in these last times, *no they are not great!* They are not great, in these poor ages of ours, I think, but little rather; an *ignarum pecus*; driven, or driving, to pasture, to market,—not at all in the heroic manner. It is in great moments only, when life and death hang in the balance that men become veracious, sincere. I for one admire veracity; it is real deeds however rude, not mimetic grimaces of deeds however elegant, that I should wish to look upon" (f. 170, about 19 Oct. 1841).

32. *Life*, III, 195.
33. *Life*, IV, 85.
34. *Works*, VI, 77.

Contributors

ARTHUR A. ADRIAN is Emeritus Professor of English, Case-Western Reserve University, and the author of *Georgina Hogarth and the Dickens Circle* and *Mark Lemon: First Editor of Punch*; he is married to VONNA H. ADRIAN, poet and Lecturer in English (retired), Case Western Reserve University and Cleveland Institute of Art.

JOHN CLUBBE is Associate Professor of English, Duke University, author of *Victorian Forerunner: The Later Career of Thomas Hood*, editor of *Selected Poems of Thomas Hood*, an assistant-editor of the Carlyle *Collected Letters*, and editor of *Two Reminiscences of Thomas Carlyle*.

DAVID J. DeLAURA is Avalon Foundation Professor in the Humanities, University of Pennsylvania, author of *Hebrew and Hellene in Victorian England: Newman, Arnold and Pater*, and editor of Newman's *Apologia Pro Vita Sua* and *Victorian Prose: A Guide to Research*.

K. J. FIELDING is Saintsbury Professor of English, University of Edinburgh, author of *Charles Dickens: A Critical Introduction*, editor of Dickens's *Speeches*, and associate-editor of Dickens's *Letters* (Pilgrim edn vol. I) and of the Carlyle *Collected Letters*.

GEORGE H. FORD is Professor of English, University of Rochester, author of *Keats and the Victorians*, *Dickens and His Readers*, and *Double Measure, A Study of the Novels and Stories of D. H. Lawrence*, and co-editor of the Norton *Hard Times* and *Bleak House*, and one of the editors of the *Norton Anthology of English Literature*.

CARLISLE MOORE is Professor of English, University of Oregon, author of the Carlyle chapter in *English Romantic Poets and Essayists*, "Carlyle and Fiction, 1822–34" (in *Nineteenth Century Studies*, ed. H. Davis *et al*), "*Sartor Resartus* and the Problem of Carlyle's 'Conversion'" (PMLA, 1955), and "The Persistence of Carlyle's 'Everlasting Yea'", MP (1957) and other studies in Romantic and Victorian literature.

MORSE PECKHAM is Distinguished Professor of English and Comparative Literature, University of South Carolina, and author of *Beyond the Tragic Vision, Man's Rage for Chaos, Art and Pornography, The Triumph of Romanticism,* and *Victorian Revolutionaries,* and editor of Darwin, Browning and Swinburne.

CHARLES RICHARD SANDERS is Emeritus Professor of English, Duke University, author of *Coleridge and the Broad Church Movement, The Strachey Family, Lytton Strachey: His Mind and Art,* editor of an abridgement of Malory's *Morte D'Arthur,* and General-editor of the Duke-Edinburgh edition of the Carlyle *Collected Letters.*

JULES P. SEIGEL is Associate Professor of English, University of Rhode Island, editor of *Thomas Carlyle: The Critical Heritage,* and author of several articles on Victorian literature.

G. ROBERT STANGE is Professor of English, Tufts University, and is author of *Matthew Arnold: The Poet as Humanist,* and editor of *The Poetry of Coleridge,* and co-editor of *Victorian Poetry and Poetics.*

RODGER L. TARR is Associate Professor of English, Illinois State University, editor of *A Bibliography of English Language Articles on Thomas Carlyle: 1900–1965,* and author of articles on Carlyle, Dickens, and related topics.

G. B. TENNYSON is Professor of English, University of California, Los Angeles, and author of *"Sartor" Called "Resartus,"* editor of *A Carlyle Reader,* and until recently of *Nineteenth-Century Fiction,* and author of the Carlyle chapter in *Victorian Prose: A Guide to Research.* He is co-editor of *Victorian Literature: Prose and Poetry.*

272

Index

Writers and their works are entered under the authors' names, although a few titles are given in addition. Other titles are of works by Carlyle. For Carlyle himself see the chronology, pp. 11–12; for topics with which he was concerned, and stylistic devices, see alphabetically separate entries. Most secondary material has been indexed, but not always repeatedly when only cited in the notes.